Centre for Educational Research and Innovation (CERI)

SOCIAL INFLUENCES ON EDUCATIONAL ATTAINMENT

Research perspectives on
Educational Equality

by
Torsten HUSÉN

RGANISATION   FOR   ECONOMIC   CO-OPERATION   AND   DEVELOPMENT
1975

*
* *

0027858

91854 370.35
CEN

PREFACE

Social equity has long been a topic for discussion and a major political issue, the scope and meaning of the concept changing from time to time and from culture to culture. To begin with the main political goal was to obtain formal rights for every Member of society to take part in voting procedures and to exploit the resources that society makes available. Gradually the concept was modified so that it denoted the equalization of opportunities for everyone to make real use of these rights, irrespective of role, sex, religion, social, economic and geographic backgrounds. The impact of policies deriving from this interpretation has been disappointingly limited, and consequently a third and current political issue has emerged in many countries today: how to ensure that social equity is really attained in terms of results, seen over the individual's whole lifetime. This is a goal that goes beyond the mere removal of obstacles to positive political measures of compensation and support, with the ultimate aim of a more equal social outcome.

The idea of equity in education has developed in similar fashion to the more general concept of social equity. The formal right to education is no longer a political issue in most countries, nor in principle is the notion of equal educational opportunities, but the different practical, philosophical and political question related to a policy of equal educational outcome in the perspective of lifelong and recurrent education is now the focus of the debate.

The following report by Professor Husén is a contribution to the analysis and clarification of this problem. Given his outstanding reputation as a scientist who has devoted much of his career to studying the relationships between education and equity, his conclusions will command widespread interest.

The central issue which emerges from Professor Husén's analysis is that the social background, education and working careers of individuals must be related in new ways in the society of the 1970s. If the destiny of all individuals is settled decisively by examinations in the education system at the age of 11 and 16, then education will be relatively powerless to overcome the disadvantages of parental and social-class background. In other words, educational opportunities must be spread over a wider span of life; must be seen as part of continuing process of development of the individual, involving work, education and leisure; and must engage the responsibilities of employers, both private and public, as well as the educational system as we understand it today. This is what is meant by a system of " recurrent education ", which is now the subject of investigation by CERI.

The conclusion that emerges is that education can play its role in equity in the future only if, beyond a period of basic education for all, new combinations of educational activity, work and leisure are developed which enable individuals to pursue their development, both in terms of income and social status, over much of their working life.

James R. Gass
Director,
Centre for Educational Research and Innovation.

TABLE OF CONTENTS

INTRODUCTION

This book is about social dimensions of scholastic attainment, which for many years has been a pervasive theme in my research. My first study of the "reserve of talent", using survey data for an almost complete age group of twenty-year-olds in Sweden, was published more than 25 years ago (Husén, 1946). As indicated later in this book, subsequent research pertaining to educational attainments and social background has cast some doubt on the concept of a limited "pool of talent" and hence on the existence of "reserve of talent" as this was understood and whose size the researchers in the 1940s and 1950s tried to estimate. Under the impact of a growing interest among policy-makers in the utilization of talent and in equality of educational opportunity, studies of the relationship between social background and educational attainment have become much more sophisticated – both conceptually and technically. Analyses of data from large-scale national and international surveys have made us aware of how closely related certain features of the formal educational systems, such as structural rigidity, diversity of programme and selectivity, are to the stratification of society at large. Whereas research relevant to the problem of equality of educational opportunity focused until recently mainly on selection for academic secondary or university education, it is now being directed at the conditions during pre-school and primary school that account for differences later in the educational career.

Until recently it has commonly been believed that inequality of life chances, say, in occupational status and earnings, could be heavily reduced by increasing equality in educational opportunities. The belief in the formal educational system as the "great equalizer" has, however, been shaken by the findings, and even more so by the interpretations of the findings of Jencks (1972) and his associates. The debate elicited by this study, as well as by the Coleman (1966) report some years earlier, has brought the research on equality to a higher level of sophistication both conceptually and methodologically.

The preoccupation with equality of educational opportunity among "progressives" or "liberals" since the time of the French Revolution is accounted for by the fact that equal educational opportunity has not been seen as a goal *per se* but as the most important step toward equalization of life chances. Horace Mann, the leading educator in the United States in the mid 19th century, hoped that education would serve as the "great equalizer". The attempt to launch massive compensatory programmes for disadvantaged children at the beginning of the 1960s stemmed from the same conviction. But the faith in what education might achieve has been challenged in recent years, both by those who believe in inherited differences as the main determiners of life chances and by those who ascribe decisive influences to the manipulation of environmental conditions. Jensen (1969 and 1973) bluntly attributes the limited success and sometimes failures of the Headstart Program to inherited differences in educability. Jencks (1972) and his associates play down genetically conditioned differences but take a fatalistic view with reference to what can be done by manipulating the educational factors. They purport to show that differences in life chances, defined by income and/or occupational status, are very weakly or, even not at all related to formal scholastic attainments. They see the role of the school mainly as that of a sorting and certification agency. Greater equality in adult life can be achieved only by public policy that directly affects income distribution and job opportunities. Marxist-oriented critics go a step further in maintaining that the role of the school in a capitalist society is mainly to prepare a docile and disciplined labour force that will fit the hierarchically structured society (Bowles, 1972; Bowles and Gintis, 1973).

If the critique launched against the futility of formal schooling is right (i.e. that education does not contribute towards equalizing life chances or "lifting" the poor from their poverty) then the matter of equalizing educational opportunities would not be regarded as an issue. Nor would it be focused on factors outside the educational realm conducive to individual or group differences in life chances. But we should keep in mind that the key criterion employed by Jencks and his associates when they talk about inequality is income, with all its inherent limitations as a measure of real level of pecuniary success, not to speal of life "success" in general.

The formal educational system is not primarily devised to maximize the income power of the individuals processed through it: it is there in its own right, as Lasch (1973a) points out in his review of Jenck's book. In the increasingly complex society of today it performs the function of enhancing the individual's "coping power", his capability to take advantage of what of what is offered — not least by public services. Coleman in his critique of Jenck's investigation points out that the major portion of his book has been devoted to the elucidation of inequalities of opportunity and not its inequalities of results (adult incomes and status) which it set out to study. Thus, the data that he and many others have presented on inequality of opportunity can be utilized for other purposes. "When re-examined from this point of view, the data indicate that those resources which increase cognitive skills and those which increase the number of years of school completed are both effective, and about equally so, in giving the capabilities that lead to prestigeful occupations and high income. It is important to note here that the criterion is not prestigeful occupations and high income, but the capabilities that lead to them because satisfaction derives from the exercise of these capabilities, and not only from the prestige or money awarded." (Coleman, 1973, p. 136).

*

The present book is a modest attempt to reconsider some of the basic concepts and to review some of the more salient findings of research that can be brought to bear on the problem of equality of educational opportunity. It does not pretend to cover the entire body of research relevant in connection, for instance the enormous literature on the nature-nurture problem. As can be seen from the list of references, however, the coverage is extensive and, as far as OECD publications are concerned, hopefully satisfactory. My main emphasis is on how access to school and school attainments is related to social background. It has not been my intention to deal with the host of intricate technical problems encountered in this field of enquiry. The only exception is the presentation of the research on the " reserve of talent ", where an account of the technical aspects is part of the historical exposition of how this research evolved.

The first two chapters deal with the theoretical implications of the main theme of this book. Chapter 1 is an attempt to clarify what is meant by equality of educational opportunity. Three different stages in the development of this concept are distinguished and certain inherent " incompatibilities " are brought out. Chapter 2 is an attempt to discuss the relationship between, on the one hand, IQ and educational attainment and, on the other, occupational success − using the Jencks study as a background. Chapter 3 sets out to demonstrate that the concept of ability has to be regarded in a sociological and not an individual-psychological context. Chapter 4 is a comprehensive review of research on the reserves of talent that has been conducted in Europe and the United States. Sweden is presented as an illustrative case of how the methodology in this particular area of study has developed. Chapter 5 demonstrates how various, mainly structural, features of the formal educational system affect educational opportunity. Particular attention is given to the problem of the comprehensive versus the selective school, which has been − and in some countries still is − the prevailing structural problem that besets the school systems of Western Europe. The social bias built into various grouping practices is pointed out. Additionally, selectivity in terms of drop-out and grade-repeating is related to social background. Whereas the focus in Chapter 5 is on the bias stemming from characteristics of the educational system as such, in Chapter 6 attention is paid particularly to the relationship between home background and educational attainment. Several pathbreaking surveys have been conducted in recent years that contribute to our understanding of how education in quite different social orders acts more as a differentiator than as an equalizer. Educational attainment is seen against home conditions, with particular reference to parental support. Finally, Chapter 7 presents conclusions and elaborates on some of the policy implications of the findings.

The first edition of this book was published in English and French, as is customary in OECD, in 1972. It was later translated into Spanish and Italian. There are two reasons for revising it some three years after it was written. The first is simply that it is now out of print. The second reason carries more weight. The book happened to appear at a time when an intense debate was beginning among academics and policy-makers about economic inequality and the role played in the modern industrialized society by social background, formal education, and IQ in determining differences in life chances. The thesis advanced in the Jensen (1969) article in the

9

Harvard Educational Review that group differences (i.e., differences between races and social classes) were mainly accounted for by genetic factors was challenged by many social scientists and geneticists alike. The literature in the wake of his article and subsequent books (Jensen, 1972 and 1973) has been enormous. The notion that IQ differences were mainly inherited elicited a debate on whether and to what extent social status in modern society is determined by IQ; in other words to what extent our society is meritocratic. (Herrnstein, 1971 and 1973).

The literature relating to both the philosophical and empirical aspects of equality in general and the equality of educational opportunity in particular, as well as to what accounts for inequalities in IQ, educational attainments, and occupational status has grown exponentially during the last few years. For instance, the debate on the technical and policy aspects of *Inequality* by Jencks and his associates (1972) has resulted in a large number of publications in both the learned journals and popular magazines.

I was in a way fortunate when I wrote the first version of this book, because at that time I did not have access to the library facilities that have later become available to me. The heated debate on the heridity/environment issue had just begun and the output of literature dealing with it was still manageable. More recently, however, I have had the privilege of devoting several months to a review of the relevant literature, and this has revealed the vast extent of empirical studies (not least from outside the Anglo-Saxon language area) published during the last 15 years or so on the relationship between home background and educational attainment.

*

I had for several years been entertaining the idea of writing a full-scale book focusing on are these problems, but it would probably not have materialised if several promoting circumstances had not occurred. When I disclosed my intention to Mr. J.R. Gass, Director of the Centre for Educational Research and Innovation (CERI) in the OECD, he suggested that I should follow up my earlier book on Social Background and Educational Career with a monograph collating all this new research and so provide a knowledge basis for national policies in this particular area. During the spring semester of 1971, I was invited to the Ontario Institute for Studies in Education (OISE) in Toronto as a Peter Sandiford Visiting Professor, and this fortunately gave me time to prepare the first draft of the major portion of it. It would be extravagant to claim complete coverage of this recent literature within the limits set for the present volume; I believe, however, that most of the important studies have been dealt with one way or another − certainly the majority of the key investigations. Hitherto, nobody so far as I know has tried to cover the relevant literature from both sides of the Atlantic.

A further circumstance enabling the realisation of my idea was an invitation to spend the academic year 1973−74 at the Center for Advanced

Study in the Behavioral Sciences at Stanford, California. Here I was provided not only with a sanctuary for further extensive reading and reflection but the opportunity to discuss the more serious of my problems with colleagues in the other social sciences and in genetics. I am most grateful to the Center for this privilege and to the Chancellor of the Swedish Universities for granting me the sabbatical leave that enabled me to enjoy it.

Now that the monograph is completed, I am glad finally to express my gratitude to Mr. Gass, Professor D. Kallen, and Dr. J. Bengtsson of CERI, who in various ways have facilitated its preparation, and to my colleagues at the OISE for the stimulating intellectual atmosphere they created. My daughter Görel Husén assisted me in preparing the bibliography.

Torsten Husén

Chapter 1

EQUALITY AS AN OBJECTIVE OF EDUCATIONAL AND SOCIAL POLICY

1. AN INTRODUCTORY HISTORICAL NOTE

"Equality" has in recent years become one of the key words in the policy debate on educational problems at both national and international level. "Equality of educational opportunity" (*Chancengleichheit, égalité des chances*), however, has not been regarded as a goal in itself, but as a means in the long-range perspective of bringing about equality of life chances. As will be enlarged on later, the classical liberal concept of equality is that all individuals should be given the same opportunity at the start of their life careers but not necessarily that this should bring about greater equality in terms of ultimate social and/or economic status. It would take us too far in this connection to spell out all the political and social implications of the modern concept of equality – let alone trace its history from the 18th century. In any case, Professor W. Sjöstrand of the University of Uppsala had already completed a historical study on equality and freedom as basic issues in Western educational philosophy (Sjöstrand, 1970 and 1973), the two concepts being as closely interdependent as those of freedom and authority.

The roots of what has been referred to as the "classical liberal" conception of "equality of educational opportunity" are to be found back in the 18th century. The famous Preamble of the American Declaration of Independence of 1776, as first drafted by Thomas Jefferson, reads in his original wording:

"We hold these truths to be sacred and undeniable; that all men are created equal and independent; that from that equal creation they derive rights inherent and inalienable, among which are the preservation of life, and liberty and the pursuit of happiness..." (Quoted after Sjöstrand, 1973, p. 51).

The ideological influences reflected in this Preamble have been studied by Sjöstrand. Evidently, when it was said that all men are created equal, the Founding Fathers meant that all men were born with the same moral and political rights and the same obligations, but not that they were endowed with equal capacities or qualifications. The interpretation of the Preamble has to be made within the context of the political philosophies of Locke, Rousseau (who in 1755 had published his treatise on the origin of inequality among men) and Helvetius.

13

Jefferson used the phrase "natural aristocracy" to characterize those who, irrespective of birth, possessed outstanding innate talents. Society should see to it that no barriers hindered the promotion of members of this natural aristocracy, they deserved a social status matching their natural talents.

Rousseau in *Le Contrat Social* in 1762 (the same year that "Emile" was published) spells out how men in the "natural" state are born equal, with the same rights within the framework of the "general will", the latter forming the basis for legislation. By means of the "social contract" the "natural equality" is transformed into moral and legal equality. Rousseau also talks explicitly about innate individual differences in qualifications. But these innate differences do not jeopardize social equality as long as society rewards men according to their merits and not according to birth and wealth. The natural aristocracy is allowed to emerge in a society that dissolves the privileges that form the basis of an "artificial aristocracy", which in modern sociological terminology would be labelled an "ascriptive aristocracy".

The classical liberal concept of equality of opportunity embodied in what is often referred to as the American Dream is epitomized in a poem by Thomas Wolfe:

> So, then, to every man his chance --
> To every man, regardless of his birth,
> His shining, golden opportunity--
> To every man the right to live,
> To work, to be himself,
> And to become
> Whatever thing his manhood and his vision
> Can combine to make him--
> This seeker,
> Is the promise of America.

At the beginning of the 18th century talent in terms of potential for outstanding performances in the arts and sciences, in politics and public office, as well as in commerce and industry began to be realized. The quest for an efficient *selectio ingeniorum* was a product of the mercantilistic era in Europe. Thus the idea among representatives of the new upward mobile class of academics, administrators and merchants that the potential for outstanding achievements was not distributed according to membership of the higher estates gained momentum. To identify and promote potential talent, wherever it could be found, began to be regarded as a means of strengthening the economic and political potential of a country (Edlung, 1947).

But a proper utilization of talent was also considered to be a means of strengthening the military potential. Gneisenau in considering the Prussian military catastrophe in 1806–07 wrote:

> How enormous are the forces sleeping undeveloped and unutilized in the bosom of a nation! When a country perishes in weakness and disgrace, in the most miserable of all villages a Caesar may tread behind his plough and an Epaminondas may make his living by his hands. (Translated from Petrat, 1969, p. 120).

14

In his book of 1912 on school reform B. Otto makes a case for the efficient utilization of "all forces, all nerves, every drop of blood and everything of mental ability which is dormant in the people... Everything that wants to be developed must be developed, otherwise the German people can never become the winner in the fierce competition now beginning between the nations ". (Quoted after Petrat, 1969, p. 212).

The Weimar Constitution of 1919 talked about the reorganization of society according to (inherited) individual capacity. This new social order should supersede the one with allocation according to socially inherited privileges. The school had as one of its major tasks to "promote talent" (*Begabtenförderung*). The newly established science of psychology was expected to provide methods whereby individual ability could properly be assessed. The constitution stated (article 146) that an educational career should be determined by "innate aptitude" (*Anlage*) and "inclination" – not by social background. The criteria for scholastic promotion should be "ability" and "will" (Petrat, 1969, p. 11-2). By introducing a system of financial aid an intensive social mobility could be promoted. The interplay of free competition and equal opportunity would see to it that the able would get access to careers that they deserved (*freie Bahn dem Tüchtigen*).

The Weimar Constitution and its initiators aired a firm belief in the liberal opportunity model. But the educators, particularly those of the élitist secondary schools, were not ready to accept any structural changes that would be conducive to the broadening of educational opportunities. Hartnacke (1917) who at the time of writing was school inspector in the city of Bremen points out that the selection and promotion of the able pupils was so important that it had to take precedence over problems of "organization and politics". What he particularly resented were the premature demands for establishing a unitary school (*Einheitsschule*). He issued a strong warning against changing the school structure so as to postpone transfer to the academic secondary school (in most cases the *Gymnasium*) until after the sixth school year. He presented some evidence which he thought supported the contention that the existing school system took adequate care of the able students. Teachers were asked to rate the mental ability (*Denkfähigkeit*) of students who were about to conclude the fourth grade of the elementary school. Hartnacke found that 11.5 per cent of those in the fee-paying group had top ratings, as compared with only 2.9 per cent in the non-feepaying group, where the majority of students came from manual working class homes. He concluded that the "broad mass from the lower classes includes only a relatively small number of children with outstanding scholastic aptitude ". (Hartnacke, 1917, p. 42). In fairness, it should be pointed out that Hartnacke was aware that children of lower class background were handicapped by a poor language culture. He did not realize, however, that whereas about half of the feepayers who were rated in the top brackets had applied for transfer, only one out of nine among the non-feepayers had done so. Thus, the overall conclusion reached by Hartnacke, and many with him, is: " We must on the whole get rid of the notion that there are masses of geniuses and talents among ordinary people ". " Revolutionizing changes " in the school structure were not called for in taking care of the relatively few cases from the bottom of the social ladder who were potential upper secondary school and university students.

15

In trying to put the problem of equality of educational opportunity into an historical perspective, it is appropriate to refer to R.H. Tawney's classical study *Equality* (first published in 1931), which was an attempt to study existing inequality in all its aspects – social, economic and political – and to recommend strategies to achieve greater equality. This discourse could not, of course, avoid taking up problems of inequality in education, particularly because it dealt with England prior to World War II. He wryly puts it: "The hereditary curse upon English education is its organization upon lines of social class... Children are apt to think of themselves as their elders show that they think of them. The public school boy is encouraged to regard himself as one of a ruling class – to acquire, in short, the aristocratic virtues of initiative and self-reliance, as well as frequently the aristocratic vices of arrogance, intellectual laziness and self-satisfaction ". (Tawney, 1951, pp. 154–5).

Tawney points out that it has been proved possible to secure for all citizens not equal health but an environment that is equally favourable to its preservation. Would it not then be possible to secure for all, not an equal culture or equal educational attainment, but "equal opportunities cultivating the process with which Nature has endowed them"? It should be noted that this was written about 1930. Tawney saw as an ideal for the British educational system a situation in which children from all walks of life went to the same school. It is an "educational monstrosity and a grave national misfortune" that children whose parents have larger bank accounts are sent to one type of school and their age-mates with parents of modest means to another.

The first large-scale attempt to elucidate empirically the extent to which equality has or has not been achieved in a particular national educational system is presented in the so-called Coleman report (Coleman, *et al.*, 1966). This extensive survey was initiated by the Civil Rights Act of 1964 in accordance with which the United States Commissioner of Education was requested to conduct a survey "concerning the lack of availability of equal educational opportunities for individuals by reason of race, color, religion, or national origin in public educational institutions at all levels in the United States" (*op. cit.*, p. 3). The survey set out mainly to determine how far the schools offer equal educational opportunities in terms of criteria (other than segregation) that are regarded as good indicators of educational quality (*ibid.*). Some of these criteria were quite tangible, such as libraries, textbooks, laboratories and the like. Others, such as curriculum offerings, grouping practices and methods of instruction, were less so. Some, finally, were rather elusive, such as teacher competence and teacher attitudes.

2. EQUALITY AT THE STARTING POINT, IN TREATMENT, AND AS A FINAL GOAL

In analysing the concept of equality of educational opportunity, the crucial point is what should be meant not only by "equality" but also by "opportunity". In this context we shall confine ourselves chiefly to discussing "opportunity"; but certain aspects of "equality" in the context of the formal educational system ought to be spelt out briefly. From the point of view of the individual, "equality" can be conceived of in three ways: (*i*) as a starting point; (*ii*) as a treatment; and (*iii*) as a final goal —or as a combination of these three.

We can think of equality as a state where all individuals *start* their educational career, their formal school career, on an equal footing. From the genetic point of view they evidently do not; but we can, at least theoretically, think of a state of affairs where all children are given exactly the same living conditions from the day of their birth. The difficult aspect of this is, of course, that they emanate from parents differently equipped genetically and therefore from the outset are subjected to different treatment.

Secondly, equality can be thought of as applied to *treatment*. Everybody, irrespective of his genetic equipment and social origin, could be thought to be treated equally in various ways. In the first place, everybody could be equal before the law. The welfare policy could be framed to guarantee everybody a minimum income or subsistence allowance. A unitary system of pre-school or regular school education could take care of all the children alike, etc. Evidently, and this is a common experience both in capitalist and socialist economies, such a system does not necessarily lead to a complete, not even to an increased, equalization among adults. When Premier Khrushchev introduced the Education Act of 1958 to the Supreme Soviet he pointed out that at the institutions of higher learning in Moscow the majority of the students came from families of functionaries or the intelligentsia. Only a minority came from peasant or manual workers' families (Sauvy, 1973). In Sweden, 20 years of a welfare policy that includes among other things child allowances and the introduction of a unitary basic school and a system of upper and post-secondary education with a student aid and tuition-free system, has only levelled out to a modest extent the differences between working-class and middle-upper-class children in educational participation (OECD, 1971; Gesser and Fasth, 1973).

Finally, equality of educational opportunity could be regarded as a *goal* or a set of guideposts in the sense that framing and implementation of educational policy should introduce measures that would contribute to an increased equalization in educational attainment. This, in its turn, would lead to a greater socio-economic equalization in terms of economic status, participation in decision-making processes that concern all citizens and so on.

In an article that spells out some of the implications of his extensive survey, Coleman (1966) raises the question of whether equality means that one wants to have equal schools (i.e., equal treatment) or equal students. He points out that his survey had focused mainly on what comes out of education in terms of student achievement in areas such as reading and arithmetic — skills that are important for success not only in further schooling but also on the labour market. This, of course, does not permit any absolute judgment about the real levels of equality or inequality of the schools the students are attending, because more of the individual differences in achievement are accounted for by their home and peer environment than by the school. However, what matters to the student " is not how 'equal' his school is, but rather whether he is equipped at the end of school to compete on an equal basis with others, whatever his social origins". (*Op. cit.*, p. 71f). Schools "are successful only insofar as they reduce the dependence of child's opportunities upon his social origins... Thus, equality of educational opportunity implies not merely 'equal' schools, but equally effective schools, whose influences will overcome the differences in the starting point of children from different social groups". (*Op. cit.*, p. 72). This implies differential pedagogical treatment.

The debate on educational opportunity elicited by the Coleman report (Coleman *et al.*, 1966) raised the analysis of the problem to a higher level of sophistication. Thus, one became aware that a basic distinction was the one between equality of opportunity and equality of results. John Rawls has in his book *A Theory of Justice* (1971) elaborated on this distinction and developed what Charles Frankel (1973) refers to as a "new" egalitarianism. The "old" one, which in the liberal vein was concerned with equality of access or equality of opportunity, advocated a policy of correction. Society had to rectify formal inequalities by providing help to the disadvantaged to overcome the hindrances or barriers that prevented them from taking advantage of, for instance, the opportunities of schooling. Rawls refers to this conception of equality (according to which careers should be open to talent on the basis of competition) as "liberal" or "democratic".

But the fact that a person is born with certain genes into a family with certain material and cultural assets is as Rawls puts it, "arbitrary from a moral point of view". The fact that some are born with a brilliant mind and others with a slow-moving one is to be ascribed to the "natural lottery". Thus, the moral problem is to "redeem" the individual who, due to this "lottery", has been born with less favourable genes and in less favourable circumstances. Society should see to it that the burdens and benefits are distributed according to each individual's abilities. This is briefly the messages of the "redemptive egalitarianism".

The redemptive philosophy has been challenged by Frankel (1973), Coleman (1973) and Bell (1973). Frankel's main objection to Rawls's theory of justice is that it "does not treat the individual as an active participant in the determination of his fate". A model of life as a lottery is not very conducive to a sense of personal responsibility. Bell (1973) looks at the equality problem in very much the same way as Frankel. But he views it also within the framework of a society where rationality, technical competence, and educated skills become more and more important and where they, since they are more sought after, are also more highly priced.

Coleman (1973) in reviewing Jencks's book poses the crucial question whether – and to what extent – equality of opportunity is an appropriate goal. Each individual is born with a highly varying set of "private resources, genetic and environmental". If nothing is done on the part of society this will result in quite unequal opportunities. Society can try to "infuse" resources selectively so as to achieve greater equality. But such a policy is faced with two problems. First, in order to compensate fully for the inequalities of private resources "the publicly-provided resources for the privately disadvantaged must be sufficient to provide to all children the same opportunity as held by the child with the greatest private resources genetic and environmental", (*op. cit.*, p. 134-5). Such extreme implementation is obviously not possible. The other problem is that an inverse policy of equality of opportunity with the aim of establishing equality of results would have disincentive effects upon parents, and this could reduce the total amount of resources available and be detrimental to a system of redistribution. This, in the long run, could lead to less favourable effects for the disadvantaged.

Coleman concludes:

For both these reasons, first because it is impossible to achieve, and second because if achieved it would lower the general level of opportunity for children, the ideal of equal opportunity is a false ideal. A society cannot make an implementationable decision to create equal opportunity for all children within it. What it must do instead is to decide what level of public resources and what imbalance of public resources it should invest to reduce the level of inequality that arises from private resources. (*Op. cit.,* p. 135).

In retrospect Coleman doubts whether public investment in bringing about equality of results more than equality of opportunity is to be preferred from the point of view of individual satisfaction. The ability to overcome obstacles may lead to at least as much satisfaction as the attainment of these goals per se.

3. MEASURES OF OPPORTUNITY AND ENVIRONMENT

The analysis below of the various conceptions of equality of educational opportunity (see p. 30 *et seq.*) imply different, or partly different, key independent variables that can be measured with various degrees of success. Some variables are important in accounting for group differences in opportunity, others for individual differences. Since, as has been pointed out by Coleman (1973), public policy is deliberately geared to affect group differences, the policy implications of the two types of variables might be quite different. The dependent criterion variable is " opportunity " which can be represented by some measure of participation rate in education or measure of disparity between various regions, social classes, individuals, etc. The following types of variables seem to fall under this heading of " opportunity ":

1. One set of variables embraces the non-scholastic, physical ones, the material circumstances. Here, we are dealing with the economic resources available to the student's family, the cost required for tuition, the geographical distance to a school and the transportation available.

2. Another set includes the physical facilities of the school, such as the quality of its plant in general, laboratories, library, texbooks, etc.

3. A third set of variables has to do with certain psychological aspects of the home environment, such as the level of the parents' aspirations with regard to the schooling of their children, their general attitude toward learning at home, and the amount of independence training, language training, and so on provided there.

4. A fourth set describes the psychological aspects of the school environment in terms of teacher competence, teacher attitudes toward differ-

ent categories of students, teacher expectations with regard to student performance and student motivation.

5. Finally, a fifth set of variables describes what in surveys conducted by the International Association for the Evaluation of Educational Achievement (I.E.A.) was referred to as "opportunity to learn" (Husén, 1967, II, p. 162 *et seq.*; Comber and Keeves, 1973, p. 158 *et seq.*). Here we are dealing solely with opportunity in the school situation, i.e., with purely pedagogical conditions in terms of how much time is allotted in the curriculum to a subject or a topic, how much time the teacher devotes to that topic and how much homework he assigns to it. This kind of opportunity was rated item by item in the mathematics and science tests by the teacher who taught the actual class. But independent ratings were also obtained from subject-matter experts who assessed the opportunity for a whole national school system.

Thus, in analysing what factors act as hindrances to the achievement of equality, we would have to make two distinctions. In the first place, we should distinguish between material and psychological barriers. There might be equal opportunity to get *access* to a certain kind of education and to pursue it in a physical formal sense: no tuition has to be paid, all costs are met from public funds, transportation is taken care of and so on. But certain psychological barriers remain even when the physical ones have been removed, and once the material conditions have been equalised, they operate with relatively greater strength. In the second place, we have to consider the entire educational environment which consists of the combined effect of both the physical and psychological conditions in the home, society at large, and the school.

As already indicated, differences in educational opportunity between, for instance, social classes or geographical regions will have to be measured, in one way or another, by participation rates at various levels in the educational system. The most comprehensive surveys, based mainly on European studies, have been carried out by the OECD in its background studies (No. 4 and 10) for the Conference on Policies for Educational Growth in 1970 (OECD, 1971). There, "educational participation" is defined as "the enrolment of persons at a given level of formal education, or the transition or retention of students from one level to the other" (OECD, 1971, p. 8). Various types of rates or ratios have been suggested depending upon what official statistics are available. These rates fall into two main categories:

1. The most obvious way of calculating participation would be to relate the enrolment to the population eligible for education at a certain stage in the system. The most accurate measure is thereby obtained by calculating the ratio for each age cohort separately, e.g., how many 6-year-olds, 7-year-olds, etc. of the total age groups are in full-time schooling. This ratio, however, does not provide a measure of the *types* of education in which students of any one age group are enrolled.

2. Another ratio is presented in Background Study No. 4 for this same OECD Conference (OECD, 1971) and is defined as the "ratio of enrolment in a given grade... at a point in time to enrolment in... a lower grade at an earlier point in time for the same cohort" (*op. cit.*, p. 9). Such a ratio, called transition rate, becomes a very good measure of participation when longitudinal statistics are available and it provides a more accurate

picture of the flow of students through the system by grade instead of by age groups (Ljung and Jansson, 1970). Particularly when the age-grade discrepancy is large, as is the case in systems with a more flexible age of school entry or with considerable grade-repeating, the transition rate is by far the best measure.

If neither population figures nor longitudinal enrolment figures are available, one could attempt to calculate the participation rate in education above the compulsory school age by using the approach adopted by IEA where a "retentivity index" was calculated for each of nine socio-economic groups among the students in the pre-university grade, most of them being 18 or 19. Since no figures on parental occupation were available for the whole population of 18-19-year-olds, the best approximation was derived from the figures for the 13-year-olds where the whole age cohort was in full-time schooling (Husén, 1967, Vol. II, p. 107 *et seq.*).

3. A third index of participation that provides not only information about access but also about selection during a given stage in the system is the "attrition rate" – the proportion of students who either repeat one or more grades during the stage or drop out from school. A beautiful example of a mapping out of this kind by relying on longitudinal statistics is afforded by *Educational Policy and Planning: France* (OECD, 1972, p. 105 *et seq.*). Another example of how attrition is related to social class is provided by the follow-up of all the fourth-graders in Stockholm over a period of five years (Svensson, 1962; Husén and Boalt, 1968).

4. CRITICISM OF SOCIAL CLASS AS A MEASURE OF EDUCATIONAL ENVIRONMENT

In studies of the degree of disparity in participation at various levels in an educational system, social class has usually been employed as a kind of overall index of social background. The most frequently used categorisation is upper, middle, and lower, which roughly correspond to the profes-sional-managerial class, semi-professional or white-collar workers and manual workers respectively. In fact, the occupation of the father is usually the information employed for this categorisation, since it is considered to be a major determinant of the social origin of the child. In surveying European studies of group disparities (OECD, 1971), Background Report No. 10 for the OECD Conference on Policies for Educational Growth (*op. cit.*, p. 93 *et seq.*) has collated classification schemes employed by the statistical ser-vices, usually within the Ministries of Education. Most classifications are based upon some kind of occupational categorisation which in turn is derived from the occupational titles. In addition to parental occupation, there is much evidence to show that parental education (e.g. number of years of formal schooling) is an important variable for which data can be collected relatively easily. In some cases attempts have been made to rank the categories according to general status, level of qualification or position in a hierarchy. Good illustrations of such categorisations are provided by several British studies, for instance one by Miller (1970) on school achievement and social class. He employs a classification scheme devised by the Registrar General's Office and used in the survey on "leavers" in 1954 (HMSO, 1954):

Non-manual Occupations
1. Professional and high administrative.
2. Managerial and executive.
3. Supervisory, white-collar.
4. Routine clerical.

Manual Occupations
5. Foreman, supervisory (manual).
6. Skilled manual.
7. Semi-skilled manual.
8. Unskilled manual.

As we shall see later in Chapter 5, in several British surveys, for instance the National Survey sponsored by the Plowden Commission (HMSO, 1967), categories 3 and 4 and 5 and 6 respectively have been amalgamated.

The International Labour Organisation (ILO) has developed a scheme with nine categories which are put in a hierarchical order according to some kind of general status criterion. This scheme was employed cross-nationally in relating home background to participation and to school achievement in the IEA project (Husén, 1967; Comber and Keeves, 1973). The categories are:

Group 1. Higher professional and technical.
Group 2. Administrators, executives, and working proprietors, large and medium-scale.
Group 3. Sub-professional and technical.
Group 4. Small working proprietors (other than in agriculture, forestry or fishing).
Group 5. Proprietors and managers in agriculture, forestry and fishing, in most instances owner and tenant operators of farm enterprises.
Group 6. Clerical and sales workers.
Group 7. Manual workers, skilled and semi-skilled.
Group 8. Labourers (hired) in agriculture, forestry, and fishing.
Group 9. Unskilled manual workers (excluding those under 8).

It is quite obvious that, by and large, this scheme reflects an occupational status hierarchy. But the difficult categories are farmers and farm workers: should they be placed before or after some other categories? Should farmers be regarded to be on a par with, say, clerical workers, or be placed before or after them? Should farm workers be put in the same category as unskilled workers or skilled workers? There are other difficulties as well as these that make the scheme hard to use cross-nationally.

In some cases the amount of formal education generally required in the various occupations is mixed with status criteria. Härnqvist (1966) who has carried out a national survey of the relationship between certain social background factors and educational choice, based on data collected by the Swedish Bureau of Census, used a five-category scheme:

A. Professionals (whose occupations almost always require a university degree), teachers, both secondary and elementary, executives, proprietors of large enterprises, civil servants, and officers in the armed forces;

B. White-collar occupations requiring formal education up to matriculation, proprietors of small or medium enterprises;
C. White-collar occupations requiring only compulsory formal schooling;
D. Farmers (owners or tenants of farm enterprises);
E. Manual workers (including farm workers).

As already said, in a large number of studies during the last few decades aimed at elucidating the relationship between social environment and educational attainments, environment has been indexed by social class. As a rule this has been a categorisation into upper, middle, and lower (working) class. The principal criteria upon which such a scheme is based are the following – the way they have been " mixed ", i.e. weighted, differs quite a lot:

1. The amount of formal education that is either required or usually attained by the holders of the various occupations.
2. Self-reported and/or assessed earnings.
3. The status attached to the respective occupations in the promotion hierarchy within businesses, the Civil Service, etc.
4. The status attached to the occupations according to some kind of prestige rating.

As is evident, these four criteria are highly intercorrelated.

All categorizations, of which some have just been illustrated, are subject to serious criticisms as composite, overall measures of environments, even more so as measures of educational environments. The social class index, which is an extremely blurred measure, is particularly open to such criticism. Anderson (1974), in issuing a warning against undue reification of social classes points out that the " variance of associated educational features is larger within so-called classes than between them ".

Several researchers in recent years have urged that social class should be dropped as a descriptive instrument. They propose instead that one should try to pinpoint those factors in the children's home backgrounds or in the wider social setting in which they are growing up that are relevant from an educational point of view. If no attempt is made to identify these relevant variables in a much more precise way and to estimate their effects, we shall not be in a position to provide research evidence that in its turn can lay the basis for programmes intended to produce improvements.

The emphasis in recent years has, therefore, been on identifying *process* variables that can be recognized as closely related to school attainments. One example is Henry's (1963) study of the so-called hidden middle-class curriculum. Another is Bernstein's (1961) on language development among lower-class children and its implications for failure in school. Bloom (1965) and his students, for example Dave (1963) and Wolf (1964), have tried to identify certain aspects of the parent-child relationship, (such as parental approval, standards of excellence and expectations) that are conducive to success in school. The development of path analysis as an analytical tool has made it possible to study the effects of more precisely circumscribed factors, not least psychological ones, and to get away from crude socioeconomic indices (see, e.g., Sewell *et al.*, 1967 and 1970; Sewell, 1971).

Miller (1970) developed an inventory that enabled him to obtain information on the children's own perceptions of their environment. He hypothesized that the inventory should comprise items tapping such variables as parental interest, goal aspirations, home relationships and parental dominance. A factor analysis of the inventory provided eight factors, of which six were positively and two were substantially negatively correlated with an overall scholastic performance criterion. These factors had throughout a much stronger correlation with school achievement, as measured by standardized achievement tests, than social class, which correlated only 0.35 with achievement. When social class was partialled out or held constant, the correlations between self-reported home environment and school performance were on average reduced only by about 0.05. Miller concludes (*op. cit.*, p. 268): " This study has suggested that less attention may well be given in the future to social class *per se* with regard to school performance. It is a crude variable of limited direct importance in the problem of school achievement".

It should, however, be pointed out that educational performance in terms of grades and scores on standardized achievement tests is not identical with other important measures of educational attainment, such as retentivity (Husén, 1967), transition rate, and attrition rate (OECD, 1971). Boalt (1947) followed a complete age cohort of children in Stockholm from grade 4 to grade 13 and related various measures of educational attainments to their social background as indexed by social class upper, middle, lower), assessed income and welfare record known or unknown. He defined " social handicap " as the partial correlation between a social background variable on the one hand and educational attainment on the other, with grades given at the previous stage held constant. The two main social background variables were social class and income. The three attainment variables were admission to academic secondary education, grade-repeating or drop-out, and grade point average. The partial correlations reflecting the amount of social handicap obtained are presented in Table 1.1.

Table 1.1 PARTIAL CORRELATIONS BETWEEN MEASURES
OF SCHOLASTIC ATTAINMENT
AND SOCIAL CLASS AND PARENTAL INCOME RESPECTIVELY

	Social class	Assessed Parental Income
Selection for junior academic secondary school (*realskola*)	0.57	0.43
Attrition (grade-repeating)	0.17	0.28
Grade point average	0.09	0.07
Selection for senior academic secondary school (*gymnasium*)		
Attrition (grade-repeating) in *gymnasium*	0.15	0.07
Grade point average in the matriculation examination (*studentexamen*)	0.12	0.07

Source: Boalt (1947).

As can be seen, social handicaps operate much more strongly in selection from one stage to another than in performance at a given level in terms of marks and ability to get promoted without grade-repeating. We therefore have to put in a *caveat* when it is suggested that we should throw out social class categorizations altogether in attempting to relate attainments to social background. Even if actual performances are weakly related to background indexed by social class, participation rates and transition rates are not. This has been shown, for instance, by Jackson and Marsden (1968).

5. EQUALIZATION INCOMPATIBILITIES

A. *Genetic Versus Acquired Inequalities*

It will be evident from what has been said above that there are certain contradictions, or incompatibilities, in the various ways in which equality of educational opportunity has been conceived. A realization of the goal of equality has to allow for the fact that, from a genetic point of view, human beings are born unequal and that, during the first years of their lives, they are brought up by parents who differ with regard not only to their genetic equipment but also to their social condition. These two sets of factors interact so as to reinforce each other, i.e. to become positively correlated.

The incompatibility between equality and inherited differences (be they mainly genetic or environmental) makes one ask to what extent equality should mean identity of treatment. Does it mean that the treatment should be identical, or should it be so geared that optimal conditions are provided for each child to develop to the limits of his capacity? Dobzhansky has recently dealt with these problems from a genetical point of view (Dobzhansky, 1973), and I myself have pointed out, in another connection, that the issue can be stated in a paradoxical way, namely that every child should have equal opportunity to be treated unequally (Husén, 1971). Such a philosophy is behind the efforts to bring about individualized instruction (cf., e.g., Bloom, 1971), but it aims at attaining greater equality of educational achievement and is by no means conducive to increased variability. One could proceed and state another paradox that is a corollary to the first one: the very fact that children from the outset are unequal enables a democratic society to give them equal opportunity to be treated differently without incurring the risk of a fully uniform society. Had they all from the beginning been genetically equal, there would still have been ample reason to treat them differently so as to bring out the variation without which the world would become a pretty unbearable place.

Dobzhansky has raised the question of whether attempts to bring about equalization in terms of treatment, particularly in the educational system, will lead to a wider or a more narrow variability in, for instance, scholastic performances. If measures are taken to remove environmental barriers that prevent the development of scholastic ability, could we then expect a shrinking variability of scholastic achievement? According to the simple model that implies that observed variance is the sum of genetic and environmental variance, the answer to this question would be "yes" (Husén, 1963). But if environment and heredity are correlated, as by all plausibility they are, the answer might be "no". Thus, the full utilization and promotion of talent by the removal of discriminatory barriers would in this case lead to a meritocratic society. Instead of having a society built on social and birth prerogatives, we would get one built on genetic prerogatives, particularly when educated ability is such a status-determining factor as it is becoming in present-day society (cf., e.g., Herrnstein, 1973).

Another incompatibility is inherent in the demands of our modern, highly-specialized and complex society with its wide range of differentiated roles (cf. Dobzhansky, 1968). Indeed, one is entitled to look into the extent to which the dynamics behind its social fabric are actually conducive to the promotion of intellectual and social differences. We do not have empirical data by means of which comparisons could be carried out between various stages in the development of, for example, European societies since the beginning of the 18th century. There are, however, indications that the variability in terms of cognitive differences that account for a major portion of scholastic attainments covered a wider range then than now. In the first place, formal schooling was the prerogative of only a small segment of the population, so it it pointless to make comparisons between then and now in terms of scholastic achievements. It would seem to make much more sense to compare two stages fairly close to each other in time in our own societies; for example, to compare the educational systems in Europe at the turn of the century with the systems that exist nowadays in terms of variability of attainments. More than 50 years ago, all the educational systems were dual-track systems with one elementary school of rather poor quality for the masses and an academic, university-preparing secondary school for the social élite. For a long time these two systems were completely separate, that is to say access to secondary education was mainly gained by attending private preparatory schools. The core problem that ought to be elucidated by a comparison between then and now, therefore, is if and how variability in scholastic attainment is affected by the setting up of a single-track system during compulsory school age.

There are indications that structural changes in the systems have narrowed down the range. When comparisons were made between comprehensive systems on the one hand and selective or dualistic systems on the other in the surveys conducted by the International Association for the Evaluation of Educational Achievement (IEA), it was found that by and large the comprehensive systems showed a lower spread of student performances (Husén, Vol. II, 1967 and 1973a). One could, of course, question whether the introduction of a single-track, unitary system is an outcome of greater homogeneity in society brought about by social change (which in its turn is an outcome of either "spontaneous" change or deliberate social policy) or if it has been conducive to such a homogeneity. Surveys carried out in Sweden (Härnqvist, 1966) indicate that structural changes of this kind, which will be more fully dealt with in Chapter 5 (p. 109 *et seq.*), are instrumental in narrowing down at least the disparity in educational participation between the various socio-economic groups.

26

B. *Equality Versus Freedom*

In his classical treatise on *Equality* R.H. Tawney (1951) deals with the time-honoured problem of equality versus freedom. He, somewhat rhetorically, poses the question: Must increased equity in distribution of benefits on the part of society inevitably "imperil the priceless heritage of freedom?". Is egalitarianism in education a peril to excellence, so that children of high calibre will be limited in their freedom to develop according to their potential by being forced to go to school with their less endowed age-mates?

Tawney points out that "when steps to diminish inequality are denounced as infringements of freedom, the first question to be answered is one that is not always asked. It is: freedom for whom?" (Tawney, 1951, p. 260). A second question is whether "the range of alternatives open to ordinary men, and the capacity of the latter to follow their own preferences in choosing between them, have or have not been increased by measures correcting inequalities or neutralizing their effects". (*Ibid.*, p. 260).

The debate about the extent to which measures taken by society to correct inequalities have limited freedom has been suffering from the confusion between having freedom to develop and acquire certain capabilities, skills and powers and the opportunity to *use* these advantages and opportunities *ad lib.* Those who talk about infringement upon freedom imply the second and not the first type of freedom.

C. *Equality Versus Efficiency*

It has been pointed out by those who have commented on the surveys conducted in the Socialist countries (see, e.g., Yanowitch and Dodge, 1969, and Sauvy, 1973) that disparity between children from various social categories, say, between those from homes of manual workers and peasants on one hand and those whose parents belong to the professional and managerial stratum (the intelligentsia or the specialists, in the Soviet terminology) tends not only to be pervasive but to increase.

There are several reasons for this. First, the rapid expansion of formal equality of educational opportunity and the fact that the great majority in, for instance, the Soviet Union will soon be able to complete a ten-year school education has strongly boosted aspirations and expectations. Accordingly, the gap between educational aspirations and actual admissions to institutions of higher learning has widened.

Secondly, in an economic order where material property or money of any significant amount cannot be passed on to the next generation, education is the best heritage that can be provided. Parents who themselves are well educated are thereby at an advantage.

Thirdly, we have the incompatibility between equality and efficiency. An economy that needs highly trained managers and technicians is not well served by a system of unspecialized general education. To counter this, one is strictly selective at the level of higher education, promotes acceptance of the best qualified applicants and thus enhances the conducive to disparity. But it is the price one has to pay for increased productivity.

D. *The " Revolution of Rising Expectations "*

The extension in time of mandatory schooling in conjunction with universal secondary schooling has tremendously affected educational aspirations, particularly in those social strata where hitherto a few years of elementary school was the only provision for those destined for manual occupations. This phenomenon has been charted by sociologists in socialist as well as capitalist countries. A comprehensive structure of elementary-cum-secondary education in both these political systems has led to rapidly rising aspirations on the part of students and their parents – even if they are still highly correlated with home background and parental occupational status.

Surveys conducted in the Soviet Union (Yanowitch and Dodge, 1968) indicate that the great majority, some 70-80 per cent of secondary school leavers, aspire to enter higher education which will admit them to the class of intelligentsia or specialists. Since this category comprizes no more than some 10-15 per cent of the total work force and the universities are admitting only 20 per cent from the secondary school 70 to 80 per cent leavers, many are bound to experience frustration because of over-ambitious expectations. Failure to get into the university is by many regarded as a "shattering of life plans", or even as a "catastrophe", to become a worker is a "temporary evil" (Yanowitch and Dodge, *op. cit.*).

In the United States and some European countries, the clash between aspirations and actual openings tends to occur at the end of first-degree studies. In a report to the OECD Directorate of Scientific Affairs, Richard B. Freeman (1974) of Harvard University under the provocative title "Investing in education: Has the bubble burst?" takes up the problem of the widening gap between the number of college graduates and the number of appropriate job openings for them in the United States.

E. *The New Intelligentsia*

In Western Europe until well into the 1950s some 2-5 per cent of an age group entered higher education. About half of this exclusive group came from the upper and middle classes. The rest had manual working class background. The recent expanded university enrollment to some 15-20 per cent of the relevant age group has mainly been to the benefit of the middle class, but has in absolute numbers considerably increased the participation of those with working class background. An improvement in chances of going to the university from about 1-2 to 5-10 per cent for working class students means a big increase in their proportion of the total enrolment. In most industrialized countries the majority of those who now enter the intelligentsia via the universities have been recruited from the lower social strata.

This phenomenon is particularly pronounced in some of the Socislist countries. The overwhelming majority of the intelligentsia in, for instance, the Soviet Union is "first-generation intelligentsia", and this has been regarded of the greatest importance in mobilizing the productive forces needed to bring society as a whole up to a new level. Furthermore, a considerable portion of the new managerial class has also emerged from workers and peasants. This new class, which according to the rhetoric has "contributed most to the advancement of the underprivileged classes", has a vested interest in seeking prerogatives. It "is as if the socialist societies were creating a new middle class, jealous of its only privilege, which is that of higher education". (Sauvy, 1973, p. 49).

F. *The Equality-Meritocracy Dilemma*

In his comprehensive attempt to depict the emerging post-industrial society Daniel Bell (1973) makes a case for a growing meritocracy. A central feature of the society that Bell envisages is the movement toward greater rationality. Instead of property and political status, systematized knowledge proper will form the basis for power and influence. He sees the ascendency of technology, the subordination of both the public and private sector to bureaucratic controls and the growing influence of professional and scientific élite as salient features of post-industrial society. The strain of bureaucratic rationality cuts across both socialist and capitalist social orders. The scientific élite is going to replace the commercial bourgeoisie as the leading class, reared in the universities. In a way, that we are heading for a meritocratic society is part of the "inner logic" of the development Bell envisions.

It would take us too far to try to resolve the dilemma that inevitably faces any highly industrialized society with an ever growing demand for highly trained manpower — be they called professionals and executives, as in the capitalist system, or specialists and functionaries, as in the socialist system. The more in demand these persons are and the more prestigious they become, the more influence they tend to accrue and, in the long run, the more subtle the rewards bestowed upon them.

Bell's prediction of an inherent and growing element of meritocracy has, however, been challenged by, for instance, Lasch (1973) who rejects some of his basic propositions on the grounds of what comes close to Marxist social philosophy.

Lasch points out that although the scientific élite might initiate ideas, the power is not with them but with the state. Lasch further tries to prove that the "new class" of technocrats can by no means be regarded as a social class. Truly, it has certain common characteristics and it certainly possesses a high degree of functional indispensability; but its members have no common interests in which political power can germinate. The rise of a group of specialists, knowledge producers and knowledge distributors to higher status does not imply that, as a class, they become more influential in a society, like the big corporations in America with their dominant influence on the country's social and economic life. Somewhat glibly, therefore, Lasch disposes of Bell's book as a *plaidoyer* for meritocracy, a "technocrat's reply to radical criticism" on behalf of the academic establishment.

Evidently, the reply to the question whether, and the extent to which, we are moving toward a meritocratic society is closely related to what kind of social philosophy will dominate the scene in the highly industrialized countries during the next few decades. For my part, having dealt with the problem at some length in another context, I would sum it up in the following way. The importance of meritocracy in the future is closely tied to the extent to which the valuation of economic growth will prevail and to the conception of what constitutes, and what is detrimental to, "progress", the "good life", or the "quality of life".

As long as educated intelligence is conceived of mainly as an invest- ment in economic growth, those who have achieved merit in this respect will tend to be singled out for special reward, that is, to be better paid and to be elevated to power and influence. (Husén, 1974, p. 173-4).

But even in the conditions that can be envisaged for a "zero-growth" social order, a complex societal machinery must be kept running. A suffi- cient number of highly skilled people is needed for manufacturing goods, providing services and administering the complex system.

The mere fact that we find meritocratic tendencies prevailing in both capitalist and socialist economies leads us to conclude that these tendencies are inherent in the highly industrialized society itself. (Husén, 1974, p. 174).

6. THE CHANGING CONCEPTION OF EDUCATIONAL EQUALITY

Professor Coleman (1968) has given a most lucid analysis of the concept of educational equality. He distinguishes four versions.

1. In pre-industrial society, with its extended family and patriarchal kinship system and the family as the unit of production and as the centre of social welfare responsibility and education, the concept had no relevance at all. Geographical, occupational and social mobility were minimal.

2. The industrial revolution changed the role of the family, which ceased to be a self-perpetuating economic unit or a training ground. Chil- dren became occupationally mobile outside the families. Training and social welfare became community responsibilities and institutions were provided where young people could learn skills that made them employable outside the family. Such elementary, tax-supported and compulsory school- ing was not universal in a strict sense, however, since it was only intended for the masses; the upper class already had a system of preparatory schools for the secondary schools and the universities, which in their turn prepared for the upper-class occupations. Thus the dual, class-linked system as, for instance, in Europe emerged.

3. Both liberals and socialists in Europe for a long time conceived of equality of opportunity as being equality of *exposure* to a given curri- culum. It was up to the child and his family to take advantage of what was offered. If he failed, he was himself to blame. Thus, the important thing from the point of view of policy-making was to construct a system in such a way that all children, irrespective of social background, would be offered equality in terms of equal and free access to education.

4. The liberal conception took the child's future for granted. The problem of assigning children to different programmes in a comprehensive system is to find programmes that will "suit the individual needs" of each

child. But the real problem is, as Coleman (1968) points out, that "what is taken for granted" is *the* problem. No guidance programme, even if it is based on the most elaborate system of testing, can predict what will "suit" a child in terms of his educational and/or occupational career. When one realizes that the essence of the problem is not the starting point but the *effects* of schooling, then one can begin to reformulate it in terms of how to bring about more equality of performance. The core of the problem, then, is whether equality should be seen as a starting point or a goal.

For the purpose of our own further discussion, we have distinguished three major stages in the development of the concept, corresponding to three more or less distinct social philosophies. These are (*a*) the conservative; (*b*) the liberal; and (*c*) the "redemptive" conception of educational equality.

A. *The Conservative Conception of Educational Equality*

The conservative conception of educational equality was prevalent in most industrialized countries until World War I. God had bestowed different amounts of talent upon each human being, and it was up to the individual to make the best possible use of that capacity. A hyper-conservative variant of this philosophy maintained that, by and large, God had given each individual the aptitudes that corresponded to the caste or social class in which he was born. The more or less tacit assumption, then, was that he had not only to make optimal use of his capacity but be content with it, because he had been given what he by birth deserved. A more liberal variant of this philosophy can be traced from the Renaissance through the 18th century, particularly during the mercantile era with its emphasis on *selectio ingeniorum* (selection of talent). This advanced the idea that it was important to search for the scarce gold of talent among the masses for the benefit of the nation's economy and the due recognition of the individual who might be thus discovered.

The policy implications of this philosophy are interesting to follow in Europe from the end of the 19th century when the changing economy led to demands for new types of marketable education. A case in point is Sweden during the 1880s. Rapid industrialization initiated a demand for adequately trained white-collar workers, particularly clerks, while self-employed persons who were running small enterprises also needed more advanced skills than those provided in the elementary school. Educational provisions that existed at the time were no more than those elementary schools, made compulsory in the 1840s, and the classical *gymnasium*, by and large unchanged since the middle of the 17th century which prepared students for the university with a curriculum that leaned heavily towards Latin and humanistic studies.

The conservative view of what needed to be done was as advanced in a brochure by a secondary school head teacher, Fredrik Andersson (Husén, 1948). He maintained that the *gymnasium* suited the needs of those who were heading for upper-class positions and the elementary school of those who belonged to the mass of manual workers in rural or urban areas. To cater for the needs of this new middle class of clerks and small entrepreneurs, he proposed a new middle school, to which the students should be allowed to transfer from the public elementary school and from which they could graduate at the age of 16 or 17, i.e., two or three years earlier than from the upper secondary school. Legislation enacted by the *Riksdag* in 1904 therefore divided the *gymnasium* into two stages and postponed the introduction of Latin in order to make room for a less humanistic curriculum during the lower stage.

A faint reminder of the conservative philosophy was given by the 1959 report of the German Commission on Education (*Deutscher Ausschuss für Bildungs- und Erziehungswesen*) which was appointed in the 1950s by the Permanent Conference of the German Ministers of Education to draw up guidelines for the further development of the school system in the Federal Republic. It had, however, no mandate from the Federal Government, for at that time it had no formal authority so far as education was concerned. In this report a common structural framework (*Rahmenplan*) was developed in which the *Volksschule*, *Mittelschule* and *Höhere Schule* were to some extent intended to serve the needs of three different social classes.

The Swedish and German examples apply to all Western highly-industrialized countries. In most cases the creation of a short non-university-preparing, selective general secondary school has been explicitly based on the perceived need for middle-level manpower.

Two so-called "Black Papers" (Cox and Dyson, 1969 and 1970) have attacked the proposed or implemented reforms in English education, particularly the attempts to abolish streaming and the eleven-plus examinations and to introduce comprehensive secondary education. It is contended that recent changes have brought about a marked decline in educational standards and that this threat to the quality of education stems from the "ideology of egalitarianism". Angus Maude in a paper (Cox and Dyson, 1969) entitled "The Egalitarian Threat" (*op. cit.*, p. 7f.) tries to make a distinction between equality of educational opportunity and egalitarianism. The egalitarian philanthropist is letting his emotions carry him away. "In the name of 'fairness' and 'social justice', sentimentality has gone far to weaken the essential toughness on which quality depends". (*Op. cit.*, p. 7). The egalitarian "instinctively dislikes any process which enables some children to emerge markedly ahead of their fellows". He therefore attempts to destroy the schools that are taking special care of the most talented students. "All kinds of education are not, as the egalitarians pretend, of equal worth and importance, nor can anything but harm come of claiming equal status for all kinds of educational institutions." Equality of opportunity is recognized as a worthy ideal which cannot, however, be achieved quickly if one wants to avoid "damaging the total quality of our society". (*Ibid.*).

In the Introduction to "Black Paper Two" (Cox and Dyson, 1970), the editors quote Maude as saying that one can have either equality *or* equality of opportunity and that one cannot have them both. In fact, the attempts to bring about equality are inimical to the attempts to achieve equality of educational opportunity.

In "In Black Paper Two" (Cox and Dyson, 1970), Szamueli makes the case that a comprehensive system that treats every student equally in terms of formal availability of education creates even *greater* inequality than the present British élistist system. What should be achieved is to provide every child with the best possible chance to develop his particular talents in an optimal way. "This", he goes on to say, "can be accomplished only by an *unequal*, differentiated educational system, which levels out the handicap created for the able pupil by the inadequacies of his family's social and economic position." (*Op. cit.*, p. 49, *et seq.*). The English grammar school has provided "countless gifted working-class children with the opportunity to break down the class barriers and achieve unrestricted scope for their talents". (*Op. cit.*, p. 50). In referring to socialist systems, such as the ones in the Soviet Union and Hungary, Szamueli contends that the attempts to create equality in education are conducive to the preservation of social and economic inequalities that exist outside the school. He presents some statistical evidence, gleaned particularly from Soviet publications, that appears to show that in the Soviet Union considerable disparities exist between, on the one hand, children whose parents are manual workers and peasants and, on the other, children from homes of the intelligentsia.

B. *The Liberal Conception of Educational Equality*

The philosophy still prevailing in the development of the concept of equality of educational opportunity is what can be termed the *liberal* one. As an illustrative case one could cite F. Berg, in the 1880s an elementary school teacher and later a Member of the Swedish *Riksdag* and for two periods Minister of Education. Berg challenged the conservative view that power and capacity had accrued to one particular social class and strongly advocated the six-year elementary school as a single-track school that would encompass children from all social classes. After the completion of the six years, they could then pursue different types of education, practical or theoretical, depending upon individual bents (Husén, 1948).

Somewhat schematically, this classical liberal philosophy could be described like this. Each individual is born with a certain, relatively constant, capacity or intelligence. The educational system should be so designed as to remove *external* barriers of an economic and/or geographical nature that prevent able students from the lower classes taking advantage of their inborn intelligence which entitles them to due social promotion. To cite one reformer who strongly influenced Berg, Count Torsten Rudenshiöld in his book on "Thoughts concerning social mobility" (*Tankar om stånds-circulationen*, 1854) developed a blueprint for a school system that would promote a maximum of social mobility by not only seeing to it that able young people from lower classes were duly promoted, but that upperclass youngsters with limited capacities should be given humble schooling and channelled into humble occupations as well! Everybody, via his education, should be given the social status to which he was entitled by his innate talent.

Several structural school reforms in Europe during this century have been guided, at least partly, by this philosophy. By extending education to more advanced levels, by making the compulsory part of it less differentiated and by making it available to children from all walks of life, one can remove the handicaps that are inherent in being born poor and living somewhere far from a school.

The 1944 Education Act in England, which made secondary school education universal and available not only to those who could afford it, was regarded by many as a democratic breakthrough. But about ten years later when a survey was made to elucidate its effects on the social structure of the enrolment for the academic secondary school, it was found (Floud *et al.*, 1956) that at least in certain regions the proportion of working-class children admitted to grammar schools was lower than before the " breakthrough ". When the economic barriers were removed and all the places were thrown open for competition within the framework of the 11-plus examinations system, children from the middle- and lower-middle-class homes were in a better position to compete than those from less privileged backgrounds and therefore achieved an increased representation. Previously, a certain quota of places had been available to those from poor backgrounds. Floud and her co-workers were the first investigators to demonstrate clearly that selectivity does not go together with equality of participation. A certain amount of social bias always goes into a selective education system (Husén, 1971).

The transition from an ascriptive society, where more advanced formal education was a prerogative of those who by birth, wealth and connections were designated for upper-class positions, to a society in which access to and promotion and reward within the educational system formally depended upon tested ability, was regarded as a tremendous step forward by means of which justice and efficiency alike were expected to be reached. In attempting to " democratize " education, objectively assessed academic ability (be it so-called intelligence test scores, achievement test scores, examination grades, or any other objective indicator of accomplishment) seemed to be the self-evident selection criterion to replace social class, economic background and personal connections.

In analysing the educational system in industrialized and technological societies, Bourdieu (1964), for example, contends that there are indications that the educational system tends to assume the function of reproduction, i.e., to preserve or even reinforce the existing structure of society instead of being an agent of social mobility for inherited ability and the motivation to use it. Other researchers, such as Jencks (1972) and Bowles (1972), have followed suit.

Recent surveys of existing research on participation rates and school achievement as related to social class (for instance, background studies to the 1970 OECD Conference on Policies for Educational Growth) OECD, 1971) provide fairly consistent evidence that extended provisions for education, and thereby increased formal accessibility to free secondary and higher education for all children of a given age, have not considerably changed the social structure of the enrolment to any great extent. Students who take advantage of the increased opportunities are already in a favoured or semi-favoured position. The same holds true for adults. Legislation enacted in Sweden by the *Riksdag* in 1966 made the *gymnasium* education (i.e. upper-secondary education qualifying for university entrance) available to adults free of charge in late afternoon or evening classes. Surveys conducted to reveal the nature of this new enrolment showed consistently that those who have taken advantage of the new opportunities are, to a large extent, youngish people on the " launching pad " at the foot of the promotion ladder who have already received a certain amount of formal education. Participation by individuals from the class of unskilled workers is minimal (Eliasson and Höglund, 1971).

What has been demonstrated by drawing upon empirical data could just as well be brought out by scrutinizing the logic behind the liberal philosophy, according to which admission and promotion in the educational system should be guided by individual capacity or aptitude and not by socio-economic background. The specific criteria of "capacity" are, by and large, grades (marks), scores and objective tests and examination results. All these criteria are to a varying extent correlated with social background. Thus, socio-economic status indices that measure either status ratings (upper, middle, or lower-class) or certain economic factors (such as income or size of family) tend to correlate between 0.2 and 0.4 with test scores and school achievement. When, however, one takes into consideration the major psychological aspects of the environment in which the child is brought up – for example the interaction between mother and child, independence training, parental support and the extent to which emulation of relevant parental behaviours is possible and rewarded (Weiss, 1970) – substantially higher correlations are obtained. Wolf (1964) and Dave (1963) found correlations which ran as high as 0.70 between certain environmental process variables on the one hand and intelligence tests and scores on standardized achievement tests on the other.

Thus, access and promotion in accordance with objectively assessed capacity within the educational system by no means exclude the influence of socio-economic factors which, according to the liberal philosophy, are discarded by employing criteria of academic merit. As long as admission to a certain type of education is generous in terms of the proportion admitted from those who apply and the attrition rate during a given stage is low, and as long as education is available to all free of charge, socio-economic background plays a somewhat less prominent role. But as soon as a competitive selection takes place, either on admission or in terms of grade-repeating and drop-out during the course, then the correlation between background and indicators of performance increases considerably. A case in point is the selection for the faculties of medicine in Sweden, which, as with all lines of study with restricted admission, is carried out on the basis of marks obtained in the *gymnasium*. With the possible exception of the intake to the training programme for psychologists, there is no other programme that is so highly selective. What is more, there is no other faculty with such a grossly unbalanced representation of the social classes (SOU, 1973.2).

In an article entitled "End of the Impossible Dream", Peter Schrag (1970) subjected the school crisis in the United States to an incisive analysis. He pointed out that the establishment of the common school has been part of the American Dream, that the schools held the promise of providing equality of educational opportunity and that they were expected to guarantee an open society unaffected by social and economic inequities. Horace Mann in the middle of the last century foresaw that a school for children from all walks of life would be "a great equalizer of the conditions of men, the balance wheel of the social machinery... It does better than disarm the poor of their hostility toward the rich: It prevents being poor..." (quoted from Schrag, 1970). Apart from being an equalizer, the educational system was seen as a prime instrument for the individual born in humble circumstances to move up the social ladder. Everybody should be given equal opportunity to achieve and to be promoted, provided he had the talent and the energy to go ahead.

Schrag observes that until about a decade ago "equality of educational opportunity" was interpreted in terms of social Darwinism: "Everyone in the jungle (or in society, or in school) was to be created equally: one standard, one set of books, one fiscal formula for children everywhere, regardless of race, creed, or color. Success went to the resourceful, the ambitious, the bright, the strong. Those who failed were stupid or shiftless, but whatever the reason, failure was the responsibility of the individual (or perhaps of his parents, poor fellow), but certainly not that of the school or the society". (*Op. cit.*, p. 70).

It has not been realized until recently that these two objectives, as they are commonly conceived, are not in fact compatible. The school cannot at the same time serve as an equalizer and as an instrument that establishes, reinforces and legitimizes distinctions. This has been brought very much to the fore by recent surveys that have tried to account for children's differences in school achievement. Their social and economic background and that of their peers account for much more of the difference in accomplishment than all the school resources together (Coleman, 1966; HMSO, 1967; Husén, 1967).

In an article dealing with the philosophical implications of the pros and cons for an open admission to university, Karabel (1972), in realizing the dilemma between selectivity on one hand and equality on the other, states the problem in the following, somewhat provocative, way:

The ideology of academic standards brilliantly reconciles two conflicting American values: equality and equality of opportunity. Through the system of public education everyone is exposed to academic standards, yet only those who succeed in meeting them advance in our competitive system. Everyone enters the educational contest, and the rules are usually applied without conscious bias. But since the affluent tend to be the most successful, the net result of the game is to perpetuate intergenerational inequality. Thus academic standards help make acceptable something which runs against the American grain: the inheritance of status. (*Op. cit.*, p. 40).

As long as we are applying one uniform, relatively linear standard (bright, average, slow learner or whatever labels we want to use), some students are, by definition, destined to fail. In developing his ideas about "mastery learning", Professor Benjamin Bloom (Block, 1971) has been questioning the whole conception of individual differences in student achievement which has been regarded as an axiomatic foundation of what has been going on in the schools, particularly during the last century, when education in developed countries has become universally available. Students are continuously judging their performances against the standards set by their teachers, peers and parents. But these standards vary, so a student who belongs to the bottom group in a school with very high standards perceives himself as a failure even if his attainments measured against some kind of national standard are far above the average. Conversely, a student with the same objective level of attainement perceives himself as a success in a school with low standards. Bloom points out that these perceptions very strongly influence student interest, attitudes and motivation, which in their turn contribute to widen and reinforce the individual differences in attainment. This is one important explanation of the fact that variability in attainment, for instance in reading, increases by grade. One of the major points in the strategy that goes under the name of "mastery learning" is to set an absolute goal in such a way that, with appropriate methods of instruction, it can be reached by the great majority of students (Block, 1971).

The rethinking about individual differences that has been going on in recent years has important practical implications. According to the "social Darwinism" view, equality had to do only with what goes *into* the system, its input resources. The question is now being asked if one should not also consider what comes *out* of the system and thereby waive the equality at the input side by providing extra resources for those who are regarded as socially and/or culturally deprived. This was, for instance, the philosophy behind the Headstart Program. Coleman (1966) has pointed out that "equality of educational opportunity implies not merely 'equal' schools but equally effective schools, whose influences will overcome the differences in the starting point of children from different social groups".

The implication in terms of policy that ensues from the rethinking of the concept of equal opportunity is that it is not very fruitful to put the responsibility for scholastic success or failure on the individual. One has to shift the burden of responsibility to the *system* — to the educational system or to society at large.

In the long run, then, it seems that the problem of achieving equality of opportunity is one of "restoring multiple options" based on different values, but values that are not ranked along only *one* dimension. Schrag puts the problem very succinctly: "By definition, no society with but one avenue of approved entry into the mainstream of dignity can be fully open. When that single instrument of entry is charged with selecting people out, and when there are no honourable alternatives for those who are selected out, we are promising to all men things that we cannot deliver". (*Op. cit.*, p. 93). No wonder, then, that we are beginning to amass so much evidence for *uniform* provision within the educational system not being the solution to a more "equal" society. To paraphrase Orwell: those who at the outset are more equal than others will take more advantage. That is the lesson learned from equalization programmes at all levels of education.

C. *A New Conception of Educational Equality*

The glaring contrast between the official rhetoric about equality of opportunity and the existing — and sometimes widening — differences in life chances has in recent years led to the emergence of a philosophy of equality of results. The problem has been clearly stated by Herbert Gans (1973) in the Preface to his book *More Equality*:

America can be described as an unequal society that would like to think of itself as egalitarian. While officially dedicated to equality of opportunity, to enabling the disadvantaged to succeed on the basis of their individual ambition and talent, America has not acted to remove group handicaps — of class, race, and sex, among others which prevent many people from actually realizing that opportunity. Rich and poor, for example, have an equal opportunity to work as common laborers, but the poor rarely obtain the education and social contacts that provide access to executive positions. Equality, therefore, cannot be defined solely in terms of opportunity; it must also be judged by *results*, by whether current inequalities of income and wealth, occupation, political power, and the like are being reduced. (*Op. cit.*, p. XI).

What it said about America applies with almost equal force to all industrialized countries, irrespective of whether they have a socialist or capitalist social order.

The decisive impetus to a new thinking over this whole issue has come from the interest being taken in pre-school education. Bloom (1964), by re-analyzing previous studies, showed that more than half the differences in performances on intelligence tests found at the end of high school could be accounted for by differences ascertained at the age of 6, i.e., at the beginning of regular schooling. Within the various social strata, the differences showed even greater stability. This meant, then, that if environmental influences were of great importance in bringing about intellectual differentiation, most of the differences were already there when the children entered elementary school. This limited the competence of the school to act as the prime equalizer; the role had, rather, to be taken over by the pre-school institutions, if there were any, to which the children of that age group had access.

A new area of research on early experience and the socialization of cognitive modes in children by means of communication and languages has been opened up by Bernstein (1961). It elucidates how language competence can act as a barrier or promoter in getting along in primary school (e.g., cf. Oevermann, 1969, and Hess and Shipman, 1965). Additionally, studies of the effect of environment on school motivation have provided yet another reason for focusing attention on the pre-school years.

Thus, equality of educational opportunity cannot be achieved simply by removing certain material barriers and by using academic ability as the democratizing criterion. The more competitive the educational system is, and the more essential formal education becomes to occupational promotion or social mobility, the more likely it is that disparities will prevail.

In his important longitudinal study of a representative sample of children followed from their birth in 1946, Douglas (1968) related parents' aspirations pertaining to the children's further education and future occupation to their social status. He consistently found that such interest was closely linked to the parents' own social background and education. The liberal conception of a mobile society where everybody would rise (or fall) to the level of his inborn capacity (as, for instance, embodied in the 1944 Education Act in England) was far away from its realization. Douglas concludes:

R.H. Tawney denounced the liberal conception of equality of educational opportunity as simply a " fraud ". It is like " the impertinent courtesy of an invitation offered to unwelcome guests, in the certainty that circumstances will prevent them from accepting ". (Tawney, 1951).

Removal of economic and social barriers which, according to the liberal philosophy, would open the gates to more advanced education for all whose natural aptitudes qualify them patently does not suffice. Inequalities in a highly selective and/or competitive system do in fact remain, or even tend to increase. The difference between comprehensive systems with a single track basic school covering the compulsory school age and those with a dual track structure, where selection in one way or another actually takes place or is prepared earlier, is that in the comprehensive system the inequalities tend to move up to the pre-university or university level. This is the case, for instance, in Japan (OECD, 1971).

It is sometimes assumed that the better educated move up the social ladder because they are the most able and that the schools and the universities sift out the best endowed and give them opportunities to rise. This is how many would wish it to be. The vigour and quality of present-day society depends on the efficiency with which the educational system sifts out the able pupils from all levels, and allows them to qualify for posts of responsibility. The evidence of this study shows how far short we are falling. While the way is, in theory, open for all those who have the ability, the influence of the family and the encouragement that the family can give are still important elements in the level of employment achieved by each individual (Douglas *et al.*, 1968, p. 90).

This another empirical test of the extent to which the liberal philosophy of equal opportunity works. Instead of saying that one had " failed " in achieving the goal set for the reform, it would perhaps have been better to admit that it is impossible to achieve a goal of equality of opportunity by means of educational reforms alone.

The results of research carried out in recent years lead one to a much more *radical conception* of equality of educational opportunity. It is not enough to establish formal equality of access to education. One has also to provide greater equality in the pre-school institutions or in the regular school for the children of various social backgrounds to *acquire* intelligence. So far as IQ differentiation is concerned, the major portion of it has occurred before the child has entered regular school. The family, and not least the peer culture, still exert a strong influence. Thus, in order to achieve greater equality in school attainment, society has to adopt special means to compensate for the deficiencies of the environment in which the child grows up, or to supplement what may have been done at home.

As we have already observed, the overriding policy problem in " democratizing " advanced education, that is to say, formal education beyond mandatory schooling, was until recently regarded as a problem of paving the entrance routes into institutions of higher education and the schools that prepared for entry into them. But one has begun to realize that equality of opportunity of access is different from equality of opportunity of success, either in school or in adult economic career; and the " corrective egalitarianism " emanating from the " liberal " thinking is now being challenged by those who, sometimes on the basis of a Marxist philosophy, advocate a " redemptive egalitarianism ".

The basic difference between the two conceptions, on the one hand the " liberal " and on the other the more " radical " or sociological, is how they view the role of the educational system. According to the former conception, which holds that the task is primarily to remove external barriers so as to make the original capacity in each child develop, success and failure in school primarily depend upon the individual student. Once the avenues have been opened up for free competition, his natural intellectual and moral resources are the decisive factors. If he fails, he has to cast the blame upon himself, because he has been given the opportunity and not taken proper advantage of it. According to the other conception, a student's success, and not least his failure, must be ascribed mainly to

39

the school situation, particularly to the way instruction is organised. The basic problem, then, turns on the extent to which the school has been able to provide the conditions conducive to satisfactory student development.

On the part of the school, such a conception implies the revision of the basic pedagogical notions. The common denominator for any such action (including remedial teaching and tutorial help) is individualization of the entire system of instruction (Block, 1971). From this it follows, then, that equality of opportunity does not mean identity of opportunity — and herein lies a fundamental problem in a modern democracy. According to the philosophy spelled out above, equality of opportunity means that every child should be given optimal opportunity to develop his personal assets as they are at the time educational treatment in a public institution begins. The objective cannot reasonably be to establish equality in the sense that all children are treated in exactly the same way. The issue could be put in a paradoxical way by saying that one should provide equal opportunity for unequal treatment so far as socially relevant differences are concerned.

Finally, then, the more radical conception of educational equality is that, in order to achieve the long-range objective of more equality in occupational career and standard of living, remdial action must be taken in the wider context within which the schools are operating — that is, society at large. Educational reform cannot be a substitute for social reform.

Chapter 2

IQ, SCHOOL ATTAINMENT,
AND OCCUPATIONAL CAREER

1. DOES IQ ACCOUNT FOR OCCUPATIONAL SUCCESS?

As has been spelt out in the previous chapter, until recently it was regarded as self-evident that increased equality of participation in further-going education, such as upper secondary schooling and undergraduate studies at university, would automatically enhance equality in occupational career and its remuneration. According to the "liberal" conception, innate intelligence, social background formal schooling, and adult success interact in the following way. Innate talent is by and large distributed randomly over social classes. In order to compensate for poor opportunities of access to higher education students from the lower classes need financial and other types of material aid. They will thereby be placed on a par with those who grew up in privileged circumstances and will be offered the opportunity to prove themselves in the ensuing competition during and after schooling. In Thomas Jefferson's terms, the "natural aristocracy", i.e., those whose innate ability justifies elevation to leading positions in society, will be sifted out by such a process.

The discovery that the removal of economic and geographical barriers and the introduction of grants for students do not affect the participation rates in such a decisive way as was anticipated has inspired a debate in which the basic assumptions in the "liberal" philosophy have been questioned.

The (more or less) inherited IQ has been assumed to bear a rather close relationship to both scholastic and occupational success (Herrnstein, 1973). The relationship between IQ and scholastic success has been thoroughly investigated, simply because intelligence tests, particularly group-administered ones, were devised in order to predict scholastic performance. No wonder, then, that these tests tend to explain between 40 and 65 per cent of the variation in scholastic attainments as measured by examinations, teacher ratings, marks, and number of years of schooling completed. The instruments by means of which pupils are selected from one level to the next in the formal educational system are derived from how they performed (or were perceived to perform by the teachers) at the earlier stages.

IQ has been assumed to be highly predictive of job success because the stratification in terms of status and salaries on the labour market is

41

pretty closely related to the level of education attained. Thus, since IQ tends to be closely related to education, and education in its turn is related to stratification in the job world, IQ can be expected to predict life success in terms of status on the labour market (Herrnstein, 1973; Eysenck, 1973). This relationship, however, has been seriously questioned by researchers coming from different disciplines and representing divergent ideologies.

We shall limit ourselves here to three contributors to the discussion on education as an equalizer of occupational status and income. Thurow (1972) points out the obvious fact that educational attainment (at least in terms of number of years of formal schooling) in the United States has become more equal in recent years. But whereas the spread of education has decreased, the spread of income has increased. Thurow advances a job-competition model as against the prevailing wage-competition model of how the labour market works. According to this model, wages are determined by the relative position of the prospective employee in the queue of applicants and by the distribution of opportunities. In an era of enrolment explosion with an ensuing tendency for an "over supply" of graduates, advanced education becomes a "defensive expenditure" to preserve one's "market share". This means that some university graduates take jobs that have been held by upper secondary school graduates who in their turn take jobs that have previously been held by elementary school graduates. In such a way differentials in earnings between various levels of formal education are preserved or sometimes even increased.

2. THE CHALLENGE BY JENCKS AND ASSOCIATES

Christopher Jencks and his associates (1972) at the Harvard Center for Educational Policy Research have launched the most massive attack on the belief in the importance of IQ and schooling for occupational success. The essential message of the research reported in *Inequality* is that eliminating inequalities of access to schooling would do very little towards eliminating differences in adult careers. If greater adult equality is to be achieved, drastic changes in the existing social order will have to be made.

This same group has made a comprehensive attempt to disentangle the factors that account for differences in adult economic and/or occupational status. The study is remarkable from at least two points of view. In the first place, it is by and large technically an outstanding piece of work. The technique of path analysis has been used in an imaginative and illustrative way. Leaving aside the main part of the monograph, in the two first technical appendices the authors reveal an impressive amount of new information through their re-analyses of data from previous studies of the heridity-environment problem and of the factors accounting for differences in adult status and income. Secondly, they arrive at the startling conclusion that family background, cognitive skills, and educational attainments (amount of formal schooling) account for a diminutive amount of the variation in adult income. This leads them to "reject the liberal notion that equalizing educational opportunity will equalize people's incomes" (*op. cit.*, p. 164). The overall conclusion in terms of the policy implications is that education cannot serve as the reform agent it was supposed to be

according to the classical liberal notion. If gre
achieved, reforms will have to be launched within th
and social welfare policy.

Needless to say, the outcomes of the Jencks'
to a controversial debate at both technical and policy
latter is concerned, the "conservatives" have taken
re-analysis of data from previous studies of the rela
and educational attainment on the one hand, and ad
income or occupational status) on the other, as a justifi
school funds. If schooling does not make much diff   ... poor,
why spend more public money on school education? Marxist critics have
interpreted the study to show that schools are instruments serving the
ruling class in capitalist societies. The school is there to process students
through a certification machinery in order to prepare them for a hierarchically structured society (Gintis, 1971; Bowles and Gintis, 1973).

But it would takes us far afield fully to discuss the implications of
the Jencks study in terms of different social philosophies. In the present
context it seems more fruitful to review some of its basic concepts, its
causal model, and its methodology at large, simply because, irrespective
of different frames of reference in terms of values, we should be able
thereby to to achieve some consensus as to the rationale for arriving at
certain conclusions. But even such a review would go beyond the scope of
this book, because the literature in the wake of the publication of the
Jencks study has been very extensive — not least as concerns the methodological issues. Apart from the standard types of review of a scholarly or
semi-scholarly character, a large number of articles have been written that
take issue with certain aspects of the Jencks methodology or with the
interpretations. Thus, the *Harvard Educational Review* devoted almost the
whole of its February 1973 issue to a series of 8 lengthy reviews by schol-
ars in educational research. It is not possible here to convey a detailed
picture of this methodological debate, but we should, perhaps, try to focus
on some of the more obvious weaknesses that have been pointed out in
the course of it.

Let us first briefly mention the data sources that were used. Jencks
and associates did not collect any original set of data, but re-analysed data
from previous survey studies, namely:

(*1*) The Coleman *et al.* survey (1966);
(*2*) Project Talent (Flanagan *et al.*, 1964);
(*3*) The National Opinion Research Center study of veterans;
(*4*) Data on the intra-generational change of occupation used by Blau
and Ducan (1967); and
(*5*) US Census data.

In the first place, only the Project Talent data are of a longitudinal
character which allows more fruitful multivariate analyses than do cross-
sectional sets of data.

Secondly, the main criterion used as a measure of adult "success"
is earnings. Apart from the fact that, for obvious reasons, this measure
could be extremely unreliable in many individual cases, it is beset with
certain shortcomings. It does not take into account, for example, regional
and age variations in income, and this helps to attenuate the correlation
between the predictors and the earnings.

that part of the adult IQ which is an effect of formal schooling *per se* is also partialled out (Husén, 1950). Furthermore, the regressing out of social background also tends to leave out a considerable part of the "effects" of school.

As has been argued in more detail elsewhere (Husén, 1974), the notion of a meritocracy determined mainly by inherited IQ rests on somewhat shaky ground. But it is another thing to make a case against the meritocracy of *educated* intelligence, which is what Jencks (1972) and his associates as well as Bowles and Gintis (1973) do. All in all, the technical limitations of the empirical studies that have been conducted so far, as well as their conceptual shortcomings, lead us to conclude in an agnostic vein.

3. DOES EDUCATION *PER SE* BEAR ANY RELATIONSHIP TO JOB SUCCESS?

Until recently differences in educational (and subsequent occupational) careers were simply assumed to be determined to a large extent by differences in (inherited) intelligence. Extensive research whereby scholastic aptitude test scores (mostly traditional intelligence test scores) were correlated with criteria of scholastic attainment (such as number of years of academic schooling, marks obtained, or level of performance in examinations) tended to show that some 50 per cent of the variance in the criterion was not attributable to the intellectual predictors (Vernon, 1950). The rest of the variance was supposed to be accounted for by, for instance, motivational factors and social background. Thus nobody, irrespective of how much weight he considered social background to carry for educational success, doubted that "intelligence" as measured by traditional so-called IQ tests was related to long-range success in a highly significant way.

But, as we have mentioned above, this notion has recently been challenged by some young American social scientists who question the whole idea that "cognitive skills" bear any substantial relationship to economic or occupational success. Jencks (1972) and his associates, among whom was Herbert Gintis (1971), have advanced the notion that cognitive skills *per se*, as measured either by IQ or by amount of formal schooling, are more or less irrelevant to economic career as measured by earnings and/or the prestige level reached in the occupational hierarchy. To be sure, IQ is correlated with both educational and occupational success almost to the same degree as is educational attainment with occupational success; but where educational success is partialled out the regression of IQ on occupational success does not amount to very much. As noted above, Bowles and Gintis (1973) obtained a beta-coefficient of only 0.13. Thus, it would seem that IQ is related to occupational success mainly through the educational system. The fact that educational attainment is substantially correlated with economic success, with IQ partialled out, is explained as a "credential effect". The content or quality of what is taught could be quite irrelevant, as employers tend to look at credentials in terms of number of years of schooling or of certificates and degrees. The credentials determine the level of employment and this, in its turn, the salary.

Bajema (1968) points out that, in spite of all the interest taken in identifying, measuring and developing the talent of a nation to its full utilization, very few, if any, follow-up studies have been made to elucidate the relationship between the methods of talent identification and the success attained by the individuals thus identified. He took advantage of data available within the framework of the Kalamazoo Fertility Study (Bajema, 1962) in which some 1,100 individuals had taken a group intelligence test while they were in the sixth grade of the public schools. Of these Bajema (1968) collected data on educational attainment and occupational status for 437 males at the time they reached the age of 45. Educational attainment was defined as number of years of formal schooling, and occupational achievement in accordance with the National Opinion Research Center occupational prestige index.

The zero order correlation were:

IQ and educational attainment	0.58
IQ and occupational prestige	0.46
Educational attainment and occupational prestige	0.63

The multiple correlation between occupational prestige and both IQ and educational attainment was 0.64, which was not significantly higher than for educational attainment alone. Bajema concludes that IQ, in spite of being substantially related to occupational prestige, operates "wholly within the school system".

This finding fits the overall conception of the relationship between IQ, schooling and occupational success that has been advanced by Jencks (1972) and his associates. In their view "schools serve primarily as selection and certification agencies, whose job is to measure and label people". Their role is "primarily to legitimize inequality, not to create it" (op. cit., p. 135). Their main point is thus that the formal educational system is there in order to sort and label people. It serve as a certification agent. The role of IQ tests is to legitimize the ensuing social and occupational stratification.

A crucial problem in taking issue with Jencks, Gintis and others is the extent to which the content of education is relevant or not to the job world. How far is what goes on in school just empty rituals in a sorting and legitimizing process?

Rather than go into the intricate technical issues associated with the problem of whether formal education or acquisition of cognitive skills is job relevant or not, it shall be enough if we point out that Jencks and his associates were confronted (as they say themselves) with an essentially American problem, whereas in Europe national certification without credentials is a widespread phenomenon. Their findings, therefore, have only a limited application outside the United States. The main objection to their logic, however, is that the tests used to assess IQ are validated against criteria of *scholastic* success. Thus, in partialling out school attainment, they also attenuate the correlation between IQ and occupational success.

The weak point in the attempt on the part of Jencks and others to demonstrate that differences in cognitive skills are either unrelated or irrelevant to the job world is the lack of empirical studies that would shed light on the content of teaching and its long-range relevancy. We shall return to this shortly.

Findings from other recent research on the relationship between educational attainments and "life chances" in terms of occupational status or earnings have also become part of the syndrome of the present "crisis" of the school as an institution. In his critical study of the "education craze" after World War II in the United States, Ivar Berg (1971) remarks on the growing tendency to link job opportunities to diplomas and degrees in spite of the fact these may be "pitifully inadequate" as preparation for jobs. In his critique of the economic "rate of return" concept of the effect of education, he shows too that there are correlates to education to which one cannot easily attach pecuniary value – for example attitudes or work-discipline. Furthermore, aggregated data with which economists have worked in their attempts to demonstrate the economic benefits of education to both the individual and the national economy disguise the effects of education in a particular occupational setting, as well as other effects it might have that could eventually be assessed at an aggregate level.

Gintis (1971), challenges the conventional wisdom which holds that "the main effect of schooling is to raise the level of cognitive development of students and that it is this increase which explains the relationship between schooling and earnings" (*op. cit.*, p. 266). He tests an "affective model" according to which the main implicit purpose of schooling is to foster a "disciplined, obedient and well-motivated workforce" (*op. cit.*, p. 267); and, as we have seen, Bowles and Gintis's (1973) view of the role of the formal educational system is explicitly conceived within the framework of Marxist social philosophy.

Gintis (1971) has spelt out the clear-cut thesis that cognitive characteristics or skills have no direct bearing on worker earnings and productivity. The school functions mainly to inculcate certain attitudes of discipline and docility and even hampers the development of characteristics such as creativity and initiative. The structure of the social relations in the formal educational system serves to prepare the individual to function routinely over sustained periods. The grading system by rewarding certain behaviour patterns and penalizing others "tends to reinforce certain modes of individual response to social situations" such as obedience and conformity. The schools are there to foster four types of personality requisites which the labour market demands: "subordinancy", "discipline", "supremacy of cognitive over affective modes of response", and "motivation according to external reward".

Gintis has also analysed empirical data for 649 National Merit Scholarship finalists as reported by Holland (1963) to see it they lend support to his "affective model" of worker competence. Two personality variables, teacher's rating of "citizenship" and student self-rating of "drive to achieve", tended to show highly significant correlations with grade point average. Gintis concludes that "grades depend primarily on affective behavior". (*Op. cit.*, p. 273).

Thus the indisputable substantial correlation between school attainment and "job success" or "job status" is accounted for simply by "assumptions of employers concerning the alleged superiorities of better-educated employees" (Berg, 1971, p. 13). Bowles and Gintis (1973) advance a similar interpretation. The cognitive skills actually produced by the school account for very little of the correlation between schooling and economic success. The major portion is due to the accreditation of individuals and the belief in credentials as such, not to the functional competence provided bu the school.

4. CONCLUDING OBSERVATIONS

Admittedly, there is not much direct evidence as to the functional skills that constitute actual job competence or the extent to which the school has been successful either in providing them or in laying the ground for their acquisition on the job. To a large extent this is due to the difficulty in obtaining criteria not only of "competence" and "success" on a particular job but of "social success" in general. Holland and his associates (1964) have criticized the tendency to overstress cognitive merits in trying to predict post-scholastic success and the use of socially irrelevant criteria in attempts to validate aptitude tests.

The "expedience" value of educational credentials for the employers also refers to the need for a device that objectively, like seniority in promotion, justifies the selection that is made. Selection according to credentials is regarded as a "fair" system with wide acceptance among both employers and employees. Since there tends to be an imbalance between occupational aspirations and the number of attractive job openings some kind of rationing is evidently necessary. Jencks and his associates point out: "But as long as some jobs are more desirable than others, rationing is needed, and credentials serve this purpose quite well", particularly since quite a few adolescents do not like to stay at school longer than necessary whereas others are willing to conform over a longer period (*op. cit.*, p. 183). There is some evidence to support this contention. For instance, the correlation between occupational aspirations and educational plans is substantially higher than that between actual occupational status and actual educational attainment. "The myth that schooling is synonymous with status is thus even more widespread than the reality" (*op. cit.*, p. 184).

Studies conducted in Sweden under the auspices of the 1957 School Commission with the aim of identifying what topics in the core subjects of the curriculum were relevant to the world of work could be cited as the most comprehensive attempt so far to define work-relevant cognitive skills (Husén and Dahllöf, 1960). Since the purpose of the studies was to identify relevant curriculum content, no data were collected on "success on the job" e.g. ratings by supervisors or earnings.

In conclusion, it is difficult to avoid an impression of confusion after all the discussion that has been going on to elucidate whether or not IQ and formal schooling make any difference in adult career. To a large extent this is due to the extremely intricate methodological problems that one is faced with, and to the shortcomings in the data, for instance the lack of longitudinal information that embraces the pre-school years, formal schooling and part of the occupational career. The analytical tools are bedevilled by obvious shortcomings; the coverage of the relevant variables is highly insufficient, and so on. These problems will be dealt with in more detail later in this book. For the moment, we can only note the existence of what Levin (1972) in his review of *Inequality* calls the "social science objectivity gap". That there should be such highly divergent inter-pretations of the existing evidence — from adherents of a more meritocratic view, on the one side, and the critics of the school as an instrument of hierarchization and credentialism on the other, is striking indeed. Even researchers analysing the same set of data have arrived at opposing con-clusions. Those with a meritocratic frame of reference tend to interpret existing relationships between cognitive competence and social status as an outcome of relevant talent that has obtained relevant preparation; the other camp sees it as an artifact of an unjustified belief in the relevance of educated talent.

Chapter 3

THE CONCEPT OF TALENT :
SOCIAL AND DIFFERENTIAL
PSYCHOLOGICAL IMPLICATIONS

1. THREE STAGES IN THE DEVELOPMENT
OF DEFINITIONS OF INTELLIGENCE

We can distinguish three stages in the development of the concept of " talent ", " ability ", or " intelligence " in the social sciences.

1. The first stage consisted of attempts to arrive at a generally acceptable *verbal* definition. Intelligence was taken to denote a fairly unitary, cognitive trait which could be objectively measured within a universal framework of valuative assessment. Representative of this conception are the papers of the symposium arranged in 1921 by the *Journal of Educational Psychology* (Vol. 12, 1921).

The majority of psychologists who have struggled to define intelligence tried to find definitions that were valid for all contexts and all times. Binet stated that it was the ability to pass critical judgments. Terman (1937) defined it as the ability to think abstractly. Köhler (1933) was of the opinion that it has to do with insight into larger contexts. Stoddard (1945) contended that it was primarily the ability to learn and to apply what had been learned, Spearman (1927) that it was the ability to educe relations and correlations, and Wechsler (1944) that it had to do with the ability to adapt means suitable to ends, to act expediently, to think rationally and to cope effectively with one's environment. Before 1940, Stern's (1935) definition that intelligence was the ability to use rational thinking in adapting adequately to new situations was the one most current in Europe.

From a common sense point of view, each of these definitions seems to be at least partly valid. They more or less cover the cognitive domain we have in mind when talking about intelligence. But they all share two weaknesses. In the first place they do not state what *media* intelligence is concerned with. Secondly, they are all related to *valuations* that are not made explicit.

2. The second stage in the development of the concept of intelligence, the stage of *operational* definition, took care of the first of these two weaknesses. Intelligence was defined in the same idiom as were the concepts

51

in physics by Bridgman in the 1930s, i.e., in terms of its measuring instruments. For example, Boring's definition of intelligence as that which is measured by intelligence tests became very widely quoted.

If a person is asked to define temperature, it is more than likely that he will say "temperature is that which we determine with the aid of a thermometer". On the other hand, he risks making himself appear ridiculous if he defines intelligence as that which is measured by a certain intelligence test. But this latter definition is in principle similar to the former, and is what is known as an operational definition. It is often objected that intelligence tests do not measure intelligence "in a deeper sense". The real significance of this objection is perhaps most apparent if we compare it with an objection made against electrical measuring instruments (ammeters, voltmeters, etc.) on the grounds that they do not measure electricity "in a deeper sense".

If we examine the procedures and instruments employed in modern psychometrics, we find that the overwhelming majority of conventional intelligence tests set out to measure things that in one way or another have to do with "symbolic" behaviour—mostly the ability to employ verbal symbols. Intelligence as conceived by most psychologists to day is undoubtedly what is measured by these tests.

Thurstone (1938) in a pioneering study administered an extensive group-test battery to college students. By means of the multiple factor analysis method he had developed he succeeded in identifying a series of group factors ("primary mental abilities"), each of which was manifest in a group of tests that were similar in content and the mental processes required. The group factors were positively correlated, which could be accounted for by a second-order factor identified as "central" or "general" intelligence (Thurstone, 1946). All the tests were administered with printed verbal instructions. Consequently, it could be assumed that the "central" factor was to some extent due to the common format in which the tests were given. For the solution, all the test exercises required "symbolic" behaviour. Hence, it may be assumed that what had been discovered was a more general ability in performing this kind of operation.

3. The third stage in the development of the concept of intelligence is represented by criterion-referenced definitions. Attempts are made thereby to render the underlying social values explicit. Obviously, in terms of value priorities, there is considerable difference between dealing with verbal symbols, like words, sentences and reading passages on the one hand, and material, tangible objects on the other.

2. INTELLIGENCE AS THE ABILITY
TO CARRY OUT ABSTRACT OPERATIONS WITH VERBAL SYMBOLS

The most significant objection that can be raised against the definitions quoted above is that they are all beset with value judgments, the significance of which is seldom made explicit. What, for instance, is meant by "thinking rationally" or by "acting adequately"? What is meant by "good response" in Thorndike's definition according to which intelligence is "the ability to give good responses from the point of view of truth"?

The critical element in all these definitions is, of course, what operationally should be meant by "good", "effective", "rational", "adequate", etc. Is it possible to formulate definitions that would bring out the general validity of these terms? Evidently, this cannot be done. A certain behaviour or a given action can be "rational", "effective", or "adequate" from one point of view and in one evaluative context, but be less rational or effective in another.

Behavioural scientists began to realize rather late that "intelligence" cannot be defined independently of criteria reflecting social value priorities. In other words, when one wishes to assess the intelligence of an individual, one cannot avoid making observations or measurements against the background of a given socio-cultural pattern. It is the system of values, norms, and rules determining human relations that above all characterizes such a pattern.

Different socio-cultural settings vary in the demands they make on intelligence or, to express this more accurately, they require not only different amounts but, particularly different *kinds* of intelligence. Consequently, each social context demands and trains just the variety of intelligence that is needed for that particular setting. Among people at the "food gathering" stage, for example, it is necessary to find and dig up roots or trap animals in order to survive. The man who possesses the greatest manual dexterity and ingenuity to make and use the tools necessary for this achieves the greatest measure of success in his social group. It is the ability to use one's hands efficiently more than the ability to think abstractly that brings such social success.

In the modern technological and complex society, it is the ability to operate with verbal and numerical symbols (letters, words, combinations of words, figures and combinations of figures) that occupies the highest position on the prestige scale, and consequently is the criterion for intelligence. In fact, a survey of all the most widely-used intelligence tests and the major studies carried out with them reveals quite clearly that their more or less implicit aim is to measure the ability to deal with symbols – and it is this that is referred to as "scholastic ability". Since adaptation to modern civilization depends to an increasing extent on such ability, and as modern technology is the outcome of such "symbolic" behaviour, it should be possible, without incurring serious objections, to define intelligence as the ability to operate symbols, not only in school but in working life and in a technological society at large. Typically enough, the most widely used intelligence tests have been validated against scholastic criteria, such as teacher ratings, grades and similar measures of attainment. The test most widely used in the United States for college entrance is not even referred to as an "intelligence test". It carries the label "Scholastic Aptitude Test".

If all this is borne in mind when group comparisons are made with respect to "intelligence", certain confusions can be avoided. It should, for instance, cause no astonishment that considerable mean score differences are found between various racial or occupational groups when they are given conventional intelligence tests. It may seem banal to point this out; nevertheless investigations are still being carried out (cf., e.g., Jensen, 1973) with the aid of such conventional intelligence tests to measure differences in "intelligence" and/or "educability" between various racial, social or occupational groups.

Lundberg (1939, p. 453) was the first to point out the vicious circle in the logic employed to prove that a test does in fact measure intelligence. Presumably, a test that is properly constructed should be able to differentiate between more or less intelligent individuals. By "more intelligent" individuals we mean those who, in *our* cultural or social pattern and with the criteria employed there, are able to get along more efficiently. The criteria of intelligence employed are based on certain socially-determined standards of judgment, such as success at school, in business, in politics, and so on.

If we define intelligence as the ability manifest in "symbolic" and particularly verbal behaviour, we must remember that the differences found to exist between, say, various occupational groups may be due to a large extent to differences in verbal experience and training that are implicit in the various forms of vocational training and in the vocations themselves. Every setting and every occupation demands a special ability and tends to promote the necessary kind of training. The scientist elaborates abstract theories; the wrestler acquires perfect muscular coordination; the instrument-maker attains a special manual dexterity. It will be readily understood that tests that are validated against criteria pertaining to one of these occupations will generally, on this account, give higher results for people who are familiar with the occupation selected. But since in modern technological society those who can employ verbal symbols most effectively are generally the most "successful", and since the increased ability to deal with verbal media implies an even greater ability to master our environment in both its animate and inanimate aspects, the ability to operate with symbols is, as a rule, more or less tacitly assumed to constitute intelligence.

Occupations that require a high degree of verbal skills are accorded the most prestige; as a rule, they are better paid and, what is more important, they require certain verbal training and skills over and above the basic education that is available to all in the primary schools. In these circumstances, it is not surprising that representatives of manual trades score lower, on the average, than do representatives of the intellectual occupations. Neither should we be astonished that those who, on average, had better school reports "get on better" than those who had worse ones.

Attempts have been made to derive certain formal characteristics from abstract intellectual operations. Intelligence has been defined as the ability to combine things in order to form new "constructions"; or the ability consciously to use our mental apparatus in order to adapt ourselves effectively to new conditions (Stern, 1935, p. 424; Spearman, 1927, p. 161 *et seq.*). Spearman considered that what was most essential for general intelligence (the *g* factor) was the ability to think in terms of relations and correlations. If we consider both the receptive and creative aspect of such operations, we could say that abstract intelligence, displayed usually through verbal media, is the ability to acquire complex information, to recognize and establish relations between its components and to communicate the outcomes.

As observed already, most so-called intelligence tests are validated against scholastic criteria, such as teacher ratings and grades. Thus, it is typical that most scholastic tests primarily measure verbal and/or numerical ability. This is the case for instance, with the widely-used Scholastic Aptitude Test (SAT) developed by the Educational Testing Service and given to the majority of applicants for college entrance in the United States.

There are many indications that scholastic ability, irrespective of how it is assessed, has increasingly become the prime factor in social promotion and success. In the introduction to the section on "School Environment" in *Equality of Educational Opportunity*, Coleman (1966) starts out with the following statement:

In the first century of this Nation's history, opportunity was associated with the frontier; the pioneer was the symbol of success. For much of the second century opportunity has been associated with expanding industrial enterprise; the self-made man has been the symbol of success. Today, opportunity must be found in a highly organized technological society; the scientist is the symbol of success *(op. cit.*, p. 36).

The "meritocratic" prospect implied in this statement has been elaborated by Daniel Bell (1973) in his book *The Coming of Post-industrial Society*. He envisages for this society a "new centrality of *theoretical* knowledge, the primacy of theory over empiricism, and the codification of knowledge into abstract systems of symbols that can be translated into many different and varied circumstances" *(op. cit.*, p. 343).

The more important formal education becomes to the individual in getting promoted in the job world and in being receptive of proper job training and retraining, the more important become the cognitive skills for getting ahead in life. Thus, educated intelligence tends to become the democratic substitute for inherited wealth and privileges of birth.

3. CRITICISM OF THE OVEREMPHASIS ON SCHOLASTIC (VERBAL) INTELLIGENCE

It is justifiable to conceive of "talent" or "intelligence" mainly as academic talent – that is, the ability to move ahead in the formal educational system? John L. Holland, former Director of Research for the National Merit Scholarship Corporation, has challenged the use of the concepts of "talent" and "loss of talent". In an article describing a "plan for practical action and research", Holland and Astin (1962) draw attention to some of the "fallacies and limitations" of the current definitions of the two concepts.

The major objection raised is that "talent" is defined in terms of school grades (marks) or aptitude test scores. Such definitions are far too narrow and to a large extent out of context. The authors propose a criterion-oriented approach which defines talent in terms of "socially relevant performance". "Talented performance, the criterion, consists in achievement or action which is judged to be of intrinsic value to the self and to society. Such a designation of talented performance, of course, requires value judgments regarding what kinds of human performance are more important to society than others. " *(op. cit.*, p. 78).

Apart from their lack of criterion-reference, the conventional scholastic aptitude tests are criticized as measures of talent because they limit themselves to *one* type of talent and leave out non-intellectual, including motivational, factors. Talented performance is said to be one that is of value to the self *and* to society. However, what is valued by the self may be quite different from what is particularly valued by society. The major point in Charles Reich's (1970) analysis of the changing value priorities among American youth is that " Consciousness II " is concerned with conformity to the values of the big organizations, of the established society, whereas "Consciousness III" has its focus on values conducive to self-realization, for instance the pursuit of interests in art and music. It is self-evident that in our present society, with its emphasis on " Consciousness II " values, the academic achievements in terms of school grades, examinations and degrees play an increasingly dominant role within the meritocratic pattern. Thus, it is not easy to make a strong case for a minimization of academic performances when defining " talent " as " socially relevant performance ".

Whereas academic ability is consistently the best predictor of academic success at subsequent levels in an educational system, doubts have been raised as to the relationship between academic ability and other socially useful talents. It is questioned why the educational system should limit itself to seek out, develop, judge and reward just academic ability, particularly in groups already rather select in terms of scholastic achievement. Holland and Nichols (1964), who studied cognitive and affective predictors of various types of extracurricular achievements among American college students, found that successful pursuits of aesthetic and social activities were poorly predicted by instruments that generally constitute scholastic aptitude test batteries.

Holland has made a case for a wider conception of talent. He and his co-workers have devised a series of instruments, both cognitive and affective, for predicting academic and extracurricular performances among students of superior scholastic aptitude. The students were among the National Merit Scholarship finalists and therefore consisted of an extremely select and academically homogeneous group – a fact that should be taken into consideration in interpreting his findings. Because of the great homogeneity in scholastic aptitude, one could expect non-intellectual variables to be much more predictive than in a representative group. This turned out to be the case. Correlations were computed between all the predictors established in the senior high-school year and seven criteria of academic and extracurricular accomplishments. Non-intellectual predictors tended to predict college extracurricular accomplishments in fields such as art, music, writing and leadership just as well as grades in high school predicted academic performance in college. Holland and Nichols themselves point out that the group they studied is far from being representative and that the findings therefore cannot be generalized to representative groups of college students. (op. cit., p. 63).

To the extent that the criticism of the concept of " talent " is valid, the concept of " loss of talent ", frequently used during the 1950s and early 60s, has its shortcomings. Holland and Astin (1962) rightly emphasize that the fact that a high-school senior with high grades or aptitude scores is not going to college does not necessarily mean that his talent or talents are " lost ". He might have another type of talent that is more developed and more cultivated by a higher level of interest and motivation than his academic potential. Furthermore, the usual conception of " loss of talent " takes for granted that the only socially useful talent is the one that helps one to go ahead in higher education. They therefore propose that loss of talent be defined as " the non-utilization of those personal capacities which

56

are necessary for the occurence of socially significant performance " (*op. cit.*, p. 79).

Again, it should be emphasized that in the modern technological society, in both socialist and capitalist systems, the ability to reach high levels of attainment in the formal educational system increasingly tends to become a prerequisite for a successful adult career according to " Consciousness II " values. Those who are able to make socially-recognized careers in fields such as art and athletics are rare exceptions. Even in the Soviet Union, a young person who sets out to become an engineer by getting into a good institute of technology has a much greater likehood of success than the one who wants to become a professional ballet dancer (Yanowitch and Dodge, 1969; Rutkewitch, 1969).

4. THE STRUCTURE OF ABILITIES

Psychological folklore distinguishes two major types of ability: practical-vocational and academic-theoretical. The former type is believed to suit manual occupations (tangible and down to-earth), whereas the latter type gets along more easily with the printed and written word and feels at home in the thin air of abstractions. The two types of ability have, furthermore, been traditionally conceived to stand in a compensatory relationship to each other. The person with an academic bent is thought to be clumsy and out of place in the world of concrete realities, while the opposite is the case among those with a practical bent. In the old Latin school many teachers advised students who were not very successful to return to the plough, behind which their future was predicted to become more successful than behind a desk.

Modern differential-psychological research has not been able to establish a compensatory relationship between so-called practical and so-called academic or scholastic ability (see e.g., Vernon, 1950; Elmgren, 1952). On the contrary, they are positively correlated, admittedly at a modest level. An individual who performs well academically (i.e., is successful in handling words, figures and abstractions) also tends to perform well in practical, concrete tasks. In our modern, complex technological society with its increasing demands on educated ability and the progressive "academization" of what formerly were unskilled occupations, we can note a tendency towards an even closer relationship between the two types of ability. This is also reflected in the programme and curricula of the secondary schools. The previously rather marked dualism between vocational and academic tracks is now yielding to a merged comprehensive programme. The development in Sweden can be cited as an illustration. For a long time admission to the *gymnasium* (the university preparing 3-year stage) required an academic curriculum during the last three grades of the 9-year comprehensive school. At any rate, the student was required to complete the academic track in grade 9 in order to qualify for *gymnasium* entrance. In order to qualify for university entrance the student then had to complete the *gymnasium*. Those who had completed the two-year continuation school or vocational courses of varying lengths were as a rule not eligible for university entrance. This has now changed, so that each of the four programmes in grade 9 qualifies for the new *gymnasium*, which is a merger of the old academic *gymnasium*, the continuation school, and the vocational schools. The new *gymnasium* in its turn qualifies for entrance to most post-secondary educational institutions – in principle at any rate, for the prospect depends in some programmes or professional graduate schools upon the ratio of applicants to the places available.

The term "ability" as used here refers mainly to scholastic ability. This is by no means an expression of arbitrary preference, for we are here dealing with ability in its relationship to the educational system and the extent to which the achievement of equality of educational opportunity in that system turns upon differences in abilities brought about by socio-economic background.

5. THE HEREDITY-ENVIRONMENT CONTROVERSY

Two hundred years ago, the French philosopher Helvétius in his famous treatise *On the Mind* put forward the fundamental proposition, later reflected in the American Declaration of Independence, that "all men are created equal". This opened up a wide field for social and, even more so, educational reformers. "L'éducation peut tout" was the principle epitomized in, for instance, Rousseau's *Emile – ou de l'Education* written at about the same time.

But the view that mental differences are largely or entirely inherited is also time-honoured and was later substantiated by empirical research. Sir Francis Galton was the first to suggest the use of standardized tests in measuring mental abilities. He was also the first to carry out studies of twins, without recognizing, however, that there were two categories of twin pairs, monozygotic (arising from the same fertilized ovum) and dizygotic (arising from two simultaneously fertilized ova).

The next "wave" of environmentalism came from behaviouristic psychology, primarily from John Watson, who in provocative statements aired a boundless optimism about what education could do. Another source of environmentalism was modern social psychology. It was no coincidence that these conceptions of the nature-nurture problem spread so easily in the United States, for they fitted the melting-pot ideology that had so strong an influence upon rhetoric in education is that country. Whether and to what extent it really influenced actual educational practices is another question.

The nature-nurture controversy is not one of the major issues to be dealt with here; but "nature", i.e., heredity as determined by genetic equipment, is conceived of as setting strict limits to educational treatment. The more genetically determined a trait (intelligence, for instance) may be, the less the likelihood that a given educational treatment will succeed upon it. This prompts us to examine some principal aspects of the problem. A focal point in the presentation that follows is the concept of "heritability" and the empirical basis for the quantitative estimations that have played such a prominent role in the debate on intellectual group differences.

As mentioned earlier, the intense emotional involvement evoked by the debate on the relative "influence" of heredity versus environment in determining human abilities stems from the far-reaching political implications of the problem.

The seemingly so academic nature-nurture controversy, which in recent years in the United States has erupted into an acidulous public debate with an immense polemic literature, might superficially appear to focus on differences in opinion about how certain group differences, especially race differences, should be interpreted. To be very specific: is the average difference of 15 IQ points between White and Black school children or between upper and lower class children, irrespective of race, mainly due to genetic or environmental factors? A tremendous amount of evidence casting light on this problem has been collected over the last two decades. Nobody who has tried to penetrate the smokescreens of the debate and get down to the facts denies that race or social class differences in the conventional IQ tests are *to some extent* conditioned by genetic differences. On balance, it cannot be claimed that the major position is genetically conditioned. Jencks (1972) and his associates have reviewed the relevant literature and taken advantage of the data that lend themselves to fruitful re-analyses. They end up with an estimate of some 45 per cent of the measured interindividual differences (*op. cit.*, p. 71). This estimation is derived from attempts to determine heretability that are based on what the authors themselves regard as a " major theoretical limitation " (*op. cit.*, p. 286), namely that genetic and environmental factors operate in an additive way – an assumption that has been doubted by both psychologists and geneticists (see, e.g., Husén, 1963; Moran, 1973). But even with an heritability index of 80 (i.e., with an estimate that 80 per cent of the individual differences in IQ are accounted for by genetic factors) a substantial margin for environmental influences remains (Bereiter, 1970).

The intense emotional involvement in the problem of the relative "influence " of genetic and environmental factors on IQ stems, as we have already remarked, from the far-reaching educational, social and – not least – political implications of the problem. This has been made explicit by several radical critics of the " IQ ideology ". The traditional liberal conception that, in a society rewarding merit, social classes sort themselves out on the basis of innate capacity has been challenged by critics like Bowles and Gintis, Jencks and his associates, and Edmonds and Moore (1973). The last two authors go so far as to characterize intelligence testing as " a political expression of these groups in society who most successfully establish behaviour they value as a measure of intelligence " (*op. cit.*, p. 12). Thus, in a way, intelligence testing can be regarded as an instrument of political oppression. Those who believe that IQ is a major determinant of social success, and mainly innate, also tend to believe that those who fail or are poor have arrived at their poor conditions because of their inferior genes.

Thus, what on the surface seems to be an academic issue, relates in fact to the struggle between two ideologies: one that wants to preserve the existing social and economic order (including education) and another that wants to bring about change.

The father of behaviourism, John Watson, once made this proposal: " Give me half-a-dozen healthy infants and my own world to bring them up in, and I will guarantee to train any or all of them to become whatever you select – doctor, lawyer, artist, engineer, tinker, tailor, beggarman, thief ". Sir Cyril Burt, who quotes this statement, says that it is

Helvétius in modern dress. This is in an article in which he deals with the problem of mental differences between children in " Black Paper Two – The Crisis in Education " (Cox and Dyson, 1970) to which we have already had cause to refer. This brochure severely criticizes recent changes in English education and accuses the school reforms, particularly the introduction of comprehensive education, of having brought about a " marked decline in standards ". The main reason given for this is that the egalitarians have not realized that their principles have "grave limitations when applied in the classroom ". Since about 80 per cent of differences in general intelligence are allegedly dependent upon heredity, and since a high level of innate ability is required to pass certain qualifying examinations, it can be concluded that social class differences (as well as regional differences) in participation in higher education mainly depend upon group differences inherited from one generation to the next. Burt estimates that the proportion of children with a professional or white-collar class background who have the innate capacity to take a university degree is about five times as high as among those whose parents are manual workers. His conclusion is: " Class differences thus become inevitable in any civilized society " (op. cit., p. 20).

Even if one goes along with Burt, however, the existing differences in participation, which in many countries are far greater than he assumes, still leave much room for an equalization policy. Until recently, participation rates in higher education in many OECD countries have been more than 25 times higher among young people with a professional or executive background than among those from working-class homes.

It should be noted that the belief that *individual* differences are mainly inherited is closely related to the belief that social class and race differences are inherited. In *Educability and Group Differences* Jensen (1973) emphasizes that it is not justifiable to generalize from *within* group to *between* group heritability. However, he is convinced that the evidence derived from within group heritability studies imposes " severe restraints on some of the most popular environmental theories of existing racial and social class differences in educational performance " (op. cit., p. 1). Considering the circumstantial evidence, a genetic explanation can, therefore, be advanced for the disparities that actually exist.

The egalitarians who want to remove or reduce disparities advance the notion that intellectual differences are, to a large extent, outcomes of differences in conditions of upbringing, culture, etc., and that education could be instrumental in reducing them. Attempts to play down the role of heredity are therefore consistent with the belief that social change could contribute to greater equality, both in educational participation and in social conditions generally. It is unnecessary here to deal comprehensively with the entire environment-vs.-heredity controversy, but it is relevant to examine a few of its principal aspects to put the problem in proper perspective.

The starting point for all attempts to estimate the " proportions " of the hereditary and environmental determinants lies with *individual differences*. We find by means of tests or other procedures of assessment that most of the personality traits under consideration show a large variability. What, at best, we can achieve is to find out the proportions of the *observed variance* (not of the absolute score on a test) within a *particular population* brought up in a *particular socio-cultural setting*, accounted for by hereditary and environmental factors respectively. If we succeed in quantifying the two types of influences, the generalizations are, of course, *limited to the population from which the sample cases are drawn*.

This means, then, that the nature-nurture problem has to do with the relative importance of genetic factors, as compared with upbringing, education, and other influences, in causing *variability* in certain traits such as intelligence or scholastic ability. Thus, about the best we can do is to determine to what extent the *rank order* in a given trait between the individuals drawn from a certain population (i.e., their *relative* positions) has been determined by the two sources of influence. This does not say anything at all about how the absolute status of the individual, let alone the group, is determined, influenced or affected by the environmental or hereditary factors.

Psychological *research on twins*, particularly for the opportunity it offers to compare monozygotic twins brought up together and apart, has come to be regarded by some as the principal key to the problem of "separating" hereditary from environmental influences on the variance of, for instance, intelligence. In fact, both Burt and Jensen have drawn almost entirely upon such studies when arriving at the conclusion that 80 per cent of the variance in measured intelligence is accounted for by innate factors (Burt, 1966; Jensen, 1969, 1972 and 1973).

The other main strategy employed in arriving at estimates of the relative influence of genetic factors on intellectual variation is comparison of biological parents with their children reared in adoptive homes, and of adoptive parents with their adopted children.

6. HERITABILITY

The concept of "heritability" has played a pivotal role in the debate that followed Jensen's 1969 article in the *Harvard Educational Review* on whether or not one can "boost" IQ. Jensen reviewed the empirical evidence, among which he attached particular weight to the analyses conducted by Cyril Burt (*op. cit.*, p. 33 *et seq.*). Statistically, heritability is the squared correlation between the genotype and the phenotype; that is, as a statistical index it tells us how much of the variance of observed differences in a particular trait is "explained" by genetic differences. The first attempt to arrive at such an index was made by Newman, Freeman and Holzinger (1937) in their classical study of identical twins partners brought up apart. Other sources of empirical evidence that have been used for arriving at estimates of heritability are comparisons between intra-pair differences among identical and fraternal twins brought up together, between genetically related and unrelated children brought up together, and between genetically related children brought up with their biological parents and in foster homes.

Those who lean toward a hereditarian view regard the index of 80 almost as a magical figure. The first one to arrive at the estimate that 80 per cent of IQ differences were genetically conditioned was Cyril Burt (1958) and his analyses are extensively referred to by Jensen. Eysenck (1973), Herrnstein (1973) and others have also accepted 80 per cent as being a more or less definitive outcome of heritability estimations. Jencks and his associates (1972), in the extensive re-analyses of data from previous studies to which we have already referred, arrived at rather conflicting results. They found that investigations of twins, and studies where comparisons had been made between unrelated children reared together and siblings reared together, both tended to yield *higher* indices of heritability in England than in the United States. They suspect that this is an effect of greater environmental similarity in England than in the United States – an explanation for which there does not seem to be any support (cf. e.g., Comber and Keeves, 1973). The twin studies cited from England, other than the one by Shields (1962), were all conducted by Burt.

Jencks and his associates, after having re-analyzed the main investigations, arrived at a heritability estimate of 45 per cent. "This estimate could easily be off by 10 per cent either way, and it might be off by as much as 20 per cent either way" (*op. cit.*, p. 71). Thus, the "sacred" figure of 80 per cent heritability of IQ is by no means consistently supported by the empirical research so far reported.

But taking all the methodological snags and the lack of representativity into account, there is evidence to support the conclusion that *in our society* genetic conditions account for about half the observed variation in cognitive competence. The qualification in italics is important because estimates of heritability are derived from observations made in a particular population and are a particular reflection of a socio-historical fact. In a population with close to zero variability in environmental conditions, heritability will be close to 100 per cent, whereas in a society with extreme social inequality and ascriptive allocation on the basis of social origin it can be expected to come close to zero. Thus, one cannot generalize from one population to another, as Jensen himself pointed out when applying heritability estimates derived from White populations to Black populations.

Furthermore, in terms of its application to specific *individuals* one great limitation of the heritability index is that it expresses an *average*. Strictly speaking it is tied to the specific populations from which it is derived and tells us nothing about the heritability within certain subpopulations or in particular individuals.

Parents with favourable genes tend to provide a somewhat more favourable milieu for their children, regardless of whether they happen to have inherited above-average genes or not. But parents with above-average genes tend to have children with above-average genes. Thus, genetically advantaged parents provide their children with the double advantage of having both favourable genes and a favourable milieu. Statistically this means that the genetic equipment tends to co-vary with the milieu. Those who have considered interaction effects have in most cases put then down to heredity. Jencks (1972) and his associates point out that, if because of some strange prejudice red-heads were banned from good education, one would after some generations find a correlation between red hair and scholastic attainment that is entirely spurious. But that is what often happens is ascribing certain attributes to heritability (Jencks, 1972, p. 66-7).

Most of the models used (and this is made explicit by Jencks and his associates) assume that the relationship between phenotype and environment is additive. This is rightly characterized as a "major theoretical limitation" (*op. cit.*, p. 266). Moran (1973) points out that the concept of heritability is "highly useful in animal breeding" where, however, the assumption that genetic and environmental affects are additive is valid. But this method of estimating heritability cannot be used for human characteristics, in which case the genetic and environmental components tend to co-vary. He specifically states that it is not applicable for heritability estimations with regard to human intelligence.

The lack of understanding of what heritability really means has contributed to a confusion of interpretations. Even if we assume that there is practically no interaction between IQ and environment and that heritability is in fact 80 per cent there is still a sizable margin for environmental "influences". Bereiter (1970) has attempted to determine the size of this margin by regarding the observed scores on an IQ test as the sum of scores of genetic and environmental factors having distributions with standard deviations of 14 and 7 IQ points respectively. Substantial differences in IQ can be accounted for by environmental factors. Thus, the finding arrived at by Skeels (1939), that on average an increase of 30 IQ points occurred when orphanage children were moved to individualized care, are in agreement with a heritability index of 80.

Again, ignoring the interaction between genetic and environmental factors and assuming that heritability is 80 per cent, Bereiter (1970) applied his model of calculating the separate effects to "Utopian environmental conditions". If by means of massive social welfare programmes and other policy actions aimed at improving conditions the average environmental standard were raised by two standard deviations and the standard deviation of these conditions were reduced to about a half, the average increase of IQ would amount to 14 points. The spread, however, would be practically the same, the standard deviation being reduced by one point only. Thus, a massive redistribution of environmental resources is not likely to change the rank order between individuals. The impact of environmental improvements affecting all the individuals, and because of redistribution measures the disadvantaged ones in particular, does not seem to affect individual differences in IQ substantially. It should be emphasized, however, that this is under the assumptions that heritability is 80 per cent and that genetic and environmental factors do not co-vary.

7. CRITICISM OF THE DATA BASE
FOR HERITABILITY ESTIMATIONS

In the critical analysis just made of the concept of "heritability" we have shown that attempts so far to estimate the amount of variance in the phenotype accounted for by the genotype have been based on the assumption of an additive relationship between environmental and genetic factors; and that certain "irrational", cumulative, relationships between genetic and environmental factors can occur — as demonstrated by the example of the red-haired children.

After having reviewed the literature arising from the debate on the heredity-environment issue one is inclined to endorse a statement made by Thomas Sowell (1973) in commenting in *Change* magazine on the famous *Harvard Education Review* debate in 1969. It is indeed to the point when he says that "the whole area of heredity, environment and testing is an almost bottomless pit of complexities" (*op. cit.*, p. 127).

The estimation made by Burt on the basis mainly of studies of monozygotic twins reared apart in England that heritability as indexed by the ratio between genotypic variance and phenotypic variance is about 80 per cent has been taken for granted without scrutiny of the data base or − in many cases − the methodology. Jencks and his associates (1972) reviewed four American, four English and two Swedish studies in which identical and fraternal twins had been compared with respect to intra-pair similarities. They found considerable differences between countries. Thus, the American studies yielded lower heritabilities than the English studies. They also examined the Newman-Freeman-Holzinger (1937) investigation in the United States, the Burt (1943 and 1966) and the Shields (1962) investigations in England, and the Juel-Nielsen (1965) study in Denmark. Burt arrives at a higher estimate of heritability than any of the others. After having reviewed the existing literature on twin studies, Jencks and his associates conclude, as we have seen above, that the heritability in IQ as determined by Stanford-Binet is around 45 per cent in the United States. On the whole, they estimate that another 20 per cent is due to the correlation between genetic and environmental influences, while 35 per cent is purely environmental.

Thus, the heritability index which has played such a prominent role in the recent heredity-environment debate is at best, as Cronbach puts it, a "socio-historic fact": it expresses the average ratio between genetic variance and genotypic variance in a particular population, in a particular situation, measured by a particular test, purportedly valid for a particular personality trait. In most cases this has been IQ as assessed by tests devised to measure and predict scholastic success. The possibility of generalizing from heritability estimations is, to say the least, limited. They have been derived mainly from twin studies many of which − and certainly the one by Burt which usually is referred to when heritability is said to be about − are not based on randomly selected pairs.

But strangely enough the data themselves, particularly from studies of separately reared monozygotic pairs, were not subjected to thorough scrutiny with particular reference to the validity of certain of the assumptions upon which the heritability estimations were based. This has recently been done by Kamin (1974) who examined the four major studies in which intra-pair similarities of separately reared identical twins were assessed and in some cases compared with intra-pair similarities for identical twins reared together as well as with fraternal twins reared together. His collated findings are presented in Table 3.1:

Table 3.1 INTRA-PAIR CORRELATIONS IN INTELLIGENCE
FOR MONOZYGOTIC TWIN PAIRS REARED IN SEPARATE MILIEUX

Investigator	Test used	Correlation	Number of pairs
Burt (1943, 1966)	Some individual intelligence test	0.86	53
Shields (1962)	Dominoes + Mill Hill, Voc. Test	0.77	37
Newman *et al.* (1937)	Standford-Binet	0.67	19
Juel-Nielsen (1965)	Wechsler	0.62	12

Source: Kamin (1974).

Burt's lack of precise information about the procedural details of his data collection is disturbing, and Kamin arrives at the harsh conclusion that the numbers he has arrived at are "simply not worthy of scientific attention" (*op. cit.*, p. 11). Shields, who has provided quite a lot of detail about the circumstances under which his data were collected, informs the reader in an appendix that in 27 cases (i.e., in the majority) the two "separated" monozygotic twins had been brought up in related branches of the parents' family. The intra-pair correlation for these 27 cases was 0.83 as compared to 0.51 the remaining 13 cases. The main snag with the Newman *et al.* (1937) study is that the test scores are correlated with age, something that confounds the observed intra-pair correlations.

There are yet other circumstances that put limits on generalizing from twin studies to the population of single-borns. Pre-natal conditions, for example, are difficult, if not impossible, to control. For representative groups of twins, both among school children and adults, it has consistently been found (Husén, 1959, 1960, 1963) that twins score about 0.25 standard deviations below the mean of single-borns on all kinds of cognitive tests, be they "pure" intelligence tests or achievement tests. This applies to both identical and fraternal twins. There is also a somewhat higher frequency of mental retardation among twins than among single-borns. One reasonable hypothesis that could be advanced as an explanation for this is the difference in pre-natal conditions, where twins have to "compete" for supplies from their mother.

Identical pairs are not treated in the same way as fraternal pairs by parents, siblings, teachers, and schoolmates. There is a strong tendency (Husén, 1959) with identical twin pairs for the two individuals to be mistaken for each other, even by parents and teachers. This means, then, that the identical partners tend to be treated much more alike by parents and teachers than are the partners in fraternal pairs. It has been shown beyond any doubt that identical pairs are not only treated more alike but usually dress more alike and want to do the same things, whereas among fraternal pairs there is about the same tendency as among siblings in general not to be dressed alike and not to do the same things. Hence, there is a clear interaction between zygosity (i.e., heredity) and environment which over time and in certain respects tends to make identical twin pairs more alike, for instance in school attainments, whereas the fraternal pairs are likely to become more differentiated with increasing age. The effect of such differential treatment is an increased difference between intra-class correlations for the respective twin categories (as can be seen from the formulae proposed) and this tends to overestimate heritability (Husén, 1963).

What environment can "achieve" is assessed by comparing identical twin pairs reared together and apart. The size of the intra-class correlations evidently depends on the degree of difference between the environments in which the partners in identical pairs adopted in separate homes have been reared. The question then arises as to what extent the differences between the homes in which the partners are reared average the same as the differences between any pairs of homes compared at random. To what extent has selective placement occurred when the twin partners are adopted in different homes? Jensen (1969, p. 51 *et seq.*) seems to have assumed that the environments of identical twins reared apart in adoptive homes were uncorrelated, and so did Burt (1970). But, as has been shown by Kamin (1974) this is not always the case.

Heritability estimations derived from twin studies should, of course, be based on *representative samples* in order to allow generalizations in the first place to twins in general and, under certain assumptions, to single-borns. Jensen's calculations of heritability were based primarily on investigations by Burt (1958, 1966) and on figures from a survey of 14 studies of identical and 11 studies of fraternal pairs collated by Erlenmeyer-Kimling and Jarvik (1963). If three large, representative twin samples are included and the correlations are weighted according to sample size, a lower median value for the identical and a higher one for the fraternal is obtained. This means that the heritability estimate obtained by Jensen (1969) is reduced from 0.80 to somewhere between 0.40 and 0.60 (Schacht-Breland, 1971).

The other main source of information drawn upon in attempts to estimate the heritability of IQ is that provided by studies of *adopted children*. In his article in the *Harvard Educational Review* Jensen makes reference to studies comparing correlations between biologically related siblings who have been brought up together and apart respectively, and between biologically unrelated children brought up together and apart. Jensen (1972, p. 124-5) gives median correlations for biological siblings reared together of about 0.50 as compared with about 0.45 for those reared apart. The corresponding correlations for children who are biologically unrelated are 0.25 and 0.00 respectively. These figures hint at the underlying "datum" from which the operation of hereditary influences has been inferred, namely that related siblings reared apart are correlated. Furthermore, studies that have focused on comparisons between adopted children and their adoptive parents, and between biological parents and their children, consistently show that the correlation is higher in the second case.

Jencks and his associates (1972) have reviewed the relevant studies of adopted children in their attempt to estimate the heritability of IQ scores. They point out that such studies are "usually rather messy", simply because of selective placement policies of adoption agencies. Legitimate middle class children are rarely placed for adoption; working class families with adopted children are not representative, etc. (*op. cit.*, p. 79-80). Kamin (1974), in his scrutiny of four major American studies of adopted children reaches the conclusion that "foster families are a very highly selected group and evidently provide a very special kind of family environment" (*op. cit.*, p. 16). After having looked at the classical studies by Freeman *et al.* (1928), Burks (1928), Leahy (1935) and Skodak and Skeels (1949), he points out, like Jensen, that adoptive parents correlate lower with their adopted children than do control parents with their own children. But a collation of the studies cited shows that the correlation between adoptive parents and their *own* children does not significantly differ from that between the adoptive parents and their adopted children. Thus, the somewhat unexpected but rather logical conclusion is that *within* adoptive homes it does not seem to make any difference whether the child is adopted or biological. There seems to be a correlation between the socioeconomic status of the biological mothers and that of the foster home. If, as is indicated by the analyses conducted by Jencks (1972) and his associates, part of the relationship between parental occupation and test scores is accounted for by genetic factors (they estimate it to be 30 per cent), then the task of disentangling how much of parent-child similarities among adopted children is due to genetic and how much to environmental factors becomes a formidable – not to say an impossible – one.

Several investigators who have tried to come to grips with the wealth of evidence on the relationship between environmental conditions and cognitive development have become convinced that these relationships are not linear but curvilinear. There are, in other words, "threshold effects". Bereiter (1970) advances a "cautious hypothesis" about this and points out that we may expect a much stronger effect from socio-economic status if we move from slum conditions to ordinary working class environment than if we move from the latter to a middle class environment. Variables such as income, quality of housing and availability of reading material are likely to be threshold variables that make no difference above a certain level. Supportive evidence at the macro-level is provided by the Six-Subject Survey conducted by the International Association for the Evaluation of Educational Achievement (cf., e.g., Comber and Keeves, 1973; Thorndike, 1973; Peaker, 1974). The industrialized countries, in spite of having most diverse educational systems, tended to bring their children up to the same average level of performance by the age of 10 or 14 when schooling is still compulsory, whereas the developing countries on average scored one to two standard deviations below the cluster of developed countries.

The fundamental assumption, behind heritability estimations based on twin research is simply that environments of dizygotic co-twins (fraternal twins brought up together) are no more dissimilar than those of monozygotic co-twins (identical twins brought up together). Excess intra-class correlations for monozygotic pairs are interpreted as genetically determined. This assumption becomes suspect, however, when viewed in the light of studies of attachment within twin pairs (Husén, 1959). Scarr (1968) studied 61 twin pairs (all girls of elementary school age) and found that monozygotic co-twins were treated more similarly than dizygotic co-twins. The question then arose as to whether this should be interpreted as conditioned by genetic factors or was an effect of greater similarity in environment. If the latter was the case one could say that the parents, in a way, "trained similarities". Scarr took advantage of 11 pairs where the parents were wrong about the zygosity of the twins in order to obtain an answer to the question whether the similarity or dissimilarity in treatment was determined by the "belief" about the zygosity, i.e., by an environmental circumstance, or by genetic relatedness. The sample was too small to provide a conclusive answer even through the analysis suggested that it was genetic relatedness that conditioned the similarity in treatment.

Several researchers have worked on the idea of the threshold effect. Scarr-Salapatek (1971), in a study of the entire population of twin pairs in the public schools of the city of Philadelphia, tested the hypothesis that environmental factors would have a stronger impact in lower socio-economic strata than in the higher ones. The evidence, however, is not entirely conclusive, probably mainly because she did not have the opportunity to diagnose the zygosity of the twins and therefore had to compare same-sex and different-sex pairs instead of fraternal and identical ones. This study, which Dobzhansky (1973) termed a "breakthrough" in research on heredity-environment conditions for cognitive development, lends some support to the interpretation that the lower mean IQ among Blacks is due mainly to their belonging to the lower socio-economic stratum. Vandenberg (1969) advances the thesis that "the ratio between heredity potential and realized ability is generally lower for Negroes than for Whites" (*op. cit.*, p. 283). Nichols studies more than 1,000 pairs of siblings, Blacks and Whites, at the age of 4. The intra-pair correlation for scores on the Stanford-Binet was 0.52 for Blacks and 0.37 for Whites. This supports the hypothesis of a lower heritability among Blacks due to environmental handicaps that suppress the realization of the genetic potential. But when sibling pairs at the age of 8-9 years were tested no difference between Black and Whites in terms of intra-pair correlations was obtained.

The rather dramatic changes in IQs which Skeels (1939) observed, when he studied children of pre-school age who were transferred from an orphanage to families where good and personal care was provided, are most likely to be accounted for by threshold effects.

8. SOCIAL MOBILITY AND CHANGES IN THE GENE POOL

In reviewing the literature dealing with such problems as differential fertility and its long-range effects on genotypic intelligence, as well as the differences in measured intelligence between social classes and races, one cannot avoid noticing the absence of any bridge of communication between the biological — in this case the genetic — and the behavioural sciences. The geneticists have not seriously questioned the instruments by means of which phenotypic intellectual competence is measured, nor have they succeeded in elucidating the genetic background of intelligence in terms of monogenic or polygenic determination. The psychologists have put in quite a lot of effort to estimate the heritability of intelligence by studying monozygotic twins brought up apart and together, and by comparing adopted children and biological children with their parents. But they have done very little to bring out the consequences of certain social mechanisms which operate in modern society, such as social mobility and geographical migration, nor have they tried to link intelligence to genetic models and mechanisms.

A.H. Halsey (1958), in a paper that unfortunately has been overlooked by almost everybody who participated in the recent debate on social class and racial differences in intelligence, looks closely at the problem of the relation between social structure and the distribution of genetic characteristics in various populations. On the basis of the assumption that intelligence is partly accounted for by genetic factors and certain assumptions about the size of sub-populations, degree of endogamy, and ease of social mobility and geographical migration, he tries to bring out the long-term consequences of two cases.

The first case is based on the assumption of a caste system with an upper caste of 10 per cent and a lower of 90 per cent. Furthermore, it assumes that intelligence is monogenic, which favours a genetic interpretation of caste differences in the long run. AA genes produce an IQ of 120, Aa genes 100 and aa genes 80. If random mating takes place within the two castes, an equilibrium of the upper caste having an IQ of 108 and the lower one of 92 will be reached. But in absolute terms there will be more high-level (AA) individuals in the lower than in the upper class.

A more interesting case, because it embodies certain mechanisms characterizing our modern society, is the one of a social class system where some selection according to inherited intelligence takes place. (It should, however, be pointed out that there are many factors other than intelligence that account for social mobility; measured intelligence, as shown in recent surveys accounts for only a modest portion of the intra-generational mobility, (see, e.g., Blau and Ducan, 1967). Assuming a ratio between upper and lower social class of 100 to 900, with a modest mobility of 10 individuals moving up and 10 moving down the social ladder and with an average IQ of 100 in both social strata, the lower class would after eight generations have decreased its IQ to 98 and the upper class would have increased it to 120. But the majority of the highly intelligent would still be found in the lower class. If, which is highly reasonable, we assume polygenic determination of intelligence, it would take many more generations to reach the equilibrium of 98 versus 120. Considering that factors other than intelligence are determining social mobility, the process of "purification" in the upper class would be considerably decelerated.

Variability in measured intelligence among subgroups can be compared with the variability in the total population from which they are drawn. The outcomes of such a comparison seen in conjunction with estimations of heritability can elucidate the plausibility of intelligence differences between social classes being mainly determined by genetic or by environmental factors.

Halsey concludes that "the relevant aspects of social structure have not been stable enough for a long enough time for the kind of polygenic process involved in human intelligence to develop class differences of the order suggested by the known social distribution of measured intelligence", (op. cit., p. 15). In a debate with Burt, Halsey (1959) concluded that the theory of inherited social class differences stands on very shaky ground.

9. COGNITIVE DIFFERENCES BY RACE AND SOCIAL CLASS

The touchy issues of whether Whites are more "intelligent" than Blacks or whether upper class students are more "intelligent" than lower class students could a priori be regarded as pseudo-problems, because the answers could logically be derived from the way the problems are posed.

We have earlier spelled out the logical consequences of the way intelligence tests are devised. Almost throughout they measure verbal ability or ability to deal with various kinds of abstractions. They are almost always validated against criteria of school achievement, such as teacher ratings, grades and examinations. All these criteria are derived from certain either generally accepted and/or dominant values. If we keep in mind that intelligence is defined by the dominant socio-cultural reference system, and that in the value structure guiding the system overriding priority has been attached to the ability to succeed in scholastic pursuits, one should not be surprised to find that upper class students have higher IQs than lower class students or that Whites perform better than Blacks.

Jensen himself quotes Duncan's (1968) study on socio-economic background and occupational achievement where it is stated that " 'intelligence' is a socially defined quality... Had the first IQ tests been devised in a hunting culture, 'general intelligence' might well have turned out to involve visual acuity and running speed, rather than vocabulary and symbol manipulation." (Quoted after Jensen, 1969, p. 14). Later Jensen (*ibid.*, p. 19) states that the " predominant importance of intelligence is derived, not from any absolute criteria or God-given desiderata, but from social demands". When dealing with the problem of race differences in IQ and scholastic achievement Jensen (1969), on the basis of empirical evidence, makes the following statement:

There is an increasing realization among students of the psychology of the disadvantaged that the discrepancy in their average performance (i.e., Black as compared to White population) cannot be completely or directly attributed to discrimination or inequalities in education. It seems not unreasonable, in view of the fact that intelligence variation has a large genetic component, to hypothesize that genetic factors may play a part in this picture (*op. cit.*, p. 82).

Existing surveys of IQ distribution show fairly consistently that Blacks score, on the average, one standard deviation below Whites on most intelligence tests, be they verbal or non-verbal. If correction is made for socioeconomic level, the difference is reduced from 15 to 11 IQ points (*ibid.*, p. 81). The Coleman survey (Coleman, *et al.*, 1966) of representative ethnic and racial groups in the United States shows that Blacks score about one standard deviation below the average for Whites throughout the entire regular school, i.e. grades 1 through 12. If 11 IQ points reflects the "true" average difference between the races (corrected for social factors), about 12 per cent of the total variance on IQ tests could be accounted for by differences between races.

The logic advanced in proving that racial differences in cognitive performance have a "large genetic component" could of course also be employed in analyzing social class differences. We consistently find that upper and middle class students score considerably higher than working class students on all kinds of tests. The difference usually amounts to 10-15 IQ points (Terman and Merrill, 1937; Husén, 1950; Anastasi, 1958).

10.   A CONCLUDING NOTE
ON THE HEREDITY-ENVIRONMENT ISSUE

In the Preface to *Genetics*, which reports proceedings of a conference under the auspices of the Russell Sage Foundation, the Social Science Research Council, and the Rockefeller University, the editor David C. Glass (1968) sums up the stance taken by the participants as follows:

Contemporary social scientists no longer adhere to a simplistic environmental determinism, just as contemporary biologists no longer embrace a genetic determinism. In both fields there is an increasing recognition of the importance of an interaction between the organism and the environment (*op. cit.*, p. V).

Anne Anastasi (1958) looked at the heredity-environment issue in the same way in a presidential address to the Division of General Psychology of the American Psychological Association ten years earlier. She did not agree with those who maintained that interest in the problem had faded away. The "heredity-environment problem is still very much alive". But its 'viability' is assured by the gradual replacement of the questions, 'Which one?' and 'How much?' by the more basic and appropriate question, 'How?' (*op. cit.*, p. 200). The task that lay ahead for research was, she envisioned, to explore the *modus operandi* of genetic and environmental factors. The traditional way of conceiving the operation of the two sets of factors has been to regard them as acting in an additive way. But geneticists, as well as others, have pointed out that such a model is not tenable. The two sets of factors interact, as has repeatedly been stressed above, along a continuum of directness. A most obvious example is the effects of discrimination against members of a social class or race in terms of opportunities for intellectual development. In the long run this will result in group differences which are correlated with genetic background without necessarily being causally affected by them. Anastasi cites Dobzhansky as presenting an even more striking illustration. Suppose that all those with blood group AB are considered aristocrats and those with blood group 0 as labourers, then blood group genes would artificially become important hereditary "determiners" of behaviour.

In order to be able to ask questions about how hereditary and environmental factors operate in moulding a particular psychological trait, it is not enough to conduct longitudinal studies of human beings developing in diverse environments. Such studies are methodologically feasible; but the much more important, and complicated, task is to link the development of, for instance, cognitive behaviour with identified genetic material, i.e., to build bridges between genetic and environmental conditions. Such endeavours have scarcely begun.

The polarization that has occurred in recent years in the scholarly community with regard to the heredity-environment issue could hardly have been predicted in 1958. Ten years later, however, the political situation had radically changed and added a dimension of applicability to research that earlier had been regarded as entirely "pure". Studies of the relative importance of heredity and environment were supposed to provide answers to problems like "Is compensatory education worthwhile?" or "Do Black children fail because of inadequacies inherent in the school, because of innate intellectual shortcomings — or for some other reason?". The overriding problem was the extent to which the formal educational system was able to rectify handicaps suffered by various minority groups, such as lower class children and children from various racial minorities.

By 1960 many people, not least the American social scientists, exhibited an almost euphoric optimism about the possibilities of a system of mass education, an optimism that was only a little affected by the search for excellence that became vociferous in the wake of the Sputnik shock at the end of the 1950s. Robert Faris (1961) in his Presidential Address to the American Sociological Association served as a spokesman for this view. It does not suffice, he said, to have a "limited stock of geniuses at the top of the productivity organization" (*op. cit.*, p. 836). By improving society you can also improve the conditions that promote the development of abilities. He noted that "a society generates its level of ability, and further, that the upper limit is unknown and distant, and best of all, that of the processes of ability are potentially subject to intentional control". (*ibid.*, p. 837); and he went on to say: "Fortunately there exists today a nation-wide enthusiasm for the development of talent resources" and it is up to the sociologists to uncover the barriers that limit the aspirations and achievements. The "boom" in formal schooling could be seen as a "potent instrument for raising the ability level of the population", something that had "spectacular implications for the future". The nation was at present "quietly lifting itself by the bootstraps to an important higher level of general ability" (*op. cit.*, p. 838).

Undeniably, it is the task of the educator to bring about worthwhile behavioural changes in a growing or even a grown-up individual. These modifications are achieved by environmental and not by genetical means, and are accessible to *direct observation and measurement*. Furthermore, as we have pointed out already, since no links between cognitive behaviour and specific genetic endowments have been identified, it would seem that the burden of proof as to how genetic factors act as restraints to educational endeavours rests with the advocate of the hereditarian, not the environmental, view. From the environmentalist's standpoint the problem could be stated as follows: Environmental influences on mental development are the only ones that can be subjected to empirical study after the conception (eventually the birth) of the individual. These influences can be assessed by two increasingly more refined techniques that are being developed in the behavioural sciences. What remains inexplicable, therefore, after the environmental factors have been assigned their "share" could fittingly, or at least conditionally, be viewed as owing to "heredity".

Chapter 4

ESTIMATING THE SIZE
OF THE " RESERVE OF TALENT "

1. THE MAJOR MOTIVES: DEMOCRATIZATION,
INTERNATIONAL COMPETITION
AND ECONOMIC DEVELOPMENT

Attempts to assess the size of the "reserve of talent" or the "pool of ability" (see, e.g. Halsey, 1961) in the 1940s and 1950s were chiefly inspired by the following motives. Several surveys of the social background of academic secondary-school graduates and university students in Europe, as well as high-school seniors and college entrants in the United States, demonstrated that there was a strikingly low participation among young people of lower-class background. Even assuming that assortive mating and correlation between innate ability and social mobility had contributed to hereditary differences between social classes, the huge discrepancies revealed by the surveys could by no means be accounted for entirely by genetic factors, i.e., differences in gene pools between the social classes. This conclusion was supported by data available from testing programmes covering complete age groups, such as military classification tests or scholastic aptitude tests given, for instance, in connection with transfer from elementary to secondary school in England, or in admitting students to college in the United States.

The existence of a "reserve of talent", defined as the remainder of those of lower class origin with superior school performances or scores on aptitude tests who did not enter higher education, was seen in several countries in the 1940s and 1950s as a striking indication of inequality of educational opportunity. The identification of talent, the assessment of the potential supply of various types of talent, and the facilitation of students from less privileged backgrounds to get into academic secondary school and into university was regarded as an act of social justice. It was felt that public action should be taken to provide economic support to those who would otherwise hesitate or refrain from realizing their potential. Such democratization of higher education and the establishment of equal access to it was the main motive behind the surveys commissioned by the Swedish Royal Commission on Student Finance (*Studentsociala Utredningen*) which submitted its main report to the Government in 1948 (SOU, 1948 a).

73

In the United States, until the early 1950s, a more individualistic approach was adopted. It was up to the individual to decide if he wanted to "make use of" his ability — in other words, whether or not he should embark upon an advanced education, which in practice meant going to college. It was also up to him or his family to finance the endeavour if he did want to go. But under the impact of increased international tensions during the Cold War, and particularly as a reaction to the "Sputnik-shock", the "search for talent" (CEEB, 1960) became a top national priority. It is typical that the first strongly implemented Federal programme (apart from the G.I. Bill) to support college attendance for needy students was provided under the misleading name of the National Defense Education Act in 1958.

William MacClelland, a pioneer in devising selection procedures for academic secondary education, in his Foreword to McIntosh's book on *Educational Guidance and the Pool of Ability* was a spokesman for prevailing concerns in Europe at the end of the 1950s. He observed that educational guidance in recent years had "acquired a new interest through its bearing upon one of the most important problems that today face modern societies — that of the pool of ability", and went on to say:

> Nations who wish to retain their places in the present ruthless world competition in scientific and other fields must make full use of the resources of talent of their citizens; and for this purpose they will have to take steps to ensure that those who have the ability to come into the pool take advantage of the appropriate educational facilities (McIntosh, 1959, p. 6).

In his chapter on "The Pool of Ability", McIntosh pointed out that it has "become increasingly evident that success in the struggles which are now taking place on the frontiers of knowledge can be achieved only by those nations which are prepared to develop and deploy the full potential of their intellectual resources" (*ibid.*, p. 162). The rapidly increased need for highly trained manpower, particularly in science and technology, and the ensuing need for better utilization of the existing pool of ability makes it a matter of high priority to "enquire into the size of this limited pool of ability." McIntosh sees the problem of devising efficient methods of selection only as part of a wider one, namely how to channel the potential ability into the "national reservoir of highly trained manpower" (*ibid.*, p. 163). One overriding purpose of educational counselling would therefore be to use intelligence and other standardized tests in such a way as to identify potential talent which could then properly be channelled into the educational manpower pool.

There was also a third important motive behind "talent hunting" and the implementation of programmes to support advanced education for able students from less privileged homes. At the OECD Policy Conference on Economic Growth and Investment in Education in 1961, the Chairman stated two reasons why governments should provide more resources for education. "The first is that mankind is entering a new and bolder environment where poverty need no longer exist and where education is the vital prerequisite for clear thinking by democratically governed peoples" (OECD, 1962, p. 5). The second factor, which was more strongly emphasized by all the participants and was regarded as the major reason for holding the conference, was that governments, when formulating their strategy for education, should take into account "that science and technology have released forces which are of staggering power and that human beings must benefit from a better education than in the past if they are to harness these forces to the well-being of their countries" (ibid., p. 5).

In Chapter 1 of Professor Svennilson's background report to the Conference on *Education and Social Welfare,* education is singled out as an important factor of production: "Economic growth is generated not only by real capital in the form of tools and machinery, but also by men. And just as technological improvements increase the efficiency of machinery, so education increases the efficiency of manpower" (OECD, 1962, p. 23). In the section on "The Pool of Ability" in his chapter on problems of policy-making, the same author makes this statement: "One thing that can be said with some confidence to those who fear the effect of quantitative expansion on quality is that there is certainly a much larger 'reservoir of ability' that has yet to be tapped. Even in the United States qualified observers would hesitate very much to say that the large section of each age group that goes to college is approximately co-extensive with those that ought to go in terms of ability. In almost all European countries the reservoir of untapped talent is much larger than in the United States" (ibid., p. 34).

Later during the same year the Committee for Scientific and Technical Personnel in the OECD organized a conference in Kungälv, Sweden, on Ability and Educational Opportunity (Halsey, 1961). A clear indication of the focus of this conference can be derived from the fact that several of the papers dealt in one way or another with the problem of "reserves of ability." Dael Wolfle (Halsey, p. 49 *et seq.*) reported on national resources of ability. P. de Wolff and K. Härnqvist presented surveys conducted in the Netherlands and Sweden and dealt extensively with the methodological problems encountered in carrying out such surveys (Halsey, *op. cit.,* p. 137, *et seq.*).

Dael Wolfle began his paper for the Kungälv conference by stating that provision for educational opportunity for everybody, irrespective of social and economic background, is inspired by a basic democratic ideal. "A free society holds as one of its basic ideals the right of each person to develop to his full capacity" (ibid., p. 49). He went on to say that this ideal has now been reinforced by economic necessity. In the main working document, which introduced the theme of the conference, the organizers stated that "countries may not be able to sustain economic growth unless all the reserves of talent in the population are actively sought out and attracted into needed educational channels" (ibid., p. 49).

In the 1950s and 1960s the serious shortage of highly trained manpower, in spite of soaring college and university enrolments, brought about a firm conviction that society had to see to it that the talent potentials (which, in fact, meant academic potential) of all individuals were brought to a maximum realization. The following quotation is typical of the rhetoric in the United States during the Cold War era: "If we as a people hope in the next few years to build a safer highway system, develop longer-range guided missiles, and construct good schools and adequate houses for all who need them, we shall be hampered less by shortage of cement, of assembly lines, or even of money than by a shortage of the necessary engineers and other technical experts" (Stice, *et al.,* 1957, p. 1).

In the Foreword to *Access to Higher Education,* a report prepared jointly by UNESCO and the International Association of Universities (Bowles, 1963), the chairman of the committee set up to advise the project recommends that pre-university education should be encouraged to expand further in order to take care of available talent:

We should cast our net wider and wider in order to identify, to catch and to bring within the scope of education all available talent, wherever it may be found. This obviously postulates universal education at the elementary level... and the provision of facilities for secondary education of sufficient amplitude to take in as large a proportion as possible of those who finish elementary schools. Out of these we must select those who show promise of being able to meet the intellectual challenge of higher education. In this way, we will be widening the opportunities for higher education but at the same time helping to raise the quality of those who are admitted to it. (*op. cit.,* p. 15).

McIntosh (1959), who in Scotland conducted one of the most comprehensive and valuable studies of the pool of ability, had no doubts in his mind about the limited size of this pool. He therefore strongly emphasized the necessity of channelling pupils who, according to the employed criteria of scholastic aptitude, held promise of successful academic careers into advanced education in order to qualify for the pool of highly trained manpower for which the need was expanding. "At the present time there appear to be good reasons for doubting whether all the requirements of the professions and industry can be met if the standards of admission continue at their present level and the social services are to expand still further" (*op. cit.,* p. 112).

The "Sputnik shock" accelerated a development which, however, had begun earlier, namely a realization that education was needed as a key production factor and that the quality of the educational system left several things to be desired. Thus, the National Science Foundation had supported surveys that aimed at mapping out the reservoir of able high-school students who were potential scientists and engineers. The National Research Councils in the United States sponsored jointly an extensive survey which was directed by Dael Wolfle (1954) who estimated that only about half the academically most able (the top 10 per cent) high-school students in terms of test scores and grades entered colleges. This figure caused quite a lot of concern in the United States and was used to substantiate the notion in many quarters that a considerable wastage of talent took place. We shall come back to Wolfle's study in our review of research on the reserves of talent to be presented later. A nationwide study in the United States was conducted in 1955 by the Educational Testing Service (ETS, 1956–57) and a questionnaire was administered to the top 3 per cent of the twelfth-graders. The top third of these were then singled out as a high-quality group for special analysis. In his study *The American High School Today,* Conant recommended certain provisions for the more able students.

*

We cannot here cover all the relevant research that pertains to the "reserves of ability", let alone the concomitant methodological problems

with which researchers have tried to come to grips. We shall confine ourselves, rather, to two main surveys in the United States – the one sponsored by the four National Research Councils at the beginning of the
1950s, and Project Talent which was launched at the beginning of the
1960s. We shall also include research carried out in Europe, the OECD
survey in Austria, and some British, French, German, Dutch, Danish and
Swedish studies.

The first large-scale, national surveys that set out to estimate the size
of the "reserves of ability" were carried out in Sweden as early as the
mid-1940s and they had a strong influence on policy making (Husén and
Boalt, 1968). It is worth mentioning that the very term "reserve of ability"
was coined by Dr. R. Edenman, who later became Minister of Education,
in an address at the Conference of the Confederation of Swedish Student
Unions in 1948. As chairman of the 1955 University Commission, Dr.
Edenman later initiated another national survey (Härnqvist, 1958) which
made a break-through in methodology. Thus, Sweden after 1945 presents
an interesting case of how survey research was part of, and had a strong
impact on, policy-making. The fact that this long series of investigations
from 1946 onwards had such an effect did not mean that they were all
commissioned as "decision-oriented" projects. On the contrary, most of
them were initiated by the researchers themselves and as we have said,
they stimulated fruitful development in methodology. After having sum-
marized the most important research on reserves of ability in the United
States and Europe it will be relevant, therefore, if we consider the development of Swedish research in this particular area in more detail.

2. ADEQUACY OF THE CONCEPT "RESERVE OF TALENT"

The rapporteur at the OECD Kungälv conference, Professor C.H. Halsey,
suggests that the metaphor "reserve of ability" or "pool of ability" should
be abandoned because it is "scientifically misleading" (Halsey, 1961, p. 23)
in that it suggests the existence of a genetically fixed amount of qualities
that set certain limits in the same strict sense as does a container from
which liquid is tapped. Furthermore, by using the phrase in the singular,
one overlooks the fact that there is "a whole range of human skills and
excellencies, literate, numerate, and manual" beside the academic ones
(*op. cit.*, p. 24).

Halsey also points out that we have now become aware that social
background or social stratification should be considered more as a major
factor determining *educability* than as a barrier to opportunity (*op. cit.*,
p. 33). This, then means that the important aspect of equality is not so
much the *formal* opportunity as the preparation the child receives to take
advantage of opportunity. Thus, the phrase 'reserve of ability' makes us
blind to the fact that ability can be generated by a concerted social and
educational policy: "... a process of economic and social development is a
process of creating ability" (*op. cit.*, p. 24).

In a paper on the pool of ability, submitted as a memorandum to the
Robbins Committee, Vernon (1963) challenged the view that "there exists
in the population a fixed distribution or 'pool' of intelligence, which limits

either the numbers of individuals capable of higher education, or the educational standards that can be achieved by groups of pupils or students of given IQ level" (*op. cit.,* p. 45). What matters here is not only the purely intellectual resources but the cultural and vocational attitudes of the home and society at large as well as the interests and motives of the individual student.

Nonetheless, since the beginning of the 1960s the term "reserve of ability" has come into extensive use in educational literature so we shall use it here — but with the caveats already expressed. The criticism that talking about "reserve of ability" in the singular limits the view to academic ability is valid; but as long as the empirical approach to the problem is made within the framework of the formal school system, and as long as success in that system is a prerequisite for social success in modern society, such a limitation of view to academic aptitude is justified.

3. SURVEYS OF THE "RESERVE OF TALENT"

A. *The Commission of Human Resources and Advanced Training Survey in the United States*

The Commission on Human Resources and Advanced Training analysed the scores on AGCT (Army General Classification Test) for freshmen at 41 colleges (Wolfle, 1954, p. 144 *et seq.*). The distributions of scores among college entrants could be related to the norms for the corresponding age groups.

A striking feature, that has later been confirmed by several other surveys, is the tremendous intellectual diversity among American college entrants. There is almost no parallel to this in the European countries with their centralized systems, uniform admission requirements, and national examinations. Some colleges were so selective as to have all their graduates above the average of the entire population of college graduates.

The Commission estimated that 59 per cent of the top 1 per cent on AGCT, 49 per cent of the top 5 per cent, and 34 per cent of the top 20 per cent graduated from college. It further estimated that 53 per cent of the high-school graduates who belonged to the top 20 per cent in terms of grade point average entered college, as compared with 17 per cent among those in the bottom 20 per cent. The fact that only about 60 per cent of the high-school graduates who scored in the top 5 per cent group on the AGCT and had grade point averages in the top 20 per cent entered college indicated that a considerable reserve of ability existed. That those who belonged to the reserve came mainly from lower socio-economic strata was made clear when educational careers were related to fathers' occupations. The Commission arrived at the estimates shown in Table 4.1.

Table 4.1 illustrates two marked tendencies. First, socio-economic selectivity operates strongly in the context of college entrance. The ability reserve is to a large extent to be found among high-school students whose fathers are farmers or manual workers, a finding that has universal application. Secondly, once the students have entered college, socio-economic background seems to play a minor role in their achieving a degree. Several other studies, some of them reported in Chapter 6, indicate that the socio-

Table 4.1 COLLEGE ENTRANCE AND COLLEGE SURVIVAL
AS RELATED TO FATHER'S OCCUPATION

Father's occupation	Percentage of high-school students who enter college	Percentage of college entrants who graduate from college
Professional and semi-professional	67	60
Managerial	50	55
White-collar workers (clerical, sales, service)	48	57
Farmer	24	44
Factory, craftsman, unskilled, etc.	26	58

Source: Wolfle, 1954.

economic barriers operate much more strongly at the entry to a certain stage than during that stage (see, e.g. Boalt, 1947).

The Commission's figures were estimates for 1952–53 built upon extrapolations from actual figures derived from 1949. Bridgman (CEEB, 1960) made a comparison between the estimates and the actual outcomes and showed that the Commission had underestimated the number of college entrants. The "enrolment explosion" turned out to be more forceful than was anticipated (see Table 4.2).

Table 4.2 ESTIMATED AND ACTUAL COLLEGE ENTRANCE

AGCT scores 118 and above (top 20 % of age cohort)	Commission estimate	Actual outcome (Bridgman)
Percentage of high-school students going into college	48	62
Percentage of college entrants in age cohort	44	58
AGCT scores 131 and above (top 6 % of age cohort)	54	69
Percentage of college entrants in age cohort	53	68

Source: CEEB, 1960.

B. *Project Talent*

One of the major objectives of Project Talent (Flanagan *et. al.,* 1964) was to survey available talent in American high schools and to provide an estimate of the available manpower pool, particularly for certain key professions. Since the survey was planned during the Sputnik era, the sponsors had such fields as science and engineering primarily in mind. The project set out to identify the aptitudes, interests, socio-economic background and motivation among high-school students and to study particularly what effects lack of interest and motivation had on further study. It is thus of the greatest interest to anyone concerned with research on the reserve of ability.

In 1960 a probability sample of 292,000 students in grades 9-12 were given aptitude, ability, achievement and interest tests. In addition the subjects had to complete a Student Information Blank. Sixty test scores were obtained. By compounding some of the tests, four categories of measurement were established to reveal General Academic Aptitude, Quantitative

ical Aptitude, and Scientific Aptitude. A follow-up by means
stionnaire was carried out one year after graduation from
about 10,000 students who were tested in grade 9 were sub-
tested in grade 12.

the 1960 seniors, 53 per cent of the male and 46 per cent of the
ale students planned to go to college immediately after having finished
high school; 49 and 35 per cent respectively actually did go; 97 per cent
of the graduates who scored in the top percentile bracket on the General
Academic Composite entered college. The corresponding figure for the
bottom percentile was 15 per cent. In the range below the medium considerably more boys than girls entered, whereas a slightly higher frequency of
boys was noted among those above medium.

There was a linear relationship between percentile rank on the aptitude
tests and college attendance one year later among the boys, whereas the
relationship was curvilinear among girls. High aptitude was equally conducive to staying on at college in both boys and girls, whereas among those
of mediocre aptitude the tendency to stay on was more marked among
boys. Among the top 2 per cent in Academic Aptitude, the drop-out rate
was only 4 per cent after one year as compared with 20-25 per cent in
the bottom third of the students. Parental occupation and education were
closely related to entering college, as can be seen from Table 4.3. The
twelfth-graders were asked how much education their parents wanted them
to have. When subsequent entrance/non-entrance to college was related to
the response, a quite close relationship was found, as shown in Table 4.4.

Table 4.3 FATHER'S OCCUPATION AND PARENTAL EDUCATION
AS RELATED TO COLLEGE ENTRANCE AMONG HIGH-SCHOOL SENIORS

In percentage

	Entered college		Did not enter college	
	Boys	Girls	Boys	Girls
Father's occupation:				
White-collar	51	54	21	22
Blue-collar	37	33	56	58
Farm	9	8	15	12
Don't know	3	5	8	8
Total	100	100	100	100
Father's education:				
College graduate or higher	20	23	6	5
High school or high school plus some college	44	43	30	30
Did not graduate from high school ..	32	29	55	56
Don't know	4	4	9	9
Total	100	100	100	100
Mother's education:				
College graduate or higher	15	17	5	4
High school or high school plus some college	57	57	41	39
Did not graduate from high school ..	25	24	46	52
Don't know	3	2	8	5
Total	100	100	100	100

Source: Flanagan *et al.* 1964.

Table 4.4 PARENTAL EDUCATION ASPIRATION
RELATED TO COLLEGE ENTRANCE

Amount of education aspired to by parents	Entered college later		Did not enter college	
	Boys	Girls	Boys	Girls
College or higher	86	77	35	20
High school or less, vocational business, junior college	8	16	43	59
Don't know	6	7	22	21
Total	100	100	100	100

Source: Flanagan et al., 1964.

Among those who scored in the top 10 per cent bracket on the academic aptitude test, 14 per cent of the boys and 22 per cent of the girls did *not* go to college if their father had not completed high school. If he had completed high school, the corresponding figures were only 3 and 4 per cent respectively. Of children of white-collar workers, 4 per cent of the boys and 8 per cent of the girls who scored in the top 10 per cent in the academic aptitude tests did not go to college. The corresponding figures for students whose fathers were blue-collar workers were 14 and 23 per cent. For those whose fathers were farm labourers, the figures were as high as 19 and 75 per cent respectively.

Thus, parental occupation and education were of great importance in influencing the decision of the very able high-school graduates whether or not to enter college.

C. The OECD Study on Austria

One study on the "latent reserves of ability" was carried out by the Psycho-Pedagogical Service of Austria under OECD auspices in 1964–65. The report (OECD, 1965) gives three reasons why the survey was launched: (1) Children from higher social strata participate more and achieve better results in school than children of the same intellectual standing from lower strata, whereas Section 26 of the Declaration of Human Rights of the United Nations asserts that every child should have access to further education, irrespective of social class, economic conditions and place of residence of parents. "Inborn abilities" should decide what find of education a child obtains. (2) Education is a decisive factor in economic growth and it is therefore in the interest of society to promote increased and equalized participation in education. (3) Promoting the development of intellectual resources strengthens a nation's capacity in international competition. Reference here is made to science and technology, space research being given as an illustration.

These motives have been quoted because they are typical of the ideas prevalent at the beginning of the 1960s as to how the "reserves of ability" should be taken care of and what equality of educational opportunity really meant.

The report distinguishes between two types of ability reserve: " The *absolute* (our underlining) reserve of ability... includes all pupils capable of graduating successfully from a school giving access to higher education, but

81

who do not apply for such scholastic training... The *relative* (our under-lining) reserve of ability... includes pupils who achieved better performances in the selection tests than the lowest 15 per cent of children examined with the aid of the same tests and who, at the time of investigation, were al-ready attending a general school " (*op. cit.*, p. 12).

The following factors are identified as conducive to further education or as barriers preventing it: (1) hereditary background; (2) sex; (3) geogra-phical factors (such as distance to school); (4) ethnic factors; (5) economic factors; (6) social factors that manifest themselves in terms of, for instance, *Bildungsdruck* (Dahrendorf, 1965) or *la famille éducogène* (OECD, 1962).

The province of Burgenland was chosen for the survey because it had the lowest participation rate of all the Austrian provinces so far as univer-sity-preparing secondary education was concerned. It could be expected, therefore, to have considerable reserves of ability. Burgenland was predom-inantly agricultural and rural, without any big cities, and this was the main reason for its low participation rate in secondary education.

The sixth school year was chosen, because transfer to academic second-ary education had by then been completed. The children were distributed as follows:

Primary school	(*Volksschule*)	50 per cent
Upper primary stream	(*Volksschul-Oberstufe* or *Hauptschule*)	40 per cent
Academic secondary school	(*Gymnasium*)	9 per cent
Special school	(*Sonderschule*)	1 per cent

Only 9 per cent had been transferred to the academic secondary school, the majority staying on in the terminal classes of the primary school. A considerable number, however, had transferred to the *Oberstufe,* a kind of middle school with a more advanced programme than was provided in the primary school.

Achievement, intelligence and personality tests were administered to the 6th-grade students. A random sample of parents were interviewed. All parents who had children in secondary schools were included.

A "cutting score" method, similar to the one employed in the 1940s by Husén (1946, 1947, 1948), was used to obtain a measure of the size of the relative reserve of ability. The general secondary school population thereby served as a reference group. The fact that the students had been admitted and were still in school after a year or two was regarded as an indication of ability to profit from academic secondary education. On the scale of the composite score, the 15th percentile was arbitrarily set as the cutting score. Those who fell below that score were considered to be intellectually unfit for that kind of study. Those who scored above the 15th percentile and who were *not* in general secondary school were con-sidered as reserves of ability. As could be expected, the major portion of the reserves (41 per cent) was found in the upper primary stream (*Oberstufe*); but even in the lower stream (the *Volksschule*), more than 5 per cent scored above the 15th percentile. A total of about 21 per cent of those who did not transfer to the general secondary school belonged to the reserve. Incidentally, much the same estimate was arrived at in the Swedish surveys in the 1940s, when about 15-20 per cent of an age group transferred to the *realskola* and 35 per cent were considered capable of passing the middle-school examination (Husén, 1948).

D. *British Surveys*

Large-scale application of group intelligence tests to school children at certain age or grade levels was introduced in England and Scotland earlier than in other West European countries. Godfrey Thomson and his students were already conducting area surveys in the 1920s. The Scottish surveys of all 11-year old pupils have become famous (Scottish Council, 1933 and 1949). Gray and Moshinsky (1936) tested some 10,000 children in London with a group test normed in the United States and came up with the result that 22 per cent had IQs of 135 and above! Burt (1943), on the basis of survey data from the 1930s, found that some 1-0.5 per cent of the total population fell within that bracket. The Barlow Committee (Vernon, 1963) estimated that 5 per cent of the entire age group had IQs of the same level as the better half of the students then at university.

In the 1950s the Scottish Council for Educational Research sponsored a study referred to above (McIntosh, 1959) which focused specification on estimating size of the pool of ability. The Crowther report presented analyses of survey data according to which the percentage of the relevant age group taking the advanced level General Certificate of Education could be raised from 9 per cent (which was the figure at the end of the 1950s) to 16 per cent (HMSO), 1959). In 1962 the Robbins Committee sponsored a survey of all the 21-year olds to determine how entry to higher education was related to social background in terms mainly of parental education and parental occupation. Finally, we should mention Furneaux's (1961) study which indicated that 20 per cent of an age group was capable of the level of attainment required for matriculation.

McIntosh's investigation of the pool of ability was conducted with the advantage of his being the Director of Education for the County of Fife in Scotland. Its particular value lay in its longitudinal character: primary school records, secondary school progress and after school careers were all studied from some 4,400 pupils. Thus, the entire secondary school record served as a criterion in assessing the validity of the selection instruments, which consisted of two intelligence tests, standardized attainment tests in English and Arithmetic, and teachers' scaled estimates of pupil attainment in these subjects. The whole battery of predictors correlated as high as 0.86 with marks obtained at the end of the third year of secondary school. On the whole, the various predictors correlated remarkably well with the criteria of success throughout the secondary school period.

The main emphasis of the McIntosh study is on detailed analyses of the predictive value of the various selection instruments. The analyses of " able leavers " and the size of the pool of ability, therefore, can be regarded as by-products of the work; nevertheless they are of particular interest in our present review. From them one could conclude (albeit somewhat irreverently) that the extremely high predictive values reflect a high degree of unanimity between teachers in the elementary and secondary school and indicated a high validity for the selection instruments in measuring docility. The tests have been validated against teacher ratings and therefore reflect teacher opinion about the nature of scholastic aptitude.

The able leavers who, in spite of high total entrance scores, did not get as far as taking a Leaving Examination, almost all came from manual workers' homes. "Without a sympathetic and encouraging home, a pupil has little chance of winning through to the Leaving Certificate Examination" (McIntosh, *op. cit.*, p. 124). There were twice as many girls as boys among the able leavers.

The pool of ability was operationally defined as the sum total of the following three groups: (1) Pupils actually attaining a School Leaving Certificate, in this case 6.3 per cent of the cohort; (2) "Able leavers" (4.3 per cent of the cohort), and (3) Pupils with high scores who did not enter higher school (0.5 per cent). Thus, the pool represented only 11.1 per cent of the entire cohort. The limited size of the pool McIntosh ascribed to the fact that the standards in the School Leaving Examination were "unnecessarily high" in demanding equally good performances in many subjects, with the result that those who were verbally oriented and had difficulty with mathematics and those who were mathematically oriented and had difficulty with languages were automatically handicapped. A revision of the criterion for academic success in secondary education seemed therefore to be overdue.

Using the combined battery of predictors as criteria of scholastic aptitude and setting a cutting score at a level that corresponded to an IQ of 110, McIntosh estimated that the pool should consist of some 16 per cent of the entire age group. McClelland (1942) in his classical study of selection for secondary education estimated that 16.7 per cent would be successful in the secondary schools of that period.

The Robbins Report *Higher Education* (HMSO, 1963) has a section on the "so-called pool of ability." As we have already mentioned, the Committee adopted a memorandum prepared by Professor Philip Vernon (1963) that attempted to arrive at conceptual clarification of this term, while Sir Eric Ashby in his introduction to a special issue of the Sociological Review (1963) on British University Education concludes that: "The glib assumptions about a genetically determined 'pool of ability' from which the better candidates can be selected by intelligence tests or by achievement in examinations, with the precision with which one can grade eggs, evaporates under the analyses reported by Vernon and Newfield" (*op. cit.*, p. 11-12). Indeed, the Robins Committee (1963) itself had remarked that "the belief that there exists some easy method of ascertaining an intelligence factor unaffected by education or background is outmoded" (quoted from Silver, 1973, p. 193).

In order to elucidate the extent to which social background was related to ease of access to higher education, the Robbins Committee sponsored a survey that was carried out in 1962. Background was defined by the status of father's occupation, social classes being grouped according to the Registrar General's system of classification. The survey covered those who at the time were 21 years old, i.e., were born in 1940-1. The ultimate relation between social class and attainment of higher education is shown in Table 4.5. This table, indeed, conveys the impression that, percentagewise, higher education is virtually a monopoly for those with a professional and managerial background. In absolute numbers they are roughly twice as many as those whose parents are manual workers – in spite of their representing less than 20 per cent of the population. The report sums up the position by saying: "The proportion of middle-class children who reach degree level

84

courses is eight times as high as the proportion from working-class homes, and even in grammar school it is twice as high " (quoted from Silver, *op. cit.,* p. 204).

Table 4.5 PROPORTION OF CHILDREN
REACHING HIGHER EDUCATION (H.E.) BY FATHER'S OCCUPATION

In percentage

Father's occupation		Full-time H.E.		No full-time H.E.	Total
		Degree level	Other		
Higher professional		33	12	55	100
Managerial and other professional		11	8	81	100
Clerical		6	4	90	100
Skilled manual		2	2	96	100
Semi- and unskilled manual		1	1	98	100
Non-manual	Boys	15	4	81	100
	Girls	9	10	81	100
Manual	Boys	3	2	95	100
	Girls	1	2	97	100
Father's age on	18 or more	32	11	57	100
completing full-	16 or 17	14	7	79	100
time education	Under 16	2	3	95	100

Source: Higher Education (The Robbins Report). London: HMSO, 1963.

E. *A French Follow-Up Study*

In 1951, seven years after an extensive national survey of the intellectual level of primary school pupils in France (Heyer *et al.,* 1950), it was decided to locate the children who in the 1944 survey had scored within the top 10 per cent and the 46th through 55th percentile respectively. The headmasters of the schools that the 6- through 12-year-olds had attended in 1944 were asked to indicate whether or not their pupils had pursued further studies after the age of 14 (when mandatory schooling terminated) and to rate them on a five-point scale from " excellent " to " bad " (*excellent* to *mauvais*). The headmasters were not told that the purpose of the study, conducted by Girard and Bastide (1954, p. 252 *et seq.*), was to trace the careers of very able and mediocre children respectively in relation to test scores 7 years earlier. Of 9,157 children who in the 1944 survey belonged to the relevant percentiles, information was obtained for 6,453 or 71 per cent of the original sample. Because of incomplete or in other respects defective information, however, a further 1,200 returns could not be used; thus, the usable questionnaire material amounted to 58 per cent. A comparison between the total 1944 sample and the subsample for which information was available in 1951 showed that the loss had not been selective with regard to age, place of residence, or socio-economic background.

It was found that scholastic success according to the ratings by teachers in the *primary* school was related to the test scores as follows:

85

Percentiles (According to test)	Excellent or good	Average	Mediocre or bad	Total
91–100	67	25	8	100
46–55	38	37	25	100

An overall picture of the extent to which the pursuit of *further studies* was related to test scores in 1944 could be obtained from the information received, even though in about 20 per cent of the cases no information was available or the child had not yet reached the age when mandatory schooling expired. It worked out thus:

Percentiles	Pursued further studies	Did not pursue further studies
91–100	73	27
46–55	47	53

Even if the researchers started their survey with the notion that the intellectual level as revealed by the test was the best predictor of scholastic career, they had to think again, because it turned out that the pursuit of studies above the mandatory school age was fairly closely related to socio-economic background and place of residence. Whereas only about half of those who 1944 scored in the top 10 per cent bracket and had parents who were farmers, rural workers or manual industrial workers went on to secondary education, almost a hundred per cent of the children of professional men, managers, and white collar workers did so. The difference was even more striking with those who had scored about average (46th through 55th percentile). (For details, see table in Bastide and Girard, 1954, p. 268).

F. *German Investigations*

Lack of *Chancengleichheit* (equality of chances) and the existence of an apparently extensive "reserve of ability" became matters of serious concern to policy makers in the Federal Republic of Germany by the middle of the 1960s. At the beginning of the decade, Edding and von Carnap (1962) published a study of the participation rates in further-going schooling (*Gymnasium, Mittelschule,* etc.) in the various Länder. Such comparisons, by implication, challenged the hereditarian view on the distribution of talent that Albert Huth (1956) had set forth some years earlier. Why, for instance, did only 4 per cent of the young people in Saarland reach the middle school certificate (*mittlere Reife*) as compared with 24 per cent in Schleswig-Holstein? Or, why did twice as many girls in Berlin as in Hamburg take the matriculation examination (*Abitur*)? Such differences obviously could not be attributed to big differences in gene pools but chiefly to variations in opportunity.

As to participation in university studies, it was notably Dahrendorf (1965) who brought the basic statistical facts out into the open. Young people whose parents were manual workers were heavily underrepresented among the students at German universities as compared with some other European countries. By the beginning of the 1960s, as Dahrendorf pointed out, roughly 50 per cent of the German work force consisted of skilled or unskilled, urban or rural labourers, while only 5 per cent of the university students came from such backgrounds. Of this 5 per cent about three quarters had parents who were highly skilled or specialized. Thus the bottom stratum of society, 25 per cent of the work force, was represented by only 1 per cent of students in the universities. The top stratum (1 per cent), on the other hand, was represented by about 25 per cent of the undergraduate population.

This disparity in the representation of the upper and lower social strata could be traced back to the moment (age 10-11) when the decision was whether or not to transfer one's child to the *Gymnasium*, the secondary academic school that would prepare him for university entry. In spite of the fact that such transfer was formally open on the basis of individual competition (the *Beschulungsfaktor*) the advantage taken of it in relation to the proportion of the total population differed widely between the social strata. Dahrendorf (1965) cites several case studies where children from professional homes transferred some 10-30 times more than those from the homes of manual workers.

The most important studies of the " reserve of ability " in Germany were undertaken from the University of Tübingen during the 1960s, when Dahrendorf led a research team that concentrated, not only on the differences between social strata in participation in advanced education, but the identification of factors that acted as a " social filter " in a system that officially was open to young people from all walks of life. In his report of this work on working class students at German universities (Dahrendorf, 1965) he concludes that it certainly does *not* give a picture of a meritocracy where people are assigned status according to IQ, schooling and diplomas. On the contrary, the universities are institutions of status confirmation, instruments of a society where status is ascribed. The family atmosphere among manual workers is not conducive to the aspirations and the support that the French refer to when they speak of " la famille éducogène." There is a feeling of remoteness towards the milieu of higher education similar to the way in which some Protestants regard life in a monastery. It is both an affective and informational remoteness, and it applies also to the *Gymnasium* with whose language-oriented curriculum working class youngsters feel no more affinity than they do with the teachers who conceive it as their role to select the " right " students.

One of the most important studies of the Tübingen group was conducted by Peisert (1967) on regional participation rates. The concept of " density of education " (*Bildungsdichte*) denoted the participation rate in a particular area, and, among other things, Peisert looked into the regional variations in the relative number of 16- to 19-year olds who were in fulltime schooling. Berlin showed a relatively high density with 20 per cent, whereas Northrhine-Westphalia came out with half that figure. The interesting analyses were those where the data were broken down by *Regierungsbezirke* (regions within *Länder*), by *Kreise* (counties within regions) and by *Gemeinde* (municipalities within counties). The lower the level of aggregation, the wider the span of " education density " :

Variation between *Länder* (states)	12- 21 % participation
Variation between *Bezirke* (regions)	10- 21 % participation
Variation between *Kreise* (counties)	3- 48 % participation
Variation between *Gemeinde* (municipalities	0-100 % participation

Peisert points out that "educational density" can be employed as an index of the level of modernization. It turned out to be highly correlated with, for instance, purchasing power and the number of hospital beds.

Since the participation rates were especially low among children whose parents were manual workers and farmers, Peisert conducted particular analyses within these categories. The farming population in the Federal Republic of Germany consisted of 9 per cent of the total population. In the regions where at least 50 per cent were employed in agriculture the education density was 2.2 per cent as compared with 14.3 for the whole country. There was also a negative correlation between "educational density" and the relative number of manual workers living in the area. When studying this relationship for metropolitan regions it was found that the correlation between "educational density" and the proportion of manual workers was 0.86 for Berlin, 0.76 for Hamburg, and 0.69 for Bremen.

Hitpass (1963) conducted surveys in industrial cities to determine the size of the reserve of ability and arrived at the conclusion that more than 4 per cent of the elementary school population (in addition to those who actually applied and were selected for further studies in the academic secondary school) belonged to it. If all these entered a university, about 50 per cent instead of 5 per cent of all such students would come from homes of manual workers.

A third group with a poor participation rate were the girls. Hannelore Gerstein (1965) made a survey in the state of Baden-Württemberg and found that, during the years 1950–64, only about 30 per cent of the matriculants from the *Gymnasium* were female.

The *Bildungskommission* of the German Council on Education (*Bildungsrat*) in 1966 commissioned a group of leading researchers in the fields of education and psychology in Germany to submit evaluative reviews on the present state of research with regard to the development of scholastic ability. One of the central issues in this connection was how hereditary and environmental factors contributed to the outcomes of school learning. The entire body of research pertaining to the relationship between ability and learning was considered to be of basic importance to the Commission, which had to advance recommendations for changes in the structure of the German school system. The core political issue was the one that faces most other countries in Western Europe: how to change the structure and the curricula so as to bring about more equality of opportunity (*Chancengleichheit*). The fifteen contributions were edited by Roth (1968), who also wrote an introduction.

Aebli (1968) emphasized that the most important reserves of ability in our society do not consist of young people who already possess all the individual psychological assets required to get along in higher education. They consist primarily of those for whom "the prerequisites must be developed." Such prerequisites are certain basic cognitive skills, attitudes, values, style of thinking, as well as some types of motivation. "Certain pedagogic and institutional measures are required in order to bring about the realization of these conditions" (*op. cit.*, p. 189).

Heckhausen (1968) in his contribution outlines four basic requirements that a school system in our society should meet. One of them is equality of opportunity (*Chancengleichheit*): "An educational system should try to observe and try to level out the inequality of opportunity that stems from the differences in socio-cultural background of the students" (*op. cit.*, p. 211. In a recent monograph, Heckhausen (1974) has analysed the concept of educational equality within the context of achievement-motivated behaviour. He points out that attempts to bring about greater equality are beset with certain dilemmas which he tries to make explicit. The school is there to impart competence and therefore tends to emphasize differences in individual achievements. Equality of attainment cannot be achieved just by equalized offerings but by increased individualization. Equality takes on another notion if it is conceived of within a criterion-referenced context, i.e., when the student is evaluated with reference to some kind of absolute standard, and not primarily ranked with his classmates.

Wilhelm Arnold (1968) refers to a series of studies which he himself had conducted on ability and educational motivation. The exposition in Roth (1968) is based upon five studies, each embracing between 40 and 77 students from grades 4, 8, and 10. Their parents were interviewed to find out what aspirations they had for sending their children to the academic secondary school (*Gymnasium* or *Oberschule*), and in the course of this a measure was derived of the interest they showed in their children's education and how well informed they were about their schools. Questionnaires and intelligence tests were administered to the children and the teachers were asked to rate their academic aptitude with particular reference to the secondary school. School marks were also available.

Arnold did not find any significant relationship between the economic status of the parents and their willingness to let their children go on to higher education. It was possible on the basis of the interviews to derive an index of motivation reflecting such willingness and an index of information which gave a measure of how much the parents knew about the school possibilities for their children, such as types of school, costs, sources of information, and monetary allowances. Arnold summed up his findings in the following statement:

"The major reason the parents were against the choice of further-going education is uncertainty, lack of information, and resignation in terms of whether the child really had the aptitude. This uncertainty is further reinforced because the teachers, lacking standards of comparison, themselves are in doubt about the aptitude of the children and — according to our criteria — therefore prefer to give discouraging advice. One reason for the negative decision about further education in the lower and middle social strata is also to be found in the lack of confidence parents have in the ability of their children to perform successfully. The image of *Gymnasium* appears to the workman is as follows: Relatively stern, alien, difficult, geared to men, frustrating and strenuous. Among the working class, as compared with other strata, the costs tend to be overestimated" (*op. cit.*, p. 362).

The motivation for sending children to the academic secondary school is highly correlated with the parents' knowledge of what that type of schooling implies. Interestingly enough, parental motivation correlated practically zero with the child's intelligence test score. Test score and teacher rating of academic aptitude correlated only 0.34.

Arnold also reports on a series of previous investigations in Germany that he and his co-workers had reviewed to obtain, among other things, an idea of the size of the reserve of ability. Their conservative estimate was that 3.5 per cent of those whose education terminated with the elementary school (*Volksschule*) possessed the aptitude to go on to academic secondary education (*höhere Schule*); a more liberal one gave 8 per cent. According to the same standards of estimation the vocational schools contributed an additional reserve that amounted to 6.6 and 9.0 per cent respectively of their enrolment.

So far no comprehensive survey based on representative national samples has been carried out in Germany. Ingenkamp (1968), on the basis of studies that he and others made of the predictive value of tests used for selecting students for the *Gymnasium,* concluded that a "considerable number of eligible children remain in the terminal classes (*Hauptschule*)" (*op. cit.,* p. 415). When standardized achievements and intelligence tests were employed as criteria of aptitude, he estimated, on the basis of several studies, that of those who scored in the top quarter between 13 and 35 per cent remained in the terminal classes of the elementary school instead of applying for transfer to the academic secondary school.

G. *Dutch Studies*

In a methodological appendix to his and Härnqvist's contribution to the Kungälv conference on ability and educational opportunity in 1961, de Wolff (Halsey, 1961, p. 147 *et seq.*) has spelt out the rationale for his analysis of data obtained from the Dutch army classification test. He began by making a distinction between the reserve of ability in a narrow and in a broad sense. The former concept includes only a limited number of factors accounting for scholastic performances – mainly cognitive factors as measured by conventional intelligence tests. The latter includes *all* relevant factors, in addition to the cognitive ones – school motivation, parental support, scholastic attitudes and so on. Following Ekman's (1949) analysis of the concept, de Wolff further distinguishes between an actual and a potential reserve of ability. The actual reserve pertains to the situation at the time when the decision about further schooling is made and various environmental factors have had time to contribute to the moulding of scholastic capacity. The potential reserve refers to an earlier situation, for instance at the beginning of regular schooling. Basically, it relates to genetic assets.

Building on a hypothesis advanced by Ekman (1949), de Wolff developed a method for assessing the reserve of ability, which was subsequently used by the Dutch Bureau of Statistics. The criterion variable was Raven's matrices which were part of the test battery given to almost complete age groups of Dutch army recruits. The distribution of test scores for each of the three social strata used in the Dutch social statistics was determined, and the participation rate by test score interval was calculated for each stratum. The so-called relative coefficient of participation for the highest social stratum was regarded as the optimal, since it was there that privileged social conditions prevailed. By these means, de Wolff was able to assess the potential reserves existing in the other social strata.

This method of de Wolff's is, indeed, a very elegant one and represents considerable progress; nevertheless it is open to certain criticisms. In the first place, the assumption that those who belong to the upper social stratum are always given opportunity to develop their scholastic aptitude according to optimal conditions can be questioned. Secondly, errors of measurement affect the estimation. Thirdly, sampling errors come into the picture because medical rejects were not included in the age groups subjected to analysis. Fourthly, data are available for men only, and the assumption is made that there are no significant sex differences in test score distributions. One could add to this list of critical points by observing that the hereditary factors, because of selective breeding, differential fertility, and so on, might be different for the three social strata.

The method developed by de Wolff was further applied to Dutch data to get a broad estimate of the reserve of ability for education at university level. Here, two additional assumptions were made : Assumption I, that the coefficient of participation could be raised half-way between the values of the two higher social strata (upper and middle class); Assumption II, that the sex ratio in enrolment would remain constant. Estimates as shown in Table 4.6 were then arrived at.

Table 4.6 THE PROPORTION OF AN AGE GROUP
IN THE NETHERLANDS ABLE TO PROFIT FROM UNIVERSITY STUDIES

In percentage

| Social class | Actual enrolment | | | Potential university population according to | | | | | |
| | | | | Assumption I | | | Assumption II | | |
	Men	Women	Total	Men	Women	Total	Men	Women	Total
Upper	26	10	18	26	10	18	26	10	18
Middle	5	1	3	10	3	7	10	2	6
Lower	1	0	0	5	2	4	5	1	3

Source: Halsey, 1961.

As can be seen, the potential university population decreases if one makes the assumption that the sex ratio will not change for some time. As a matter of fact, it has changed somewhat since the 1950s when the data were collected (see below). Furthermore, the actual enrolment has increased and passed the somewhat conservative participation ratio estimated more than ten years ago.

The question as to the size of " unutilized talent ", and, conversely, to what extent the " reserve " was exhausted, has often been raised in European countries that had a large increase in university enrolment in the 1950s and 1960s. Spitz (1959) confronted university enrolment data from the Central Planning Bureau in the Hague with test data for almost complete age groups of young males in the Dutch Armed Forces. A previous study by Daniëls and Albinski (1958), which he criticises, was based on test data for university entrants alone. The investigators, employing a cutting score method, estimated that a minimum IQ of 121 for men and 135 for women would be required for university studies. One has, to take into account not only those who are in the system of higher education but those who for various reasons do not enter it. Information on their intellectual capacity can be obtained by drawing upon data from the military testing.

Spitz makes the assumption that young people from the upper social stratum are given optimal opportunity, both financially and culturally, to proceed with their education. Thus, the question becomes: How many lower-stratum students above a certain minimum level of capacity, estimated from data for upper-stratum students, are intellectually capable of profiting from higher education? For each of the three main social strata Spitz calculated the percentage that scored above the minimum for university entrance and hence could estimate the size of the "reserve of talent". He also calculated a participation ratio – the number who entered higher education in relation to available talent. Striking differences were found between the three social strata and also between men and women. In the middle of the 1950s the latter had a participation rate of 19 per cent. By 1970 the participation rate among women had increased to only 21 per cent, in spite of a total enrolment increase by several hundred per cent since the 1950s. This shows the inertia of the system in terms of broadening opportunities for all categories. Spitz estimated that university enrolment could be doubled without lowering the intellectual level of the entrants, i.e. that it could be raised from 2.5 per cent of the relevant age groups to 5.4 per cent. In fact, the increase up to 1970 turned out to be much larger and amounted to 11 per cent of the relevant age groups. Professor Denis Kallen (personal communication) gives assurance that the intellectual standard has not decreased.

In a contribution to the 1962 *Yearbook of Education* Spitz (1962) dwells further on the methodological problems of estimating the reserves for higher education. At this juncture he could refer to the method developed by de Wolff (1961) and presented at the OECD conference at Kungälv. The "talent-limit" or cut-off score method is, indeed, a very arbitrary one in making reserve estimations. But another objection, already raised by Ekman (1949), is that aptitude for advanced studies is a multi-dimensional one. It is constituted not just by "pure" intelligence but depends on social skills, motivation, health, social background and so on. The upper social stratum in the tripartite stratification can be used as a reference group where optimal conditions for opportunities to enter and complete higher education are given. From here, reserve estimations for the two other strata can be made under the assumption that the same conditions, by means of some Utopian change of society, were offered to them.

The Dutch Armed Forces had given Raven's matrices (a non-verbal reasoning test) to almost complete age groups of 18-year old draftees. On the basis of the distribution of standard scores within each of the three main social strata Spitz (1962) was then able to calculate transition and completion probabilities according to the method developed by Härnqvist (1958) and de Wolff (1961). *Transition probability* is the student's chance of attaining the next stage in the educational hierarchy after having completed the previous one. *Completion probability* is his chance of completing the stage successfully once he has entered it. If follow-up data are available these probabilities can be calculated exactly. Spitz points out that transition probabilities tend to be more strongly affected by the child's home background than the completion probabilities. This is in agreement with the findings reported by Boalt (1947) from a follow-up of an age cohort in Stockholm, where the social handicap coefficient was higher for the selection from elementary to academic secondary school than for grade point average, grade-repeating or drop-out once transfer had taken place.

In the 1960s a large talent research programme under the directorship of F. van Heek of Leiden University was carried out (van Heek, 1968).

The aim was to identify the factors that underlie the observed differences of participation in Dutch education by the various social groups and to explore the possibilities of modifying this participation by changing school and teaching variables. The obstacles to equal participation seemed to be strongest at the transfer from primary school to academic secondary school and to be much less powerful once access had been gained to this type of education. The project therefore concentrated on the transfer from primary to secondary and on the progressive selection taking place during primary education. A set of hypotheses was developed concerning the participation of the different social groups in education, the different attitudes toward possible future changes in participation rates, and the consequences of these changes for the educational system and for society at large. Over the years a good deal of research has been carried out to test these hypotheses. This has included analysis of the socio-economic situation, in particular of adults from lower social strata who had achieved rapid social promotion; an assessment of the "talent reserves"; a psychological analysis of the inter-action between social background, educational choice and ability; and a study of the relationship between parents' social background, attitudes and so on and their children's school careers. Of the findings from these studies the following deserve particular mention.

1. Regional differences in participation in academic secondary school are strongly correlated with the regional occupational structure of the population, but differences within one and the same occupational group can be accounted for by differences in parental education.

2. There is no substantial reserve of highly gifted children for academic secondary schools (" gifted " being those whose chances of success are high). There is, however, a reserve of moderately-gifted pupils (those whose chances of completing this type of school successfully are moderate).

3. For the moderately gifted, participation in academic secondary school is strongly related to parental education and to the social origin of the mother. Family budget, parental attitude towards education, and the frequency of their contacts with school seem to have no impact.

4. If the educational level of the father is kept constant, "white-collar " and " manual " workers send their children in equal proportions to academic secondary school.

A pilot project carried out in a number of primary schools, however, gave strong support to the view that these findings should not lead to discouragement. In an eight-week " activation " programme, it appeared possible to increase considerably both the measured intelligence and the achievement of children of manual workers. The report on van Heek's talent research programme concludes with the proposal that special schools should be opened for children from disadvantaged groups, offering both pre-primary and primary education, so as to activate their potential talents.

H. *Danish Surveys*

In 1965 and 1968 the Danish National Institute of Social Research conducted two major surveys with the broad aim of elucidating the situation of young people at an age of 14-20. Representative samples were drawn from the target populations of 14-20 and 14-year olds. The surveys focused particularly on the education and the career opportunities of young people.

These aspects of the surveys have been dealt with by Hansen (1971) and Örum (1971). Both authors, particularly Örum, also considered the problems of reserves of ability.

Hansen (1971) devoted one section of the report on his survey to the reserve of ability problem (*op. cit.,* p. 42 *et seq.*). Like Ekman (1951), he made a distinction between potential and actual reserve of ability, the former being realized under socio-economic conditions that determine the development of children of upper or upper middle class background, the latter being available under conditions present in a class-stratified society where only a minority grows up in very privileged conditions. The actual reserve, then, consists of youngsters, mostly of lower-class background who, according to some valid criterion, have the ability and/or motivation to profit from higher education, particularly at the pre-university level (*gymnasium*), but who have not had the opportunity to do so.

When the 1965 sample of 14-20-year olds was asked what occupation they would choose if they could decide what they would most like to become, 64 per cent of the youngsters with professional and managerial background indicated occupations that require at least the completion of upper secondary school, whereas 23 per cent among those whose fathers were craftsmen or skilled workers and only 16 per cent among those of with unskilled fathers made this choice. Only 14 per cent of the first group indicated occupations that did not require any further general education but just the completion of statutory elementary schooling and some vocational training. The corresponding percentages for the two latter groups were 46 and 49 respectively. Since the majority of the youngsters were about to complete, or had already completed, their school education, these findings support the theory advanced by several educational sociologists (see, e.g., Breton, 1970b or Bowles and Gintisi 1973) that the school serves as a stratification instrument in moulding the occupational aspirations of its students.

A simple vocabulary test was used as a rough measure of scholastic ability. Cautions in interpreting the findings were expressed by Örum (1971). Nevertheless, by using the cutting-score approach, he estimated that the intake to the upper-secondary school (*gymnasium*) could be doubled without lowering the intellectual requirements. This is in accordance with the findings of similar surveys in Sweden (Husén, 1948) and Austria (OECD, 1965).

Whereas the Hansen (1971) survey included a stratified random sample from the whole age range 14-20, the Örum (1971) study, which was conducted in 1968, comprised only 14-year olds who will be followed up until the age of 20. The base sample consisted of a 4 per cent random national sample that included 152 classes with 3,151 7th-grade students. The major purpose of the 1971 publication was to elucidate the relationship between social background, ability and educational attainment on the completion of compulsory schooling which takes place at the age of 14. The follow-up part of the study is planned to continue until 1975. Until then, it will not be possible to assess relative importance of the various background factors that have influenced the educational and occupational careers before the age of 20.

The socio-economic groups, into which the sample was broken down were:

i) Professional, managerial, civil servants
ii) Middle management
iii) Supervisors
iv) Clerks, craftsmen, and skilled workers
v) Unskilled workers.

Three types of ability measures were used: (1) a group test of general intelligence; (2) a test of spatial ability; and (3) a test of inductive ability (number series). The difference in mean score between children with professional and managerial background and those whose parents were unskilled workers amounted to one standard deviation on the verbal test, 0.8 on the test of inductive ability, and 0.6 on the test of spatial ability. The difference between those whose parents had passed matriculation examination and those who had only 7 years of elementary schooling was 0.9 of one standard deviation.

Örum (1971) showed that, in spite of the large difference in the proportion between socio-economic groups (i) and (v) (81 versus 25 per cent transferred to, or chose, the academic track in the secondary school) the same standards in terms of intelligence test scores had been applied. The lowest decile among those admitted was even higher in group (i) than in group (v). Therefore, no more in terms of at least verbal intelligence was required from lower-class students than from upper or middle class. This only proves, of course, that the intelligence test alone did not account for differences between the socio-economic groups in transfer to (or selection for) academic secondary education. Since intelligence tests in the first place were not employed as selection criteria, and since differences in intelligence test scores at most account for half the variance in scholastic achievement, social class bias in terms of non-cognitive factors may very well have entered into the selection procedure. But the percentage of those admitted to the academic secondary school decreased with falling socio-economic status (from I to V) within the respective test score intervals. As can be seen from Table 4.7, this is particularly striking for students with average verbal intelligence for whom social background appears to have great influence.

Table 4.7 ENROLMENT
IN THE ACADEMIC SECONDARY SCHOOL PROGRAMME
AMONG DANISH 14-YEAR OLDS,
BY SOCIAL BACKGROUND AND TEST PERFORMANCE

Test score interval	Social background				
	High I	II	III	IV	Low V
− 24	−	(0)	(0)	(0)	(0)
25–34	(0)	(0)	2	5	2
35–34	(8)	(22)	17	10	9
45–54	74	61	46	36	28
55–64	96	82	68	72	59
65–74	97	95	93	93	(69)
75 −	−	(100)	(100)	(100)	−

Note: Percentages in brackets are based on less than 25 cases.
Source: Örum, 1971.

I. Swedish Research on the " Reserve of Ability "

Before surveying the research conducted in Sweden in the 1940s and 1950s with the specific aim of estimating the size of the " reserve of ability " we shall briefly review some studies of social class " representation " at the secondary and university levels, since it was these studies that brought about an awareness of the existence of a " reserve ".

It has already been observed that, since the middle of the 1940s, research on the " reserves of ability " has been concomitant with the Swedish school reforms (Husén and Boalt, 1968). The 1950 Education Bill, which introduced the comprehensive school on a pilot basis, made reference to surveys carried out by Husén (1946, 1947, and 1948) and Boalt (1947), designed to assess the proportion of an age group capable of passing both the middle school and the matriculation examination.

Several Royal Commissions dealing with various aspects of Swedish education during the 1940s and 1950s either sponsored surveys or drew upon information already available to elucidate the extent to which students from different home backgrounds (defined either by social class or by parental occupational status) participated in academic secondary and university education. Most of these surveys focused on how students reaching the matriculation examination or entering the university were recruited from various social strata – usually defined as upper, middle, or lower class.

The 1940 Royal Commission, which had the formidable mandate of drawing up a blue-print for revising the structure and content of the entire primary and secondary system, followed up an age-cohort of students who had entered various types of junior academic secondary schools, with particular reference to the four- and five-year *realskola.* The issue over which the Commission was split was whether the transfer from primary to academic secondary school should occur for all children after grade 6, when they would go to the four-year *realskola,* or whether some (allegedly the more able) should be allowed to transfer immediately after grade 4 to the five-year *realskola* (Husén, 1962). The various characteristics of these two types of school had then to be elucidated, among other things the socio-economic factors behind their respective enrolments. The Commission studied the whole population of students who enrolled in the various types of *realskola* as well as the *gymnasium* and followed them up until 1944. The enrolment by social class is shown in Table 4.8.

Table 4.8 SWEDISH SECONDARY SCHOOL ENROLMENT
IN 1938 BY SOCIAL CLASS

In percentage

Social class	Five-year state *Realskola*	Four-year state *Realskola*	Four-year municipal *Realskola*	State *Gymnasium*	Social class distribution among population
Upper	18	9	7	28	5
Middle	58	55	50	61	38
Lower	24	36	43	11	57

Source: SOU 1944:21, Government Printing Office.

96

Still in 1940s, the Royal Commission on Student Aid sponsored a study of the social background of secondary school matriculants and university students carried out by S. Moberg and C.E. Quensel (1949). They arrived at the percentage shown in Table 4.9. Later, Moberg (1951) conducted a thorough follow-through for three age groups of matriculants and studied their university and occupational careers in relation to their social background and school marks.

Table 4.9 SWEDISH SECONDARY SCHOOL
MATRICULANTS AND UNIVERSITY
STUDENTS IN THE 1940s BY SOCIAL CLASS

		In percentage
Social class	Students registered for matriculation examination	Students enrolled at the University
Upper	51	58
Middle	42	36
Lower	7	6
Total	100	100

Source: SOU 1948:42, Government Printing Office, p. 31.

In a follow-up study by Husén (1950, 1969) in which the entire male population of the city of Malmö was traced from the third grade of elementary school (age 10) via induction to military service (age 20) to occupational status at 35, it was shown that enrolment in the academic type of secondary school was very unequally distributed through the social strata. The percentage of further schooling within the four socio-economic groups into which the population had been divided are shown in Table 4.10.

Table 4.10 TRANSFER RATE TO ACADEMIC SECONDARY EDUCATION
IN THE CITY OF MALMÖ FROM 1938 TO 1948 BY SOCIAL CLASS

Social class	Further education		
	In secondary academic school	In *Realskola* only	In *Gymnasium* (per cent)
Upper	85	24	61
Middle	40	30	10
Upper-lower	22	13	9
Lower-lower	12	9	3

Source: Husén, 1950.

What has become recognized as the classical survey of migration in relation to social and geographical background, education and tested intelligence was conducted in Sweden by Neymak (1961). This investigation was based on a 10 per cent sample of the total age group of conscripts, comprising practically all males born in Sweden in 1928. The first set of data

97

was collected in 1948. The number of sons from various occupational categories who had taken the university-qualifying matriculation examination or the examination from the *realskola* (lower secondary school) varies quite a lot, as can be seen from Table 4.11.

Table 4.11 NUMBER OF SONS OF VARIOUS OCCUPATIONAL CATEGORIES GOING TO ACADEMIC TYPE OF SECONDARY SCHOOL
(Investigation based on 10 per cent sample of all 20-year-olds born in 1928)

In percentage

	Proportion having passed matriculation examination	Proportion having passed middle-school examination
A. Farmers:		
1. Farm owners	2	3
2. Tenant farmers	2	2
B. Small-farm owners:		
1. Farming, gardening, forestry, etc.	0	0
2. Farm labourers with smallholdings	1	1
C. Fishermen	0	0
D. Small merchants	11	21
E. Small manufacturers and artisans	9	9
F. Building contractors	9	13
G. Repairmen	0	9
H. Taxi owners, etc.	2	13
I. Civil servants:		
1. With university training	80	11.5
2. Other specialised training	53	21.5
J. Managers	70	17
K. Middle and low grades of managerial posts	23	34.5
L. Supervisors and technicians:		
1. In public service with assignments not requiring advanced general education	15	35
2. Privately employed	8	20
3. Foremen	3.5	14
M. Salesmen	2	8
N. Workers in public services:		
1. Firemen, policemen, coastguards, etc.	2	23
2. Traffic workers (railway, bus, tramway), postmen	5	9.5
O. Skilled workers in industry:		
1. Construction workers	2.5	7.5
2. Craftsmen (skilled carpenters, mechanics, etc.)	3	12
P. Semi- or unskilled construction workers:		
1. In public services	1.5	13
2. Road workers, railway workers	0	1.5
3. Construction workers (building industry)	0	3
Q. Workers in industry of other categories than O and P	1	5
R. Forestry workers	0	2
S. Farm labourers (other than B.2 above)	0.5	1
T. Workers in transport and distributive trades ...	0	3
U. General labourers	3	3

Sources: Neymark, 1952, and 1961.

Findings such as those presented in this Table, showing a high "over-representation" of students from upper or middle class homes in the academic type of secondary school and among entrants to the university, naturally give rise to the question of the extent to which a "talent reserve" existed in the lower social strata. There was no reason to believe that the working class (more than half the population) was unable to provide more than 10 per cent of the university students, while the upper class (less than 10 per cent of the adult population) produced from three to give times as many.

Moberg (1951) showed that the proportion of students from lower social class taking the matriculation examination had been fairly constant between 1910 and 1943. Even if we assume that social mobility might have brought about a higher level of potential (hereditary) scholastic aptitude in the middle and upper classes, the difference in enrolment between them and the lower class must be accounted for by other factors, such as the earning power of the family, the level of educational aspiration of the parents, and their attitudes towards higher education.

*

It is of interest now to take a look at the series of Swedish studies to which we have already referred — those that, from the mid-1940s, set out to estimate the actual size of the "talent reserve", or the potential academic population. To make possible an investigation of the size of the potential academic secondary school or the potential university population, two conditions have to be met. First, comparable measures of ability, such as intelligence test scores, achievement test scores, or standardized school marks, have to be available for representative samples. Secondly, the system of registration should enable follow-up studies for a number of years. The first condition is self-evident, since no dependable estimates can be made unless ability data for representative samples of individuals are available. However, an estimate must be based also upon a follow-up of the sample from the moment in the school career when organizational differentiation begins until schooling itself is finished.

The whole age group of conscripts for military service, 20 years old, provided the data for the first comprehensive investigation in this field in 1945 (Husén, 1946). Complete information was collected for 44,011 individuals who comprised more than 95 per cent of the total male population born in 1925. The conscripts were given a group intelligence test composed of eight sub-tests, most of them verbal in content. The tested population was broken down according to formal education into the following sub-groups: elementary school only; middle school (realskola) without leaving examination; middle school with leaving examination; university-preparing school (gymnasium) without leaving examination; university-preparing school with leaving examination; and university studies.

The test score distribution for each group was determined, as was a series of measures of spread, such as the 10th percentile, the lower quartile, the higher quartile, and the 90th percentile. The potential academically talented school population was estimated in the following way. A comparison was made between those who had reached the middle school examina-

99

tion and those who had dropped out, mainly because of failure to meet the academic requirements. Only 50 per cent of the intake in the *realskola* reached the leaving examination in due time. Another 10-15 per cent repeated one or more grades. The number of students not being promoted at the end of the spring semester was on average 10 per cent. If one were to omit those who score below the 10th percentile in the leaving examination, one would have to omit also some of those with low intelligence who, by coaching or other means, had " survived " the *realskola* and managed to pass the final examination. A cutting score at the 10th percentile for those who had reached the leaving examination divided the distribution of those who did not into equal halves which corresponded to the opinion held by some investigators that about half the failures in the *realskola* were caused by lack of intelligence and the other half by non-intellectual factors. Applying this cutting score to the distribution of the total age group and the sub-group with elementary schooling only, we found that 33 per cent of the total age group scored an IQ of 107 or above, which implies that the *realskola* had intellectual requirements that would fit the best-endowed third of an age group. About 20 per cent with elementary schooling only had scores above an IQ of 107. They therefore constituted the " reserve of ability " so far as the junior academic secondary school was concerned.

Applying the same procedure to those who entered *gymnasium,* we found that 14 per cent of the age group would have the intellectual capacity to pass the matriculation examination (*studentexamen*). We could then determine how many of the tested group with formal schooling above the cutting scores for the middle school examination and the *studentexamen* had the potential to profit from further education. In this event, it turned out that less than half of those having these scores in the total age group had actually proceeded to more advanced education. Only about a third reached the *studentexamen*, which indicated that the potential university population was considerable.

The same methodology was applied when replication studies were carried out on the age groups from 1946 through 1948. Thus, four age groups, making a total of around 175,000 individuals, were tested and school records collected (Husén, 1946, 1947, 1948 and SNS, 1950). It should be pointed out that the intelligence test employed was completely changed after 1947. The findings for the four age groups are presented in Table 4.12.

Since, at the end of the 1940s, the number of students actually taking the matriculation examination was about 5 per cent of their age group, one might say that the " talent reserve " consisted of at least as many as those who passed it and, in the majority of cases, went on to university. The same conclusion applies to those who passed the junior secondary school examination. This would indicate, then, that a tremedous talent reserve, mainly in the lower social classes, was not being used for the types of occupation for which the academic schools give the basic preparation. However, even among social scientists, some doubts were expressed about the existence of a substantial "reserve of ability." The fact that only 1/2 per cent of the children of manual workers reached as far as the matriculation examination did not shake the conviction that the reserves were small (Quensel, 1949).

Table 4.12 ESTIMATE OF THE NUMBER OF INDIVIDUALS
WITHIN TOTAL AGE GROUPS CAPABLE OF PASSING
LOWER SECONDARY SCHOOL (*Realskola*) EXAMINATION
AND UNIVERSITY ENTRANCE EXAMINATION (*Studentexamen*)

In percentage

Age group	Proportion of individuals above test score limit			
	for lower secondary school examination		for university entrance (matriculation) examination	
	Within total age group	Among those with elementary schooling only	Within total age group	Among those with elementary schooling only
1945	33	22	14	5
1946	32	20	13	5
1947	32	19	12	4
1948	33	22	13	5

Sources: Husén, 1946, 1947, 1948; SNS, 1950.

The methodology that has been briefly described here for estimating the relative number of academically talented young people and assessing the extent of a reserve of such talent that lies unused has several weaknesses. These we will consider in turn.

To start with, the lack of reliability of the test used as a measure of ability constituted a source of error. The distribution of scores for those who have passed a certain type of schooling and those who have not entered it will overlap more than would the distributions of the "true" scores because the error variance increases the overlap. This means, then, that the number of those with lower schooling who pass the critical score can be inflated by insufficient test reliability.

A much more important source of error, however, was pointed out and analysed by Ekman (1949). A group intelligence test is far from perfectly correlated with either the level of formal schooling reached or the criteria of success in the academic school. Under favourable circumstances, the correlation ceiling is about +0.70, which means that about half of the variance in school performance can be accounted for by factors measured by intelligence tests. Ekman (1949) showed that lack of validity is a much more important source of error than lack of reliability in that it will considerably increase the overlap between the distributions of the sub-groups and therefore contribute to an over-estimate of the size of the talent reserve.

A third source of error was the following. The test was administered at the age of 20, i.e., after the differentiation in various types of schooling had taken place. Those who had gone far enough to reach the *gymnasium,* or had passed the matriculation examination, were tested either when still in school or immediately after having finished it, whereas those who had left after completing elementary school only (age 13-15) were at a disadvantage, since the skills measured by the paper-and-pencil tests could have become "rusty" over the years. In a ten-year follow-up study it was shown that the academic type of schooling leading to *studentexamen* improved the IQ by at least ten points (Husén, 1950). Härnqvist (1959), employing a more adequate method, estimated the rise in IQ to be about fifteen points.

This source of error tends to reduce considerably the overlap between the distributions compared and would contribute to an underestimate of the intellectual reserve. It is therefore highly desirable to measure intellectual capacity *before* any differentiation in formal schooling has taken place.

To meet these criticisms in advance, one should, then, make these qualifications:

(1) A reserve in a *wide* sense should be distinguished from a reserve in a *narrow* sense. In talking about a reserve in a wide sense, we include *all* the factors (cognitive and non-cognitive) that are related to success and failure in the academic type of schooling. In the above-mentioned studies we were able to cover only cognitive factors, and the estimates are therefore limited to reserves in the narrow sense. It has been suggested that this should be called the "intelligence reserve".

(2) A "*potential* reserve" should be distinguished from an "*actual* reserve". In tests administered at the age of 20, part of the individual differences are due to variations in formal schooling and to other experiences during the interval between leaving school and the point in time when the test is administered. The ideal conditions for a study of the size of the "talent reserve" would therefore have to include access to data pertaining to intelligence and school performances at the ages of, say, 7–10, and thereafter a follow-up of the students until the age of 20 or 21, when the students have completed the upper secondary school.

Before leaving this particular topic, we should, perhaps, take note of some findings from a ten-year follow-up study in the city of Malmö cited above (Husén, 1950 and 1969). The school careers for an almost complete age group of about 700 boys were followed from the age of 10 to 20. A group intelligence test was administered at both ends of the follow-up period. The group was divided into four social strata: upper, middle, upper-lower, lower-lower. The number of secondary school entrants (in per cent) within each social stratum with an IQ above 100 or rated "above average" by the teachers is given in Table 4.13.

Table 4.13 PERCENTAGE OF STUDENTS
ENTERING ACADEMIC SECONDARY EDUCATION
in the city of Malmö, by social class, IQ and teacher ratings

	Upper	Middle	Upper-Lower	Lower-Lower
IQ above 100	77	17	12	5
Scholastic aptitude above average according to teacher ratings	78	22	12	10

Source: Husén, 1950.

The most significant empirical contribution to Swedish research on the size of the talent reserve has been made by Härnqvist who conducted a survey on the reserve of ability for higher education for the 1955 Royal Commission on University Reform (Härnqvist, 1958). In this, he was able to draw upon theoretical conceptions derived from previous research, particularly by Ekman (1949). But he himself made several new contributions to conceptualization and methodology in this field. Thanks to the effectiveness of registration of census data, he could draw samples at several points in time for which retrospective data were already available and thus did not have to wait for results of follow-up enquiries.

The school records of two large samples were retrospectively studied: one that completed the fourth grade of the elementary school in 1945 and the other that completed the penultimate grade (eight school year) in the *realskola* in 1949. The sampling technique employed was stratified cluster sampling with systematic selection within strata. The elementary school group contained a quarter of the fourth grade classes in Sweden, a total of about 10,000 boys. Since Härnqvist wanted to use the test data obtained during induction to military service, this sample was confined to boys. The *realskola* group contained 3,600 boys and 2,800 girls. School marks were available for the end of the fourth grade in the elementary schools and for the *realskola* group.

Härnqvist adopted a modification of a method proposed by Ekman (1951) which he called the "probability" method (see Halsey, 1961, p. 147, *et seq*). Its essential points are these:

1. The assumption is made that all upper class children who have the necessary minimum capacity to profit from academic secondary school education actually get the opportunity to go there. Previous studies by Husén (1950) and Neymark (1952) had shown that in the 1940s about 85 per cent of the upper class and upper middle class children had obtained some secondary academic type of schooling and about 60 to 65 per cent of that group had passed the university-qualifying matriculation examination at 19-20. There were even rare cases with an IQ below 100 who had succeeded in getting into the *gymnasium*. The probability that, under optimal conditions, a student at a certain ability level will transfer to the academic type of school is therefore determined by the percentage of boys at the same ability level within the upper social stratum who actually transferred.

2. The number of students at various initial levels (according to school marks) is multiplied by the probability computed at each initial level from social stratum 1. This yields an estimate of the number of students in social strata 2 and 3 (middle and lower) who, given the opportunities of those in the upper stratum, would have the potential for transfer to academic education.

3. The "probability" that a student, having embarked upon academic education, will pursue his education to a leaving examination is derived from data available for social class 1 (upper). The assumption is, then, that in social class 1 it is optimal conditions that keep the student in school and prevent him from dropping out.

4. The numbers of students in the middle and lower classes calculated by the process in (2) are multiplied by the probabilities arrived at by (3). This yields estimates of how many students there are in social classes 2 and 3 who have the capacity to pursue their studies to the leaving examination, given the opportunities of social class 1.

5. The numbers arrived at by the calculation in (4) are then totalled and reduced by the number of students who actually reached the school-leaving examination. The resultant figure is the estimate of the talent reserve. According to Ekman's (1951) terminology, this is an estimate of the "potential reserve in the wider sense."

One table from Härnqvist's survey (which is reviewed in Husén and Boalt, 1968) is presented by way of illustrating how the probability of

103

students being transferred from one level of formal schooling to another were calculated. Table 4.14 illustrates the probabilities for transfer from *realskola* to the upper stage of secondary academic school (*gymnasium*).

No less than 61 per cent of the students in the upper stratum had passed the matriculation examination which gave admission to the university, as compared with only 4 per cent in the entire sample. We notice that the probability of getting a higher education with a relatively low grade-point average is much higher for children from the upper class than for children from the rest of the population.

Using the procedure described above, Härnqvist arrived at the following results:

Number of students in an age group:

1. having actually passed university admission (matriculation) examination, ... 8.2%
2. having passed leaving examination from *realskola* but, according to estimates, capable of passing university admission examination, ... 4.1%
3. having not even been transferred to *realskola* but, according to estimates, capable of passing the university admission examination (matriculation examination), ... 15.5%
4. having passed leaving examination from *realskola* but, according to estimates, not capable of passing university admission examination, ... 6.5%
5. having not been transferred to *realskola* but, according to estimates, capable of passing the leaving examination from *realskola,* and 17.1%
6. not capable of passing leaving examination from *realskola* ... 48.6%

   Total 100.0%

According to Härnqvist's method of estimation, therefore, about a quarter of the boys within an age group (categories 1-3 above) had the potential to pass the university admission examination. Since only about 8 per cent of an age group actually passed it in 1956, the potential university reserve in a wide sense was, then, about one fifth of the age group. The potential reserve in the wider sense would have been about one third of the age group. In conclusion, then, Sweden at the beginning of the 1950s did not develop even half of its intellectual potential or even one third of its potential university population.

The crucial question in discussing the validity of the results obtained in this study is the extent to which the basic assumption itself is valid. One might question the assumption that, given the environment of the upper class, the young people now in the middle and lower classes (with the same initial capacity in terms of school marks) would, in fact, proceed to the academic type of secondary school and pursue their studies there as assiduously as most upper and upper middle class students do. To be fully valid, this assumption must presuppose an almost perfectly egalitarian society for more than one generation. Research on educational motivation and aspirations has shown that attitudes towards higher education, such as willingness to encourage one's children into it and the setting of a relatively high level of aspiration, are not as closely related to the economic as to the educational background of parents. For example, 68 per cent of the sons

Table 4.14 FREQUENCY OF TRANSFER TO " GYMNASIUM" AND OF PASSING MATRICULATION EXAMINATION BY SOCIAL CLASS AND GRADE POINTS

Sum of grades	Upper-class			Middle and lower-class			Entire sample		
	Total sub-group	Transferred	Passed university admission examination	Total sub-group	Transferred	Passed university admission examination	Total sub-group	Transferred	Passed university admission examination
	1	2	3	4	5	6	7	8	9
10.5	28	6	6	101	8	4	129	14	10
11.0–13.0	167	82	52	403	70	37	570	152	89
13.5–15.5	269	160	116	679	176	123	948	336	239
16.0–18.0	250	202	162	577	236	198	827	438	360
18.5–20.5	175	148	138	323	168	148	498	316	286
21.0–23.0	107	103	98	214	145	140	321	248	238
23.5–25.5	49	46	46	135	98	94	184	144	140
26.0–28.0	31	31	31	63	53	53	94	84	84
28.5	14	14	14	16	16	16	30	30	30
Total	1,090	792	663	2,511	970	813	3,601	1,762	1,476

Source: Härnqvist, 1958.

of graduates pass the matriculation examination to university. The corresponding figure for the rest of the occupations included in the upper social stratum is 42 per cent. In her study of *Bildungsabstinenz* ("educational abstinence") among manual workers Susanne Grimm (1966) particularly emphasizes the influence of certain socio-cultural factors, such as parental education, rearing practices, the acquisition of language skills and achievement motivation.

As an estimate of the talent reserve in Swedish society, as at present constituted, the figures quoted above overrate the resources; but in a Utopia, where all parents share not only upper class economic privileges but upper class attitudes and aspirations as well, they would probably give a fair statement of the position.

4. WILL THE POOL OF TALENT SOON BE EXHAUSTED?

Those who advocate a status quo for the educational system and who also tend to favour a selective school structure that channels only an élite to more advanced levels often (somewhat rhetorically) raise the question whether the pool of talent will suffice in an era like ours when enrolment at advanced levels is increasing. They foresee a lowering of standards as a result of expanded access to higher education (see, e.g. Cox and Dyson, 1969).

In another publication I have dealt at some length with various aspects of the question whether the opening up of new opportunities and broadening of enrolment leads to a lowering of standards (Husén, 1974b). The fact that in some countries the total enrolment to upper secondary education and to first-degree courses at the university level has increased by more than 400 per cent (OECD, 1971) and that the proportion of young people from lower class homes going to university has increased from about 1-2 to close on 10 per cent may well make one ask if the "reserve of talent" has been tapped to the bottom.

Before examining some empirical evidence we should be clear that a reply to the question posed in the title to this section will depend upon how static one's conception of talent is. Those who express worries about exhausted intellectual resources and inflated standards tend in most cases to be believers in inherited talent, i.e. to conceive of talent as a fixed genetic asset that cannot be improved except by eugenic measures. Those who take a more environmentalistic point of view, on the other hand, hold that the available capital of talent can be considerably improved and/or expanded by redesigning and improving the circumstances in which young people grow up.

There are three sources of evidence to suggest that the pool of talent is to some extent expandable:

(1) Follow-up studies which have compared students who went on to advanced formal education with those of the same initial intellectual standing who did not, indicate that IQ can be considerably "improved" by further education (see, e.g., Husén, 1950 and 1969).

(2) Cross-sectional studies of age cohorts with regard to IQ and achievement level consistently indicate an improved standard of performance.

106

The Scottish surveys in the 1930s and 1940s are cases in point (Scottish Council, 1937 and 1949). National surveys of childrens' achievement in reading at 11 over the years 1948 to 1964 in England indicate "a remarkable improvement in standards" (HMSO, 1967, p. 260). Surveys in major cities in the United States, however, show a decline in mean achievement scores in the 1960s. During the last decades, a considerable reshuffling of the structure of enrolment has occurred as a result of the influx of poor minority families which in some cities (for instance in the borough of Manhattan) now make up the majority.

(3) The average levels of performance on IQ and achievement tests have been compared over a long time span during which high school enrolment has increased. One should in this connection refer to Finch's (1946) study in the United States. He plotted the mean IQs of high school students in all the research studies that had been done from 1916 to the early 1940s against the time axis. There was a tendency of increased IQ among these students in spite of a spectacular increase in the percentage of the relevant age cohort that enrolled.

The Robbins Committee conducted a survey of the 21-year-olds in England and concluded: "In short we think there is no risk that within the next twenty years the growth in the proportion of young people with qualifications and aptitudes suitable for entry to higher education will be restrained by a shortage of potential ability" (quoted after Silver, 1973, p. 198). "If there is to be talk of a pool of ability, it must be of a pool which surpasses the widow's cruse in the Old Testament, in that when more is taken for higher education in one generation more will tend to be available in the next" (op. cit., p. 198).

The Presidential Address that Robert Faris (1961) delivered to the American Sociological Society in 1961 can be cited as an illustration of how some social scientists on both sides of the Atlantic have viewed the problem of proper utilization of talent. This address was entitled "Reflections on the Ability Dimension in Human Society" and it made a case for mass higher education. Modern society cannot do any longer with only a "limited stock of geniuses at the top of the productivity organisation" (op. cit., p. 836). The security and power of advanced nations "lie not in buried gold but mainly in the accumulated capital of collective ability" (op. cit., p. 837). Faris' main point was that "a society generates its level of ability" and "that the upper limit is unknown and distant, and best of all, that the processes of ability are potentially subject to intentional control". Institutional schooling is the main instrument for raising the ability level of the entire population. Faris was convinced that the "educational boom" prevailing at the beginning of the 1960s had "spectacular implications for the future" (op. cit., p. 839).

The hopes for what formal education can do are high: "What is happening at the present time is that the nation is quietly lifting itself by the boot-straps to an important higher level of general ability" (op. cit., p. 838). Such a statement was more likely to have been made by a sociologist in the United States at that time. In Europe a similar view was being expressed in connection with research on the reserves of ability (Husén, 1951). The majority of those involved in the debate on school reforms, however, were convinced that the pool was fixed, in the last run being determined by the gene pool.

Chapter 5

STRUCTURE AND SELECTIVITY OF EDUCATIONAL SYSTEMS AS RESTRAINTS ON EQUALITY

1. THE PROBLEM OF DUALISM IN EUROPEAN SCHOOL SYSTEMS

The formal educational systems in most European countries have for a long time consisted of two distinct sub-systems: a public primary school for all (or almost all) the children up to the age of 10 to 12, and a secondary school for an intellectual and social élite. This legacy from an ascriptive society still looms large, and the overriding problem in recent attempts to bring about reforms has been how to integrate horizontally and vertically the various types of school that cover the mandatory attendance period into a one type school, be it called a comprehensive or not.

The dualism that until recently prevailed meant that transfer from the middle grades of the primary school, say after grade 4 or 5, could only be to the academic, university-preparing secondary school. Everybody was fully aware that those who transferred to the more prestigious secondary school were heading for the better paid and more highly esteemed jobs. Those who remained in the terminal grades of the primary school were as a rule destined for manual labour.

A system whereby students were selected for academic tracks of study as early as 10 or 12, and (even more important) where decisions had to be made *for* them that had decisive consequences throughout their life career, has been a major issue in European school policy for decades. The prime motive behind the quest for "democratization" of further-going education has been the opening up of careers to talent from all walks of life. But the demand for highly trained manpower in a society on the verge of having more people in service than in manufacturing occupations and the need to boost economic growth have also been stimulants to this quest, particularly in the 1960s.

In this chapter we shall mainly deal with two problem areas that both pertain to structural and selective restraints on equality of educational opportunity. After some introductory observations on selectivity versus comprehensiveness in educational provisions, we shall first examine educational attainments and aspirations in selective and comprehensive systems. Secondly, we shall try to identify the selective barriers that exist and indicate some of their effects in terms of built-in social bias.

The introduction of a mandatory elementary school for the masses in many industrialized countries in the middle of the 19th century accentuated the problem of dualism which still characterizes most school systems. The result was two systems running partly parallel to each other: on the one hand, the compulsory, elementary schools with varying lengths of attendance for the masses; on the other, the secondary schools which essentially prepare for the university with a programme of a humanistic-classical type and with an enrolment less than 10 per cent of an age group consisting mainly of upper and upper-middle-class children. For a long time in most countries there was no bridge at all to enable transfer between the common elementary school and the academic secondary school. The families who wanted their children to enter the secondary school had to send them to special, mostly private, preparatory schools. In Sweden, for instance, there was no linkage between the two school types until 1894, when new regulations provided for transfer from the better public elementary school to the first grade of the state secondary school.

As already said, a fundamental policy problem in many European countries during the last few decades has been how to reorganize the educational system so as to abolish the dualism between the common elementary school and the academic secondary school up to the age of, say, 15 or 16. The obstacle at the heart of this has been the long-established existence of separate types of schools for children from different social classes. The urgency of the problem has been enhanced by the following trends. First of all, economic growth and the complexity of modern technological society have pressed for prolonged education (mandatory or not) for all young people — regardless of whether it be provided in an extended elementary school or partly taken care of within the structure of a secondary school. Secondly, the rapidly expanding demand for skilled manpower has put pressure on the school systems to increase their intake at the secondary level. Thirdly, and this is an important concomitant of the democratization of secondary and higher education, the " consumption " of or " social demand " for education has increased tremendously.

Prolonged school attendance, however, gives rise to considerable structural problems which all have to do with the linkage between primary and secondary school. Until now the " primary school " in most Western European countries (irrespective of whether it formally consisted of six, seven, eight or nine grades) has had to see many of its best students transferred to the academic secondary school after four to six grades. In effect, therefore, a primary school in most cases has been an institution that accommodates the first four to six grades, while the secondary school follows by accommodating grades 5-6 to 13. Because of the overlapping grades, the two types of school run partly parallel to each other. Since entry to the academic secondary school in some countries takes place at the age of 10-12, prolonged mandatory school attendance has resulted in an increased number of parallel grades in the two types of school. This means that in several countries an increasing number of young people in the age range of 10-15 have come to be taught in schools that have quite disparate objectives. Efforts to establish greater equality of educational opportunity, which is itself part of a social welfare policy that attempts to create greater social equality, has naturally generated demands for a more unified school organization. In this context it is pertinent to recall that the Swedish Minister of Education, in the terms of reference he gave to the 1940 Royal Commission, underlined the dilemma posed by a continually enlarged system of parallel schools (Husén, 1962). The same problem has impressed itself on committees assigned to deal with organizational matters in, for instance, England, France, and the Federal Republic of Germany (see, for example, OECD, 1971b and 1972).

When we examine how various countries have worked out a linkage between the primary and the secondary school, we can distinguish three main lines of approach:

1. Until recently the public school system in many European countries, such as England, France, and Germany, consisted of two almost completely separate sub-systems: a primary school for all, or for the majority, up to the age of 10–12, and a secondary school that socially, and to a large extent intellectually also, was fairly selective. (A private sub-system, such as the independent so-called Public Schools and the 'private' preparatory schools in England or the Catholic schools in France, catered for a minority and covered both the elementary and secondary level). Transfers from primary to secondary school occurred with few exceptions at the ages of 10–12. Some students never attended public primary schools but went to private preparatory ones. For the majority of students in most of these countries, such a system meant that the parents had to make an irrevocable educational decision which had important career implications for their children young as they were at the time. Those who transferred to the secondary school were bound for white-collar occupations at a professional and semi-professional level. Those who did not go beyond primary school were heading for manual occupations.

Structural reforms projected or implemented in countries like England, France and Germany have considerably modified, or are intended to modify, the systems to the extent of permitting the age range from 11 to 13–15 to become what in the French reform of 1959 was referred to as an "observation stage" (*cycle d'observation*) so that a definitive categorization of students may be postponed. Further, new types of upper-secondary school have sprung up alongside the traditional types with their humanistic curriculum with the result that the classical pre-university school no longer holds the monopoly for entry into the professions.

2. For a long time there was no provision for secondary education apart from the pre-university *Gymnasium*-type school; but, at the turn of the century, various types of "middle schools" were established in several countries as a preparation for white-collar jobs, for instance for office clerks. The middle school was then sometimes made into a precursor of the upper secondary school. Thus, for instance in Sweden, provisions were made for such a sequence on two occasions – by the Education Act of 1904 when the *gymnasium* was divided into two levels (a *realskola* with its own middle-school examination and a four-year *gymnasium*) and by the Education Act of 1927 when those who obtained the middle-school certificate at municipal middle schools were granted entry into the university-preparing *gymnasium*. Other examples of middle schools being established with a profile of their own are provided by Denmark and the Netherlands. In the Netherlands a "bridge-year", which coincides with grade 7 and age 12–13, was introduced in the late 1960s.

3. The third approach to the problem is found in countries with secondary schools that are comprehensive both as regards enrolment, which

is mandatory for all up to a certain age, and curricula, which are vocational as well as preparing for university entrance. The organization of secondary education in the United States derives from two historical determinants: unlike Europe, there was no parallel-school tradition except in the old colonies (Cremin, 1970). American education had to meet particular demands of society at an earlier stage than was the case in Europe. It was expected to socialize immigrants and to satisfy the needs of a rapidly industrialized job world. Secondary schools had therefore to be created to cater for all kinds and degrees of ability.

The corollary of lessened social, and to some extent intellectual, selectivity is that much of the subject matter that in the first two types of system is taught at the upper secondary school level has been moved up to the post-secondary level. Thus, the first two years of college in the United States, or in some places all four years, offer programmes of study that are equivalent to the terminal classes at the French *lycée* or the German *Gymnasium*.

2. EDUCATIONAL ATTAINMENTS AND ASPIRATIONS IN SELECTIVE AND COMPREHENSIVE SYSTEMS

A. *Quantity Versus Quality*

There is a widespread belief that the broadening of opportunities for upper secondary education that has taken place on both sides of the Atlantic has resulted in a sizable lowering of standards. More, it is said, means worse. Now, if we are properly to assess the effects of recent changes on what the systems " produce ", we must first make certain basic distinctions. Evidently, one cannot expect a system that takes care of 100 per cent of a nation's young people to bring them up to the same level of academic performance as a system which is both academically and socially selective and takes care of, say, 5 to 15 per cent — which, until recently, was the proportion of the relevant age group that went to the academic secondary school. The same applies to comparisons made at the post-secondary level. There are two points here that, in my view, have been overlooked. Firstly, a comparison between, for instance, American college freshmen, who comprise about 50 per cent of their age group, and the small group of European academic upper-secondary graduates who, after selection and screening, in most countries comprise only 5-15 per cent of theirs, is not very informative. Secondly, the price paid in the European system at the secondary stage (in terms of loss of talent by built-in social bias, grade-repeating, drop-out and so on) for the high quality of those who manage to survive the system and complete the course is rather high. It is by no means self-evident in evaluating an educational system that one should confine oneself to the *end-products* and, by the same token, disregard the price that has been paid for them. In evaluations that provide a basis for policy decisions, the evaluative criteria are too rarely made explicit.

An illustration of the latter point is provided by the introduction of the comprehensive school in Sweden on a pilot basis, for which provision was made by the Swedish *Riksdag* in the Education Act of 1950. The Bill presented to Parliament stated that "practical experiments" pertaining to the proper structure of the comprehensive school, such as different teaching and grouping practices, would have to be carried out during a ten-year period. The Act itself stated that the comprehensive school should be considered for universal introduction "according to the extent that the aimed experimental programmes prove its suitability". The quoted passage had been inserted to satisfy the conservative members of the *ad hoc* education committee in the *Riksdag* who wanted the experiments devoted entirely to a comparison between the existing secondary schools of the selective type (*realskola*) and the unified comprehensive school.

As a result of this, evaluation of the comprehensive school experiments by means of continuous comparisons with the existing, selective, academic school was thought to be one of the overriding tasks for the National Board of Education's Department of School Experimentation (Husén, 1962). Yearly surveys were carried out by means of which students in the upper grades of the comprehensive school were compared with those at the same grade level in the *realskola*. Steps were taken to secure comparability in terms of social background and tested intelligence. The criterion variables were mainly standardized achievement tests. But it did not occur to those involved that the evaluation had omitted any measure of the price paid for the end products. For instance, only about 50 per cent of the students selected for the *realskola* reached the goal, i.e., passed the final examination, in due time. The drop-out rate amounted to more than 30 per cent. Both grade-repeating and drop-outs were correlated with social background, which meant that the price was also paid in terms of social bias (Husén and Boalt, 1968). Moreover, no systematic attempt was made to evaluate the two systems in terms of the objectives stated in their curricula which were, of course, different. Nobody seemed to question the logic of trying to evaluate them in terms of a common set of criteria. Some proponents of school reform contended that social objectives, such as the enhancement of equality of opportunity, were more important than purely pedagogical ones, such as the imparting of certain quantities of knowledge. Most of those who were involved in the debate seemed to assume that cognitive competence achieved at the end of the junior secondary stage was the main criterion, maybe the only one, according to which the "efficiency" of the two types of schools should be evaluated.

B. *Educational Aspirations in Selective and Comprehensive Systems.*

An "enrolment explosion" at one level of an educational system seems to elicit a delayed explosion at the next level, which in its turn is conducive to another delayed explosion at the third level. For instance, the enrolment curve in Sweden for the junior secondary school from 1950 to 1960 was repeated in the senior secondary school from 1960 to 1970 and again at the post-secondary level from the beginning of the 1960s onward. The opening up of opportunities at one level increases the social demand for education at the next level. Evidence for this comes from a national survey carried out by Härnqvist (1966).

The Swedish Bureau of Census, which is reponsible for the collection of educational statistics, conducted a survey in 1961 comprising a 10 per cent stratified random sample of all students born in 1948. This survey was the first in a series at five-yearly intervals. Their major purpose has been to obtain follow-up information that can be stored in data banks and used for evaluations of the reforms in school structure that took place in the 1950s and 1960s (Svensson, 1971).

The great majority of students in the 1961 survey was enrolled in grade 6 in the comprehensive school or in the corresponding grade in the *folkskola*, the elementary school, which still existed in about half the districts where transfers could be made to the academic secondary school. Information was obtained on school marks, scores on standardized achievement tests (which were given to all students in grades 2, 4 and 6 at the end of the school year) and the occupation and education of parents. Additionally, all students in the sample completed a questionnaire about their interests, plans for further education, choice of future occupation, and their attitude towards school. They also took a group intelligence test.

Since by the time of data collection about half the school districts had introduced the nine-year comprehensive school, this was a unique opportunity for making comparisons between the two school systems — referred to below as "comprehensive" and "parallel".

The students were divided by parental occupation into the following categories:

(a) Professional (with university degrees), executives, proprietors of large enterprises.
(b) White-collar occupations requiring formal education up to matriculation, proprietors of medium and small enterprises.
(c) White-collar occupations requiring no particular formal education beyond elementary school.
(d) Farmers (owners or tenants of farming enterprises).
(e) Manual workers.
(f) No information.

Students' plans as to their future education were related to social background in both kinds of district. The choice for the academic stream in a "parallel" district was quite clear-cut: it meant transfer from the traditional elementary school, before finishing its full course, to the academic secondary school. In the "comprehensive" districts, however, the academic choice was not so simple. At that time it meant taking two foreign languages (English and German) instead of only one or none, and normally a transfer to a class within the grade where students with academic choices were all grouped together. Future educational aspirations were assessed by asking the students if they planned to sit for the matriculation examination that qualified for university entrance.

The number of students (in per cent) who said they would whose academic programmes after grade 6 was:

	Comprehensive	Parallel
Boys	58	42
Girls	66	51

Academic choices were 15–16 per cent more frequent in the "comprehensive" than in the "parallel" districts. This raises questions of interpre-

114

tation. To what extent was the difference due to differences in school structure *per se*? Had the introduction of an elective system stimulated an interest in further-going studies to a greater extent than the selective system that required transfer to another type of school? Or was the difference in aspirations mainly accounted for by differences in the structure of the enrolment between the two systems? There might be, for instance, socio-economic differences between the two systems. It could be that the "comprehensive" school districts, being more urbanized and modern, enrolled students with a more favourable attitude towards academic education. In fact, it was found (and for details in this, as in other respects, the reader is referred to Härnqvist, 1966) that the "parallel" districts were less urbanized than the "comprehensive" ones and had twice as many students whose parents were farmers. Socio-economic background, as defined by the lettered categories listed above, had therefore to be kept under control. In doing so, it was found that academic choices in all occupational categories were more frequent among students from "comprehensive" districts (see table 5.1). Keeping father's occupation under control, we find that the differences between the categories are much smaller than those between the two types of district, wherein the most striking difference is that between students whose parents are farmers. This confirms the contention that the introduction of comprehensive education at secondary level has considerably broadened the opportunities for students in rural areas (Husén, 1962).

Table 5.1 NUMBER OF ACADEMIC CHOICES
AT THE END OF GRADE 6 BY SOCIAL BACKGROUND
AND TYPE OF SCHOOL DISTRICT

In percentage

Socio-economic group	Boys		Girls		Total
	Compre-hensive	Parallel	Compre-hensive	Parallel	
Professionals, etc. ..	92	87	94	92	91
Higher white-collar, etc.	85	72	91	83	82
Lower white-collar, etc.	68	54	72	65	63
Farmers	43	26	72	41	38
Manual workers	45	32	53	40	41
No information	59	38	62	45	47
Total	58	42	66	51	52

Source: Härnqvist, 1966.

Still one possible lack of comparability had yet to be tested. Could a "two-language programme" during grades 7–9 of the comprehensive school be regarded as comparable in academic content with the parallel *realskola* studies? Another test of the effect of the comprehensive school on attitudes towards further academic studies was made by asking sixth graders if they felt they would be capable of qualifying for university entrance by

115

taking the matriculation examination when they reached grade 12 or 13. The numbers (in per cent) who answered "yes" were:

Boys		Girls	
Compre-hensive	Parallel	Compre-hensive	Parallel
27	15	28	17

Almost twice as many students in the "comprehensive" as in the "parallel" districts, therefore, envisaged matriculation. To what extent could this be due to differences in socio-economic structure of the two types of district? Comparisons had, once again, to be made within each of the socio-economic categories, with the result set out in Table 5.2. Here it will be seen that, with social background under control, students in "comprehensive" districts much more frequently contemplated matriculation than did those in "parallel" districts.

Table 5.2 NUMBER OF STUDENTS ANTICIPATING
THAT THEY WILL QUALIFY FOR MATRICULATION

Socio-economic group	Boys		Girls		Total
	Compre-hensive	Parallel	Compre-hensive	Parallel	
Professionals, etc. ..	79	58	73	65	68
Higher white-collar .	50	41	51	48	47
Lower white-collar .	32	20	33	20	25
Farmers	12	5	18	8	8
Manual workers.....	13	8	16	9	11
No information	31	11	30	11	18
Total	27	15	28	17	20

This is further support for the view that the introduction of a comprehensive system at secondary level broadens the opportunities particularly for children from rural areas and for those whose parents are manual workers.

C. *A Case Study of the Effects of Various Differentiation Milieux*

In 1950 local Boards of Education in Sweden were invited by the Government to participate in a pilot programme for which the *Riksdag* made provision in the Education Act of that year (Husén, 1962). The city Council of Stockholm joined it in 1955, introducing it first in the southern part of the city. The dual system was kept for some time in the northern part. On the South Side, transfer to an academic secondary school could not take place until after grade 6, whereas on the North Side it was possible after grade 4. This meant, in effect, that there was a basic six-year school on the South Side. At the end of the sixth grade, students could either transfer to the three-year academic programme provided in their own school

116

or to a separate three-year *realskola*, a type of junior secondary school that had existed for some years.

This set-up provided the opportunity for a unique kind of survey because comparisons could be made between students who had passed through various types of school structure.

Three different structures could be compared in grades 5 and 6:

1. On the South Side, entirely undifferentiated elementary school classes in grades 5 and 6 where no transfer or allocation to programme took place after grade 4.
2. "Positively differentiated", that is selected classes, on the North Side, where selection on the basis of school marks equalized on the basis of standardized achievement tests took place after grade 4. These classes are referred to as "plus-select".
3. "Negatively differentiated" or "minus-select" classes on the North Side. These consisted of reconstructed grade 5 and 6 classes that had lost their able students by transfer to the academic secondary schools.

The structural arrangements in grades 7 and 8 were of even greater interest. Here comparisons could be made between four types of "plus select" classes, namely:

1. Students on the North Side who had transferred to the academic (5-year) school after grade 4.
2. Students on the South Side who had transferred to the academic (3-year) school after grade 6.
3. Students on the South Side who had transferred to the three-year academic programme within their own school.
4. Students on the South Side attending three pilot 9-year schools and who had opted for the academic programme.

Finally, comparisons could be made between students in the grade 9 programme, which prepared for *gymnasium* entrance, and students in three different academic *realskola* programmes.

The entire grade 4 population consisted of about 11,000 students in some 350 classes. A sample of about 25 per cent was included in a 5-year follow-up. Achievement tests in reading, writing, mathematics and English were administered on five occasions. Additionally, a group intelligence test given at the end of grade 4 was used as a control variable in making the various groups comparable by means of analysis of co-variance.

In the context of the social selectivity of the dual system as compared to the comprehensive, Table 5.3 is of particular interest because it shows how the degree of selectivity affects the social class composition of the enrolment. The three socio-economic groups are the ones used in the election statistics by the Swedish Bureau of Census and correspond roughly to upper, middle and lower (working) class. The proportions in the so-called "base population" are given at the top of Table 5.3. Fourteen per cent of the parents belonged to the managerial, professional and large proprietors group, 39 per cent to what in broad terms could be referred to as white-collar workers, including semi-professionals, while 47 per cent were manual workers. The 5-year *realskola*, which drew most of its enrolment from grade 4, was the most selective and had the lowest representation of students with a working-class background. The 3-year *realskola* was less selective and had a higher representation of students with lower-class background. The most striking difference is the one found in the comprehensive school between enrolment in the academic programme and in the "practical" programme. It strongly confirms Breton's (1970b) theory, substantiated by a large-scale survey in Canada, of the role secondary school programmes play in moulding student educational aspirations in relation to their background. Lastly, the "minus-select" classes became progressively more negatively differentiated in terms of social class composition.

The majority of the secondary school teachers felt that it was much easier to teach classes of the *realskola* type or the two foreign-language type in grades 7 and 8 than undifferentiated classes at the same level. This could be explained to some extent by the heterogeneity of social class in the comprehensive school as compared with the academic secondary school where the initial homogeneity was augmented by drop-out of students from less motivated backgrounds — facts that must have some relevance to the great resistance met by the Education Act of 1962 when it prohibited organizational differentiation before grade 9.

Table 5.3 ENROLMENT BY SOCIAL CLASS
IN THE VARIOUS TYPES OF SCHOOLS FOLLOWED UP IN STOCKHOLM,
1955–1960

In percentage

Student population	Social class	Grade				
		4	6	7	8	9
"Base" population (entire age cohort)	Upper	14				
	Middle	39				
	Lower	47				
5-Year *realskola* (traditional)	Upper		35	36	37	24
	Middle		46	40	40	31
	Lower		19	24	23	45
3-Year *realskola* (new set-up)	Upper			11	13	13
	Middle			49	49	29
	Lower			40	38	48
Combined *realskola* and elementary school (3-year)	Upper			13	14	10
	Middle			40	38	38
	Lower			47	48	42
Two-language upper section of experimental comprehensive school	Upper			12	13	15
	Middle			51	53	43
	Lower			37	34	42
One or no-language upper section of experimental comprehensive school	Upper			4	2	
	Middle			31	28	
	Lower			65	70	
Undifferentiated middle section (South side)	Upper		7			
	Middle		34			
	Lower		59			
"Minus-select" classes (North side)	Upper		10	7	4	
	Middle		38	31	31	
	Lower		52	62	65	

1. Transfer to the academic upper-secondary school (*gymnasium*) took place after grade 8.
Source: Svensson, 1962.

The main conclusions of this North Side/South Side survey in Stockholm as far as cognitive skills are concerned were the following. In grades

5 and 6 organizational differentiation did not significantly affect students from middle and upper class homes, but had a significant effect on those with a lower class background. Those who were admitted to the selective 5-year *realskola* from working class homes developed better cognitive skills than those of the same background who were in undifferentiated grades 5 and 6, or who spent these two grades in "minus-select" classes. The undifferentiated classes tended to develop more favourably than did the "minus-select" ones. By and large, the differences between the various differentiation milieux tended to decrease and even disappear when allowance was made (as was the case in all comparisons) for social class and initial IQ differences. The investigation suggested that organizational differentiation does not have the great effect on the cognitive outcomes of instruction that some had claimed in the debate.

Dahllöf (1971) has subjected the Stockholm survey to a critical scrutiny from a methodological point of view. In the first place he showed that if one takes into consideration the direction in which the (mostly non-significant) differences go, the knowledge increments in the "plus-select" classes tend to be larger than in the "minus-select" ones, something which Svensson (1962) also emphasized. A major criticism that Dahllöf levels against the investigation is that it does not take into account the "process variables", i.e., the variables that characterize the teaching-learning process in the classroom. Thus, the amount of instructional exposure (i.e., time) in the subject areas included in the comparisons was not considered in spite of the fact that it varied between the school types. Finally, he questioned the adequacy of the achievement tests employed. These were originally devised for a representative population of fourth-graders. Several tests displayed "ceiling effects", that is, they did not differentiate sufficiently among the most able students and this, of course, tended to lower the average score among the students in the "plus-select" classes. This effect was seen particularly in grade 6.

3. SELECTIVE BARRIERS WITHIN THE EDUCATIONAL SYSTEM

A. *Structural Barriers*

There are certain barriers or screening devices built into the educational system. By being part of its structure, these prevent ability from being adequately fostered. One can distinguish four major locations for such barriers:

1. In the selection of students for academic secondary education or for institutions of higher learning.
2. In the screening in terms of grade-repeating and drop-out that takes place during a given stage.
3. In grouping practices, such as "streaming" or "tracking", that tend to bias against students with a particular background.
4. In curriculum practices that prevent the promotion of certain types of talent or students with certain backgrounds.

It is convenient to review research pertaining to these built-in barriers or screens under three main headings:

119

(i) *Organizational differentiation.* That is, the structure of the education system as it concerns the age level and the extent to which
the schools are organizationally differentiated. The overriding
problem in Europe during the last few decades has been how to
accommodate the exploding enrolment at post-primary level within
a system that can provide enough flexibility and diversity. The
dual or parallel system is not able to make adequate provision
for this; the political issue, therefore, has been *if, when,* and *to
what extent* the system should " go comprehensive ". Concomitant
with this problem is the question of the age or grade level at
which the final selection of " academic " students should take
place and the implications of this being done at an early or a
late stage.

(ii) *Grade-repeating and drop-out as related to social background.* The
major problem in establishing equality of opportunity is often seen
to lie in the provision of equal access to a certain type of education. The barriers that have to be overcome in achieving this are
often formidable ones indeed. This is reflected in the substantial
correlations between, for instance, admission to academic secondary school and social background. Even among students who
have been admitted there is often a differential failure rate in
relation to social background. Several extensive surveys have
followed the flow of students through the various stages of the
formal school system and have tried to identify factors that
operate as screening devices in terms of grade-repeating and/or
drop-out.

The fact that a striking imbalance exists between the various socio-
economic groups when it comes to participation in upper-secondary and
higher education, and the differences in educational attainment observable
even in the first years of regular schooling, together raise the question of
how far one is justified in talking about " barriers " that prevent children
from certain social strata or geographical areas from going to more advanced education and whether one should not rather consider the extent
to which the institution, i.e., the school itself, should be changed in order
to reduce this bias against students from the lower classes.

(iii) *Educational programmes, curriculum and grouping practices.* These
are interrelated and can act as obstacles to the development of
certain types of ability or exercise bias against students with a
particular social background. The same applies to certain methods
of instruction.

B. *Organizational Differentiation*

A catchword in the vigorous debate that arose from the preparations
for changing the structure of the Swedish school system in the years 1948–
1962 was " differentiation ". What the word, in fact, signified was whether
a person was for or against different tracks or programmes according to
level of academic performance at the upper stage (grades 7 and 8 particular)
in the comprehensive nine-year school (Husén, 1962). The basic issue in
this differentiation debate was the extent to which the traditional, prestige-

loaded, selective academic secondary school should be preserved within the organization for schools. As is often the case with words that are used to denote emotionally loaded issues, the meaning became rather blurred. Some clarification may, therefore, be useful here.

It is pertinent to distinguish between organizational, or external, differentiation on the one hand and pedagogical, or internal, differentiation on the other. Organizational differentiation is reflected in the structure of the school system as determined by legislative action in parliament or a central school board. The structure, as it concerns types of school, tracks or programmes, is to a large extent determined by historical conditions and by the social stratification of the society in which the educational system operates.

The main types of organizational differentiation are:

1. *Differentiation according to type of school.* There is considerable variation in the reputation or status of different types of schools. Those of high repute attract applicants and this enables them to be more or less restrictive in their admission policy and to educate a small elite heading for the more advanced and more highly esteemed occupations. This has, for instance, been exemplified by the so-called eleven-plus examination in England (which, after the 1944 Education Act, was the screening device for selection to grammar school) and by the various selection procedures for the *Gymnasium* in the Federal Republic of Germany (Yates and Pidgeon, 1957; Vernon, 1957; Roth, 1968).

2. *Differentiation according to line of study or tracks.* Students may be assigned to one of several different tracks of study in a single school. These tracks are kept more or less separate in respect of curricula and instruction. Examples of this kind of differentiation are the comprehensive secondary schools in England (where the tripartite system, previously accommodated in different types of school, is now provided in one) and the Swedish *gymnasium* (where all the programmes — academic, semi-vocational and vocational — are provided by the same school and by the same teaching staff).

3. "*Homogeneous grouping*" (Yates, 1966) or "*streaming*". This means that students at the same grade level are grouped according to some criterion of academic performance, such as IQ or grade point average, in parallel classes. Usually there is only limited transfer between various streams and this takes place mostly from the more able to the less able streams. The students are taught all school subjects, or at least the academic ones, within their own streams. One example of this kind of differentiation is "streaming" in the British schools where it seems to have been general practice, at least until the middle of the 1960s (Jackson, 1965).

4. *Ability grouping or "setting"* whereby students in the same grade are grouped according to their performances in certain subjects only and are regrouped for other subjects. This has been common practice for a long time in the American high schools (Conant, 1959). During the pilot period of the Swedish comprehensive schools, students in the upper section (grades 7 and 8 mostly) were ability-grouped in, for instance, English (as a foreign language) and in mathematics according to their performance in these

subjects, but they were taught other subjects together with their ordinary classmates. This kind of arrangement is sometimes referred to as "sectioning". Grouping problems as they present themselves at the international level have been extensively considered in a UNESCO publication edited by Yates (1966), who also reviews the relevant research literature up to 1965. Other reviews are those by Ekstrom (1959), Borg (1965), Dahllöf (1971), and Findley (1973).

The practices referred to as "pedagogical differentiation" all occur within the framework of a given class and need not have anything to do with the structure or organization of a particular school or school system. They could therefore be referred to as "individualization" and be defined by the methods of instruction employed. It is up to the school, and in practice therefore the teacher, to organize the work in terms of sub-groups, independent assignments, and individual tutorials within the confines of his or her own class.

C.   Social and Intellectual Selectivity Within the Systems

All types of educational system are, in fact, more or less selective, be it in terms of entrance requirements or screening practices at the various stages, such as non-promotion, grade-repeating, or drop-out. But systems vary widely in how they employ these practices which, in most cases, only apply seriously at secondary level. In some systems there are practically no enrolment restrictions during mandatory school age. This is the case in countries where there is a common basic school which covers the entire period of mandatory attendance. When it comes to the choice of optional programmes or subjects, it is up to the student and his parents and not to the school to make the choice.

Petrat (1969) conducted a survey in three *Kreise* (counties) in the *Land* of Schleswig-Holstein in the Federal Republic of Germany. He obtained lists of two age corhorts of children who, in 1955 and 1958 respectively, had qualified for entrance to secondary academic school (*Realschule* or *Gymnasium*). He then followed them up through grades 10 and 13 respectively and used the combination of a longitudinal and a cross-sectional approach.

In grade 7 the students were distributed in three different types of school: (1) Terminal grades of the elementary school (*Hauptschule*), (2) Middle school (*Realschule*) which brought them to a middle school leaving certificate, and (3) *Gymnasium*, which was a nine-year school leading to the matriculation examination (*Abitur*) which qualifies for university entrance. Table 5.4 gives the proportion of students to be found in grade 7 in each of the three types of schools by parental occupation. The range for the three *Kreise* is also indicated.

The overwhelming majority of the children whose parents were civil servants, professionals and executives were in the *Gymnasium*, whereas an equally impressive majority of children, whose fathers were workers, were in the *Hauptschule*. Petrat's interpretation of these differences in participation was somewhat speculative. He thought that the "ahistoric lifestyle" of the social strata that were underrepresented was a reflection of the modern "consumer society". An unwillingness to delay gratification was seen as a major cause of the "educational abstinence" among workers.

Table 5.4 DISTRIBUTION OF STUDENTS IN GRADE 7
AMONG THE THREE MAIN TYPES OF SCHOOLS IN THREE COUNTIES
IN THE STATE OF SCHLESWIG-HOLSTEIN
(*by parental occupation*)

In percentage

Category of parental occupation	*Hauptschule* (a continuation of *Volksschule* until end of mandatory schooling)	*Realschule*	*Gymnasium*
Farm workers	89–97	3–11	0
Blue-collar workers in industry and craftsmen	62–79	19–31	2–7
White collar workers	30–41	39–48	17–26
Civil servants, executives, professionals	0–4	0–20	79–96

Source: Petrat, 1959, p. 89.

Petrat (1969) also analysed grade-repeating or drop-out in relation to social background. This relationship was particularly strong in the *Gymnasium*. The attrition rate during the first four years of *Gymnasium* was on average 22 per cent. The proportion varied from about 12-24 per cent in the top social stratum to 33 to 40 per cent in the bottom stratum.

A comprehensive study of students who dropped out from the *Gymnasium* in the Land of Baden-Württemberg was made by H. Peisert and R. Dahrendorf (1967). They used available statistics for this particular type of school to elucidate the proportion of drop-outs over the ten-year period 1953–1963 and made special investigations in some schools by means of student interviews. It was quite clearly brought out that early leaving before the *Abitur* was related to both social background and institutional factors. The drop-out patterns varied from school to school. About 40 per cent of the intake to the *Gymnasium* at the age of 10 (including the grade-repeaters) completed the course of study and passed the *Abitur*. This figure varied from 84 per cent of those whose fathers were civil servants to 24 per cent of those with a working class background. Since, in terms of intellectual qualifications at the age of entry, these groups did not differ very much, one might conclude that there was a considerable reserve of talent among those who dropped out.

Systems also differ enormously in non-promotion and grade-repeating practices that are employed as early as at elementary or basic school level. In France, for example, roughly one-third of the children repeat the first grade of the *école primaire* (OECD, 1971b). In the United States and the Scandinavian countries, grade-repeating during the first 6–9 years of schooling is almost non-existent.

In his monograph on students of working class background in German universities (to which we have already referred in the context of 'reserve of ability') Dahrendorf (1965) tentatively advances a theory about the operation of the "social filter" which brings about a glaring disparity in participation all the way from entry to the *Gymnasium* to university graduation. In addition to the syndrome of "deferred gratification" (the tendency to shy away from long-range investments such as in education) he advances the explanatory concept of "social distance" – the psychological remoteness of universities from the mentality of ordinary workers — to which we have already drawn attention. The school also, particularly the secondary school, serves as a selecting and promoting instrument dominated by middle class values which are alien to the working class students. The very model of the time-honoured *humanistisches Gymnasium* with its emphasis on classical languages and abstract verbal achievement denies the values they hold, while the teachers, who are the guardians of these traditions, inadvertently serve as gate-keepers tending to admit those students whose background is more compatible with the milieu they themselves represent.

As already observed, until the 1960s transfer from primary to secondary school in most Western European countries took place at the age of 10–12. Selectivity on grounds both of ability and of social background (two sets of criteria that are correlated) was relatively severe. The introduction of the *cycle d'orientation* and, later, the *collège d'enseignement secondaire* in France were attempts to establish more flexibility and less social bias at this stage. The *Strukturplan* submitted by the *Deutscher Bildungsrat* (1970) must also be regarded as an important step towards the introduction of the kind of flexibility provided by a comprehensive school (*Gesamtschule*). The Committee explicitly talks about an *Orientierungsphase* (*op. cit.*, p. 73).

For a long time educators were hardly aware of the fact that all kinds of educational selection, which allegedly are carried out on the basis of intellectual proficiency only, are correlated with social background (Husén, 1971). This meant that the more selective an educational system was in terms of conventional academic criteria (school marks, examinations, and test scores), the greater was the imbalance between students from different social strata, for the criteria of school performance are correlated with most of the criteria of social status (see, e.g., Fraser, 1959). Thus, if one sets out to " do justice " to all children by seeing to it that they are promoted strictly according to academic criteria or IQ and regardless of their social origin, the inevitable result is that their social background comes nevertheless into the reckoning.

It has been emphasized repeatedly that policy decisions about the reorganization of school structure, for instance decisions to " go comprehensive ", should be based on adequate and conclusive evidence provided by research. Adherents to the bipartite or parallel system and those in favour of an unselective, comprehensive system both unanimously endorse the idea that, before policy-makers decide to make a change, evidence showing whether or not this change would bring an improvement in " standard " must be presented. But, as pointed out above, the crucial question which unfortunately is seldom, if ever, made explicit is: What criteria should be chosen as indicators of the " efficiency " or " adequacy " of the different systems? Those in favour of a parallel, selective system tend to choose the attainments of the group that represents the *end-product* of the academic programme and to disregard the rest; those in favour of a unified comprehensive system prefer as their criterion the attainments of *all who enter the system* and would also include outcomes other than the purely academic or cognitive ones — for instance, attitudes, interests, motivation to pursue further studies, and so on. In this way, the *choice of criteria of evaluation* reflects differences of opinion between " élitists " and egalitarians ". But even if agreement could be reached on a uniform set of criteria to evaluate the two systems, there would still be difficulty in reaching a consensus about the *specific*, concrete criteria that should be employed to assess student attainments. How much emphasis should be placed on the learning of "hard facts" as compared with the mastery of such skills as the ability to study indepently? How should received knowledge be weighed in comparison with the ability to learn new things? What importance should be given to non-cognitive attainments such as ability to cooperate or to take responsibility? Adherents to the bipartite system tend to appreciate skills and non-cognitive outcomes less than do those in the comprehensive camp.

The comprehensive-versus-selective-school issue provides another illustration of the problem first pointed out by Gunnar Myrdal in the 1930s and recently taken up by him again (Myrdal, 1969), namely the place of implicit values in social science research. It would take us too far afield to enlarge upon this matter here, so let us leave it with the observation that the social scientist is guided by his own value priorities – not only when choosing problems to investigate, but in selecting his criterion variables also. This, however, should certainly not imply that those engaged in such research are so wedded to their value premises that they are content to work in solipsistic isolation from each other. We shall come back to this problem in our final chapter when we discuss the conclusions of research into what causes individual differences.

The intensive debate focused on surveys and experiments carried out in connection with the structural change of the Swedish school system did much to air this matter of values in social science research. When the 1946 Royal Commission submitted its main report to the government in 1948 and recommended a nine-year comprehensive school that would replace all other school types covering the mandatory school age, its recommendations were partly based on extensive studies of the development of scholastic abilities from 7-16 years of age (Elmgren, 1952). Everybody who participated in the ensuing debate, pro or con, was convinced that scholastic aptitude was to a large extent inherited and that it could be assessed in a valid way at the age of 11 or 12 – that is, when transfer to the academic secondary school used to take place. Nevertheless, the Commission opposed the idea of selecting students for the academic type of school or programme at that early age chiefly because this would "deprive" the other programmes of their "proper share" of talent and eventually deny the manual occupations the spokesmen they needed (SOU, 1948:27; cf. Husén, 1962).

Unfortunately, both those who favoured and those who were against later differentiation confused diagnosis with prognosis. It is one thing to measure actual ability, for instance to assess the child's verbal IQ at 11; it is quite another to use the score for predictive purposes, e.g., as an aptitude index. A composite of measures of home environment predicts attainments in the academic secondary school better than IQ and similar indices do (see, for example, Fraser, 1959). But so far nobody has suggested that some kind of social background index should be employed in selecting children for academic secondary education!

D. *Selection for and Screening during Secondary Education*

Selectivity has been, and still is, a predominant feature of all educational systems, particularly those that operate "dually". Students are selected for academic secondary education on the basis of some criterion of scholastic ability, such as marks, examinations, and test scores, and there is screening of those admitted during the course. Grade-repeating and drop-out, especially the former, has been very prevalent, and still is, in some countries. A Royal Commission in England (HMSO, 1954) showed that, in the middle 1950s, more than one-third of the students who, after careful scrutiny, had been admitted to the grammar school either did not obtain a final certificate or failed to get enough passes. About half of the students in the first five grades of the primary school in France repeat at least one grade (OECD, 1971b). In France too, in spite of the selection and grade-repeating that occurs in the *lycée*, about one-third fails in the last grade of the academic secondary school (*ibid.*).

It is not possible here to present a complete conspectus of the vast amount of research that has been directed at the effects of selectivity on educational opportunity; purpose will be served well, however, if we look briefly at some of the more typical studies that focus mainly on educational attainment and social class. The follow-up of a representative intake to the grammar school in the United Kingdom (HMSO, 1954) has already been mentioned; to this should be added the regional surveys by Floud, *et al.*, (1956) in England and the Fraser study (1959) in Scotland of the relationship between school performances and conditions in the home. Girard (1963) and his associates have conducted surveys on grade-repeating, drop-out, and social background in France. The social factors affecting school attainments have been considered by the German *Bildungskommission* in the report on ability and learning edited by Roth (1968). The equality of opportunity aspect of the Swedish school reform stimulated a series of surveys beginning with Boalt (1947) and Husén (1948), and research in Sweden up to 1966 has been reviewed by Husén and Boalt (1968). A background paper on group disparities in educational participation was prepared by the OECD (1971) for its policy conference in 1970. Additionally, extensive statistics on disparities due to socio-economic background have been collected, most of them referring to higher education. In what follows, some of the findings of this research will be presented in two sections, one concerning itself with the relationship between social class and selection for academic education, and the other with the relationship between social class and screening during a given course of study, with particular reference to grade-repeating.

A complete survey of all the 11,000 fourth-grade students in the city of Stockholm provided the basis for the follow-up study to which we have already given some attention (Svensson, 1962). Another special study was carried out on the 6,000 students from the North Side who had the choice either of competing for entry into the academic secondary school or of proceeding to the terminal classes of the compulsory elementary school. Scores on achievement and intelligence tests, school marks and social background information were available. The categorization in three socio-economic groups, as developed by the Swedish Bureau of Census, was employed. The distribution of social classes represented by the students who were admitted to the five-year *realskola* was compared with the same phenomenon for those who continued in the terminal classes of the elementary school (Table 5.5). The difference between the distribution for the upper (professional, managerial, etc.) and the lower group (manual workers) is highly significant. It should be pointed out that a transfer to the academic secondary school had no financial implications for the individual student or his parents. No tuition fees had to be paid, and the social benefits were the same as for the elementary school. The differences between those who transferred and those who continued could be accounted for by a combination of home background (and the motivational factors that go with it) and academic aptitude as measured by school marks equalized by standardized achievement tests.

Table 5.5 SOCIAL CLASS DISTRIBUTION
OF STUDENTS WHO WERE ADMITTED
TO THE ACADEMIC SECONDARY SCHOOL
AFTER GRADE 4 AND OF THOSE WHO CONTINUED
IN THE TERMINAL CLASSES
OF THE ELEMENTARY SCHOOL

(*The entire fourth-grade population on the North Side
of the city of Stockholm, spring semester, 1955. n = 5366*)

In percentage

Social class	Number of students continuing in elementary school	Number of students admitted to secondary school
1	10.4	34.3
2	37.6	46.2
3	52.00	19.5
Total	100.0	100.0

Source: Svensson, 1962.

Table 5.5 poses two questions, namely: What are the more specific factors that underlie the under-representation of social class 3 students in the secondary academic school? and: What kind of social bias may have gone into the selection procedure? It was clearly worth looking into this more closely, for as many as 43 per cent of the applicants from social class 3 were not accepted into the secondary school, while only 32 per cent of class 1 failed in this respect.

Table 5.6 APPLICANTS FOR ADMISSION
TO ACADEMIC SECONDARY SCHOOL,
BY SOCIAL CLASS AND ABILITY LEVEL
ACCORDING TO INTELLIGENCE TEST

In percentage

Social class	Ability level on stanine (9-point standard) scale (intelligence test)								
	9	8	7	6	5	4	3	2	1
1	87	89	82	82	70	58	47	21	14
2	85	77	74	59	47	36	20	13	7
3	66	72	45	40	24	18	8	7	5

Sources: Husén, 1967 and Svensson, 1962.

Three measures of intellectual capacity were available: intelligence test scores, achievement test scores in the three R's, and school marks. Each of these was converted into a nine-point scale with the top 4 per cent of the total population in group 9, the next 7 per cent in group 8, and so on. Details of the analysis have been presented elsewhere (OECD, 1967), and we shall confine ourselves here to relating the intelligence test score to incidence of application and rejection in the various social classes. The outcome is much the same when the achievement test scores or school marks are employed as a criterion of scholastic ability (Table 5.6).

Table 5.7 NUMBER OF REJECTED APPLICANTS TO SECONDARY SCHOOL BY SOCIAL CLASS AND ABILITY LEVEL ACCORDING TO INTELLIGENCE TEST

In percentage

Social class	Ability level (intelligence test)								
	9	8	7	6	5	4	3	2	1
1	6	20	18	36	52	69	69	(80)	(100)
2	6	23	33	50	60	68	79	(100)	(75)
3	13	30	31	43	37	61	82	(54)	(100)

Sources: Husén, 1967 and Svensson, 1962.

In the first place, we note on every ability level a consistently lower number of applicants from socio-economic class 3 than from classes 1 and 2. The difference is not very great among the 11 per cent most able (levels 9 and 8), but it is striking among students of average or close to average ability. Thus, about two three times as many from class 1 as from class 3 applied at levels 6 and 5. Considering the low application rate in class 3, one could expect the rejection rate to be lower there than in classes 1 and 2. As can be seen in Table 5.6, this is not the case. The difference in rejection rate tends to be higher among the more able than among the less able. Thus social handicap operates not only in building up the level of educational aspiration but also in translating the aspiration into action, i.e., by applying for entry to academic education.

Similar findings were reported by Härnqvist and Grahm (1963) who conducted a comprehensive national survey of three groups of students in three different choice situations in secondary school: (*1*) the choice between proceeding to the senior secondary school (*gymnasium*) or going out to work after completion of the junior secondary school; (*2*) the choice between different programmes at the beginning of the senior secondary school; and (*3*) the choice between different tracks or programmes during the two last years in the senior secondary school. The choices were related to student attitudes, school marks, and social background.

In this connection we shall limit ourselves to the findings pertaining to transfer/non-transfer to the senior secondary school. Table 5.8 shows that this differed between various types of urbanized areas where the junior secondary schools were located. It should be noted, however, that the percentages do not reflect differences between students from rural and from highly urbanized areas since the major part of differentiation due to urbanization had taken place at entry to the junior secondary school.

Table 5.8 TRANSFER FROM JUNIOR SECONDARY
TO SENIOR SECONDARY SCHOOL BY TYPE OF URBANIZATION

In percentage

	Boys	Girls
Large cities and university cities	82	68
Large industrial cities	72	46
Old gymnasium towns	69	50
Towns in norther Sweden (Norrland)	61	48

Source: Härnqvist and Grahm. 1963.

As can be seen from Table 5.9, transfer is closely related to socioeconomic status and parental education. The previous tendency among middle and upper class students was to transfer from the penultimate grade in the junior school to the first grade in the four-year *gymnasium*, whereas the practice of taking the leaving examination from the junior secondary school before transferring to the senior secondary was an outcome of broadened possibilities for pre-university education for those who attended municipal middle schools.

Table 5.9 DISTRIBUTION BY SOCIAL CLASS AND FATHER'S EDUCATION
OF BOYS INTENDING AND NOT INTENDING
TO ENTER SENIOR SECONDARY SCHOOL (*gymnasium*)

In percentage

	In terminal grade of junior secondary school		In penultimate grade of junior secondary school	
	Intend to enter immediately	Do not intend to enter immediately	Intend to enter immediately	Do not intend to enter immediately
Social class				
1	28	11	53	13
2	48	50	31	47
3	40	32	10	38
No information ...	4	7	6	3
Total	100	100	100	100
Father's education				
University	10	2	26	2
Senior secondary ..	11	4	16	7
Junior secondary ..	12	10	16	13
Elementary	61	76	35	34
No information ...	6	8	8	6
Total	100	100	100	100

Source: Härnqvist and Grahm. 1963.

In view of the fact that transfer from the second highest grade in the junior secondary to the senior secondary school was the traditional pattern in the social strata from which most senior secondary school students had been drawn, the two columns on the right of Table 5.9 are the most interesting ones. About half the boys who intended to transfer immediately were from social class 1 as compared with only 10 per cent from class 3. The father's education is also highly correlated with immediate transfer to the senior secondary school.

Härnqvist (Härnqvist and Grahm, 1963, p. 46) sums up the effect of geographical and social factors affecting the choice of further education thus: "The direct effects consist of economic obstacles in the way of continued school attendance, and obstacles in the form of great distances to educational institutions. The indirect effects could be associated with differences in the value attached to further education among parents of different social status. Since social classes are geographically unevenly distributed, geographically determined differences may be operating. Still more subtle is the way that conciousness of social status may influence the student's self-appraisal and level of aspiration, thus leading to a choice of more modest types of education, even when intellectual capacity is excellent, and the economic and social barriers are surmountable".

E. *Grade-repeating and Drop-out*

As already suggested, one could hypothesize from the concept of academic ability that grade-repeating would, as would all other selective measures, be correlated with social background. Hence the individual costs of grade-repeating are particularly heavy for students of lower class origin. Boalt (1947), in his survey of an age cohort of Stockholm students who were followed up for ten years, was able to show that screening in terms of grade-repeating and drop-out was indeed so correlated.

The considerable social cost of screening is the principal reason for concern in countries where grade-repeating has been frequent. Frommberger (1954) conducted a survey of grade-repeaters in West Germany, and Undeutsch (1955, 1960) made *das Sitzenbleiberelend* ("grade-repeating misery") an object of studies and conferences. In France, grade-repeating as early as in the first five years of elementary schooling on average delayed the students by 1.5 school years (OECD, 1971b).

Until recently, grade-repeating was standard practice in elementary schools in all European countries and up to 1914 it was apparently quite common in the United States. E.L. Thorndike (1113) questioned its value as an instrument of "individualizing" instruction so as to get the majority of the students up to an acceptable standard. It is reasonable to assume that this practice is closely associated with heterogeneity of student enrolment, particularly social heterogeneity. Since the main approach in instruction is the "frontal" one (i.e., the teacher addresses the entire class), the ensuing differences in students' performances can be remedied either by having those who lag behind repeat the class or by setting up some kind of streaming or tracking system (Jackson, 1965).

The French educational system shows how a screening with a built-in social bias can operate as early as at elementary level. In the OECD's report, *Educational Policy and Planning: France* (OECD, 1972a), statistical survey data have been brought together to elucidate enrolment ratios, grade-repeating, drop-outs, and examination ratios as related to social

130

background. This reveals a remarkable degree of grade-repeating – even in the first grade of the *école primaire* where it hits 35 per cent of the boys and 30 per cent of the girls. The frequencies for the next four grades vary between 18 and 24 per cent. This accounts for the fact that it takes on the average six and a half years to complete the 5-year course. Only 24 per cent of the boys and 27 per cent of the girls complete it in the scheduled time. Thus as many as 21 per cent of the boys are 3-5 years over age when they transfer to the secondary school.

One could expect grade-repeating and the ensuing over-age to influence the likelihood of getting into the more attractive streams of secondary education, particularly in the *lycée*. Even there, in spite of the selection that takes place on entry, grade-repeating goes on, affecting 15 per cent of the *6ème* and close to a third of those in the terminal class (the *baccalauréat* year). In 1962, Girard and Bastide (OECD, 1971) conducted a survey of the students leaving CM2 (the fifth grade of *primaire*) who should have reached *second degré* of the secondary school by 1966. Fifty-five per cent of the primary school-leavers entered either a CEG (a secondary school with a general syllabus) or a *lycée* (with a more academic one). Only 18 per cent were found in the *seconde* five years later.

One of the outcomes of grade-repeating at secondary level as well as during the primary school is a high frequency of over-age in the terminal class, for instance in the *lycée*. Those who have got there without grade-repeating should be 17, but in fact only a third of the terminal students are of this age or younger, whereas another third are 1 year older than they should be and the final third 2 years over age. The attrition taking place in both the primary and the secondary schools is socially selective and is another illustration of the role that the school plays in allocating people to various social strata. The social stratification procedure is already effective at the primary stage. According to a survey by Girard and associates (1963), children with the following backgrounds were of normal age, i.e., 11 or under, when they had reached grade 5:

	Per cent
Agricultural workers	27
Farmers	41
Manual workers	36
Clerical staff	48
Junior executives	71
Professionals and	
industrial entrepreneurs	69
Senior executives	76

The students included in the survey were rated by their teachers as to scholastic ability. Thirty-five per cent of those whose parents were classified as manual workers were rated as "excellent" or "good" as compared with 64 per cent of those with junior executive background. According to another survey conducted by Girard (1953) in the Seine Department, 54 per cent of the children who completed the *école primaire* had working class backgrounds. The corresponding figure for the *6ème* (the first grade) in the *lycée* was only 10 per cent. The number of children with professional, civil service or managerial background in the *5ème* was 3 per cent, whereas in the *6ème* they amounted to 57 per cent.

By and large, in most West European industrial countries before the enrolment explosion and the restructuring of secondary education, the representation of social class 3 (mainly manual workers) in the junior academic secondary school was around 10 per cent, whereas it accounted for about half the students in the first grades of the primary school. But even after secondary education became general and the various programmes began to be integrated within a more unified system, the "tracking" of the students implied an allocation according to social origin. In the survey conducted by Girard *et al.* (1963), students with a working class background accounted for 40 per cent of the entire *6ème* population as compared with 12 per cent with a managerial or professional background. But in the selective *lycée* the former group accounted for 24 per cent and the latter for 30 per cent at the *6ème* level. In the primary terminal classes (completing compulsory education), 49 per cent were of working class origin as compared with 2 per cent from a managerial or professional background.

A British Royal Commission in the 1950s conducted a study on failures, particularly "early leavers", in the grammar schools. The students admitted to these schools had been carefully selected on the basis of the so-called 11+ examinations which allegedly provide a fair diagnosis of scholastic ability in 90 per cent of the cases (see, e.g., Vernon, 1957). At the end of the follow-up period, 37 per cent of the total enrolment were regarded as failures by the Committee on one or more of three counts: they had not completed the five-year course, they had not gained any certificates or they had gained a certificate with less than three passes. Attainment in grammar school was related to performance in the entrance examinations and social background. The results are shown in Table 5.10.

Table 5.10 FAILURE RATE AMONG BRITISH GRAMMAR SCHOOL STUDENTS
BY ENTRANCE QUALIFICATIONS
AND SOCIAL BACKGROUND

In percentage

Paternal social status	Entrance standing		
	Best third	Middle third	Lowest third
Professional and managerial	10	25	34
Clerical	19	32	42
Semi-skilled workers	38	58	62
Unskilled workers	54	62	76

Source: Early Leaving. London: HMSO, 1954.

The most striking finding in this table is that among the students who, according to entrance examinations, belong to the *top* third, four or five times as many working class children failed as those from a professional or managerial background. This is another indication of the school's role as a social stratifier. Even if a student of lower class background has qualified for entry to a school or a programme that is considered to be geared to the needs of children with a privileged background or has traditionally enrolled students from such a background, he apparently has difficulty in remaining in that school or programme. In his classical book on *Equality*, written around 1930, Tawney (1951) attacked the liberal concept of formal equality of access to education, referring to it as "the impertinent courtesy of an invitation offered to unwelcome guests".

A Swedish survey conducted in the 1950s (Orring, 1959) illustrates the relationship between social class and screening by grade-repeating. One fifth of the total national enrolment into the five-year junior secondary school was followed up, and the proportion of the original intake that was still enrolled at a certain grade level – and which reflected both grade-repeating and drop-out – was calculated. Sixty per cent of the students from socio-economic class 1 (highest) reached the final grade without delay, as compared with 48 per cent in class 3 (lowest). The difference between its classes was greater for drop-outs (which during the first three years meant going back to elementary school) than for grade-repeaters.

F. "*Educational Abstinence*"

In conducting a study of "educational abstinence" among workers in Germany, Suzanne Grim (1966) set out to test the following four hypotheses, the first of which relates to the material conditions of the workers while the other three relate to psychological barriers:

1. Workers avoid sending their children to further-going (academic) schools because of lack of financial means.
2. Workers let their children remain in the *Volksschule* (primary school) because they are uninformed about further-going education and the occupations to which it leads ("information distance").
3. Workers shun upward social mobility via the school system because of social inhibitions ("affective distance") towards advanced education as well as towards the social strata to which such education gives access.
4. Workers let their children remain in the *Volksschule* because they live in conditions that are not conducive to planning ahead.

On the basis of responses to six interview questions about their concern for the education of their child, whether they would contact the teacher to discuss educational plans and the like for him, the parents concerned were divided into three groups corresponding to levels of aspiration. They were asked what they knew about the middle school, the *gymnasium*, and the university. On the whole they were better informed about the first of these than the other two. But the most interesting finding, which confirmed the hypothesis about "information distance", was that parents in the best informed group had only half the "information distance", that is, they knew twice as much as those in the two other groups.

The workers who tended to send their children to academic secondary schools, and who thereby "deviate" from the norm of sticking to the *Volksschule* and entering a *Beruf* (occupation), were characterized by a small or moderate "affective distance". The result is a reduced "information distance" and forward planning for the child's education, together

133

with a willingness to take the financial risks. All of this together constitutes what Grimm calls "deviant educational behaviour".

On the results of her interviews, Grimm tried to identify what social factors were prevalent among those who exhibited such deviant educational behaviour. Her findings were: (*1*) They tended to identify themselves with groups or individuals on a higher level in the status hierarchy, such as teachers. About one third of the "deviants" had fathers who had moved downward from the middle class. (*2*) The "deviants" were successful in their occupations. The majority were highly skilled workers, masters or supervisors. (*3*) Their own ambitions had in one way or another been thwarted, and they had transferred their former hopes for themselves to their children.

Chapter 6

IMPACT OF BACKGROUND FACTORS
ON EDUCATIONAL ATTAINMENT

In this chapter we shall look at some of the major studies that have shed light on background factors related to educational attainment and performance. On the whole we shall move from nationwide surveys, where participation in further-going education has been related to crude background factors such as rural-urban residence and social class, to studies aimed at identifying more specific and circumscribed background factors that account for differences in amount of formal schooling attained and cognitive skills achieved. There are several surveys that pertain to career decisions and the role played by the school *vis-à-vis* teenage children. In the 1960s several studies of career plans among young people in the East European countries, particularly in the Soviet Union, were published (see e.g. Yanowitch and Dodge, 1968). These reports provide us with an opportunity to examine the relationship between educational and occupational aspirations and attainments, on the one hand, and home background on the other in a social order different from that in the West European countries and the United States where previously the bulk of the empirical studies on this subject had been carried out.

1. SOCIO-ECOLOGICAL FACTORS

We referred earlier to surveys conducted in the Federal Republic of Germany by Edding and van Carnap (1962) and by Peisert (1967), which were focused on regional disparities in participation in upper secondary and higher education. In the United States, Nam (1968) and his associates used national data from the Current Population Survey in 1965 to analyse drop-out from high school with regard to the joint and separate effects of race, socio-economic status, religion, sex and place of residence. Later Nam (1971) analysed data for OECD.

A. *National Surveys*

National surveys consistently show that in most countries there are disparities between rural and urban areas in the matter of educational

135

participation. The OECD (1971a) collated a comprehensive set of statistics relating to this situation in its Member countries for the 1970 Conference on Policies for Educational Growth. Data by region were available for 15 countries at two points in time. In at least 12, regional disparities seemed to be of the same order on both occasions or showed a tendency to widen at the secondary level. The latter case applied, for instance, in Canada, France and Sweden. Coefficients of variation were used as relative measures of variability between regions or provinces. However, it was overlooked in this report that the tendency towards an increased participation gap between regions could very well be an artifact of migration from rural to urban areas. Those who migrate have had more education than those who remain and tend, of course, to pass on this privilege to their children (Neymark, 1961).

In several countries, though, the picture is not as clear-cut as it used to be. Previously, there was a progressively diminishing participation rate from big cities, through middle-sized cities, small cities and villages down to sparsely populated rural areas (Husén, 1948). But now in the United States, for instance, one finds the highest participation rates in the urban fringes. In Denmark they are higher in the provincial cities than in the larger capital, Copenhagen.

Douglas (1964) found great differences in the availability of grammar school places as between regions in the United Kingdom. Wales had places for 33.5 per cent of an age group of primary school-leavers as compared with 18.9 per cent in the south of England, which had a higher percentage of salaried workers and a higher mean score on the scholastic ability test. Where grammar school places were in short supply, middle class children appeared to be awarded the same number as they obtained in areas where the availability was good. It was the working class children who suffered most from the increased competition.

B. *The 1970 OECD Participation Survey*

As a preparation for the 1970 Conference on Policies for Educational Growth, the OECD Secretariat compiled a background study of disparities in educational participation due, among other things, to the socio-economic background of students (OECD, 1971a).

Data on socio-economic disparities were available for seven OECD countries – Denmark, France, Germany, the Netherlands, Norway, England and the United States. The following statistics illustrate the occurrence of such disparities as they concern secondary education. In France participation at secondary level approached 100 per cent, but great socio-economic disparities existed as between the various tracks and programmes. Children from homes of professionals and executives had participation rates of only 20 to 30 per cent in the *collèges d'enseignement général* (CEG), as compared with 60 to 80 per cent in the classical streams of the more highly regarded *lycées*. According to a German study reported in " *Die höhere Schule* ", students whose parents were themselves university graduates increased their representation in the 9-year *Gymnasium* from less than 10 per cent at the beginning of the nine-year course to 35 per cent in the graduating class, while representation by the children of workers (not foremen and skilled workers) decreased from 31 to 2 per cent. In the Netherlands, the ratio of admissions among 12-year-olds to the academic secondary schools increased over a five-year period from 45 to 67 per cent in the upper stratum, but only from 4 to 7 per cent in the lower stratum. A study in England by Westergaard and Little (OECD, 1967) showed that among 11 to 13-year-old boys born in the late 1930s, 62 per cent with professional and managerial background had been to grammar school as compared with only 7 per cent of those whose parents were unskilled workers. By the age of 17, 43 per cent of the former group and only 1.5 per cent of the latter were still at grammar school.

The 1971 OECD participation survey has a section which, country by country, compares the socio-economic distribution of university students with that of males in the labour force (OECD, 1971a). By the arrangement of these statistics in a diagram showing the percentages of participation by student background and the composition of the labour force at two points in time, one is given a picture of the extent to which changes in participation in higher education have taken place. The report expresses the *caveat* that this type of representation does not take into account shifts in social class distribution over time. Since in the more industrialized countries there is a tendency towards an increase in the managerial and professional groups and a decrease in the number of manual workers, the change might seem to widen the participation gap because of a considerable increase in the upper stratum and a slight decrease in the lower one. All of these OECD statistics, like most produced by other surveys, are limited to participation by the crude index of socio-economic status. In offering an explanation for the differences in participation, the 1971 report points out: " The relationship between socio-economic factors and school participation may be not so much an economic relationship as one which accounts for differences in life styles and mobility aspirations ". (*op. cit.,* p. 80).

2. HOME BACKGROUND AND SCHOOL PERFORMANCE

A. *Various Types of Home Variables*

An extensive research has identified a number of social variables associated with educational career. Most of these, however, are distal and not proximal measures of how social background actually works. Social class, for instance, is a very crude overall background index. It is a composite of economic, status, and qualification measurements. It does not tell us in a concrete way *how* a particular child from a particular social stratum is treated by his parents or what kinds of psychological *processes* are promoting or acting as obstacles to success in education. Hence, our consideration of most of the research reported in this chapter must be regarded as no more than an attempt to obtain an over-all descriptive picture and to identify only the major relevant independent variables.

We are, therefore, far from the stage when we can begin to analyse causally how the variables act and interact. The vigorous debate, for example, that followed the publication of the Coleman report (Coleman, *et. al.,* 1966, OE, 1970; Mosteller and Moynihan, 1971) and, a few years later, the report by Jencks (1972) and his associates, shows what difficulties are encountered in disentangling the "effects" of home background and school resources in accounting for individual differences in student achievement. New analytical tools, such as path analysis, have not substantially lessened the dilemma the researcher faces in trying to establish causal relationships between background factors, schooling, and occupational career. In his comments on a series of papers given at a United States Office of Education conference on the effect of the teacher (OE, 1970), Coleman suggests that longitudinal data should be employed to come to grips with the enormous problem of separating effects due to student and to school differences (*op. cit.,* p. 175).

In an article on dimensions of inequality, Tretheway (Fensham, 1970) distinguishes between the following types of social variables that survey research conducted so far has shown to be more or less correlated with educational opportunity:

1. Family-related variables, such as socio-economic status, income, parental education and parental attitudes towards education.
2. Neighbourhood variables, such as geographical location and the sub-culture of the neighbourhood community.
3. Ethnic variables, such as levels of education open to or aspired to by different ethnic groups.
4. Religious variables, such as education open to or aspired to by different religious groups.
5. School-related variables, such as school facilities, teacher competence, programmes available.
6. Peer group variables, such as attitudes of age-mates to schooling, teachers, and authority.

He could have added sex as one further dimension of inequality, since in most countries there are considerable sex differences in educational participation to the disadvantage of girls.

In her study of "educational abstinence" among manual workers, to which we have already referred, Susanne Grimm (1966) discerns three groups of factors that may cause it:

1. socio-economic factors, such as parental occupation, size of family, access to private tutoring;
2. socio-cultural factors, such as parental formal education, rearing practices, the possibility to acquire language skills, achievement motivation; and
3. socio-ecological factors which relate to the area of residence, such as urban versus rural, slum versus suburban upper-middle class, or the distance away of the relevant educational institution.

This study was focused mainly on psychological barriers and was largely based on personal interviews with the parents.

In trying to determine the implications of the influence of the school for future research and policy, Gagné (OE, 1970) outlines a model of the educational process which, apart from genetic factors, distinguishes between two types of "input" variables – proximal and distal. The former are defined as "those human actions which transform distal input variables into proximal inputs". The latter comprise home environment, community, peer culture, and school resources. Gagné points out that the major

138

difficulty in interpreting the results of the many surveys that have been published is that "they deal with distal and correlated measures, and fail to use proximal measures" (*op. cit.,* p. 170). This applies to opportunities provided by both the home and the school. Socio-economic status as a measure of home opportunities is such a crude distal measure because it does not provide any close or accurate description of what *actually happens* with the child in the home, what positive actions are taken by the parents in bringing the child up and preparing or not preparing him for school entry. Similarly, measures of school resources such as laboratory facilities or teacher competence do not tell us very much of "those human actions which transform the raw materials of input into opportunities for learning... Seldom do we find ... measures of process which are direct, in the sense that they indicate the nature of teacher activities" (*ibid.*).

In commenting on the United States Office of Education conference at which several of the studies to which Gagné referred were presented, Coleman (OE, 1970) takes the same position. The present data sources do not provide very much information about what kinds of specific factors are conducive to changes in student achievement. Coleman also points out that research programmes, if they are to be useful as part of the knowledge basis for policy decisions, should be designed with respect to the actual problems on which these decisions have to be taken. He points out that problems pertaining, for instance, to teacher selection may not be answered within the same research programme as problems related to teacher behaviour in the classroom. The same, it seems to me, applies to problems of establishing greater equality of educational opportunity. For a long time the policy implications of consistent research findings of social class difference in participation in secondary and tertiary education were construed as lying mainly in the economic field. Since the most tangible difference between social classes was economic means, the solutions to inequalities in educational participation were therefore sought in providing grants or other instruments of financial support for students who came from backgrounds with low participation rates. It has since been found that financial steps to equalize opportunities for formal accessibility do not have the desired effect, so attention is now being drawn to the proximal or process variables – that is, how, exactly, children in the different social strata are brought up and what kinds and amounts of "preparation" for entry into the regular schools are being provided in the various types of home.

B. *The Fraser Study (Scotland)*

Having emphasized the need for "proximal" studies, that is the need to identify specific variables that describe the psychological atmosphere at home conducive to school success, we must here single out the investigation conducted by Elisabeth Fraser, *Home Environment and the School* (1959), for it was the first major study that attempted to relate the total effect of the home environment, not just some kind of socio-economic index, to scholastic performance. Nearly all the other investigators, both prior to her study and after, have limited themselves to some kind of easily available index of parental occupational status or parental education or to some kind of socio-economic classification (mostly in terms of the upper, middle and lower classes). No previous study, therefore, had provided such an extensive "coverage" of the home milieu as hers, together with a series of psychological variables.

Elizabeth Fraser's investigation comprised 408 Aberdeen children who had been transferred from primary schools to 10 different secondary schools and were followed from the age of 12 1/2 to 13 1/2. Two intelligence tests and one achievement test in English were administered. Home environment was assessed by personal interviews with the parents. Four aspects of the environment were considered in these interviews: (1) cultural (parental education and parental reading habits); (2) material (income, parental occupation, family size, living space); (3) attitudinal (parental attitude, including encouragement, towards the child's educational and vocational career); and (4) the degree of abnormality in home background (for example, the general quality of the home, whether or not it was "broken", if the mother went out to work, and so on).

Scaled school marks over IQ were used as the main criterion of scholastic achievement, and each environmental indicator was correlated with this and with IQ. Finally, a multiple correlation between all the indicators, IQ and school marks was computed. The findings are shown in Table 6.1.

Table 6.1 CORRELATIONS BETWEEN ENVIRONMENTAL INDICATORS ON THE ONE HAND AND IQ AND SCHOOL MARKS ON THE OTHER AMONG SECONDARY SCHOOL STUDENTS IN ABERDEEN

Environmental indicator	IQ	Criterion (scaled school marks)
Parental education	0.42	0.49
Parental book reading	0.28	0.33
Parental magazine and newspaper reading	0.38	0.40
Income	0.35	0.44
Family size	−0.40	−0.46
Living space	0.36	0.45
Parental attitude towards education	0.30	0.39
Parental encouragement	0.60	0.66
General impression of home	0.39	0.46
All environmental indicators (multiple correlation)	0.69	0.75

Source: Fraser, 1959.

It should be noted that parental encouragement (a typical "process variable" for which the quest has been strong in recent years among educational researchers) correlates much higher with both IQ and scholastic achievement than do any of the other environmental variables. Later, Dave (1963) and Wolf (1964) were able to show that psychological variables characterizing supportive action by parents correlate very highly with test scores (intelligence and achievement). It should also be noted that all environmental indicators tend to correlate higher with scholastic performance than with IQ, which reflects among other things that they are all loaded with non-cognitive factors. Finally, one should observe that indicators of material conditions do not correlate lower than those that measure psychological processes.

Fraser draws the following conclusion: "There is little doubt that if some account were taken of a child's home background when trying to forecast his future scholastic success, this would add to the predictive efficiency of intelligence and other standardized tests" (*op. cit.*, p. 73). However, she stops short of recommending that social indicators should be used as predictors to improve the accuracy of secondary school selection procedures. It is interesting to observe how psychologists who regard it as part of their professional function to recommend improved *techniques* for prediction come to realize at a certain point that such improvements can make explicit underlying values that they have not been aware of. They then hesitate to advocate them. In this particular case, the task was to discover how social factors might operate to handicap children in their educational career. Social handicap, then, was seen as a correlation between performance and social background when inborn intelligence was kept under control. The fact that a crude measure of supportive action on the part of the parents correlated as high as 0.60 with IQ casts some doubt on the conception of the educability handicap as something mainly attributable to inherited intelligence (cf. Jensen, 1972).

C. *Australian Studies*

In the previously cited collection of Australian studies on inequalities in education edited by Fensham (1970), one of the contributors, F.J. Hunt, points out: "Unequal participation in education is probably the most comprehensively surveyed social aspect of education and inequalities have been revealed in every society that has been studied, and in relation to a wide range of other variables" (*op. cit.*, p. 42).

In Australia several surveys have been conducted with the primary aim of elucidating the social determinants of educational inequalities. Others have revealed such inequalities as a by-product of studies with different primary aims. Hunt mentions some examples in his chapter, and five relevant empirical studies are presented in other contributions to Fensham's (1970) compilation. From these sources we learn, for instance, that metropolitan and rural areas differ substantially in participation. A survey in Victoria showed that around 1960, 22 per cent of the metropolitan children remained in the secondary school in the matriculation year as compared with 11 per cent of the rural children. Ethnicity was another factor of importance. Only 1 per cent of the Australian-born youth had less than 6 years of education as compared with 24 per cent of those who had immigrated. Among the immigrants themselves wide differences were found as to the completion of secondary schooling. Whereas 20 per cent of British immigrants had completed secondary school, only 6 per cent of those with a Greek and 3 per cent of those with an Italian background had reached thus far (Fensham, 1970). Radford (1962) carried out a survey that elucidated the relationship between schooling and the occupational status of parents in Australia. Unskilled and semi-skilled workers, who accounted for 33 per cent of the population, contributed only 8 per cent of university entrants. The figures were exactly the reverse for the professional and higher administrative occupations.

Another survey was carried out in five secondary schools in the Melbourne area selected in a way that would bring out certain contrasting features with regard to enrolment and resources. Two were independent schools – one highly respected with an established tradition of educating distinguished people for public life, another similar but with more modest resources. The other three were governmental high schools drawing their students from very diverse areas. One of them had dilapidated premises but a "strong corporate spirit" and recruited its students from a "good" area. All five schools were compared in terms of finance, teacher quality, class size and so on, and, on the basis of a combination of quality measurements, the author arrived at the following conclusion: "... a child will have the best chance of academic success if he is sent to a major independent school, almost as good a chance if he goes to a well-established government high school in a good area, and the worst chance at a northern or inner suburban high school". These outcomes reflect to a very high degree the socio-economic differences between the areas of location, so it is not possible to establish to what extent the schools themselves had contributed to differences in quality of their end-products. The survey suggests that the "metropolitan schools are merely perpetuating existing inequalities" (Fensham, 1970, p. 82).

3. SOME NATIONAL AND INTERNATIONAL SURVEYS

A. *A British Longitudinal Survey*

If one wants to establish causal relationships between background factors (in the home and/or in society at large) and educational opportunity and attainment, follow-up studies over a long period, beginning with the pre-school years, are of immense value. J.W.B. Douglas and his associates (1964 and 1968) have conducted investigations with this advantage. Their studies are without doubt the most important of those that, with a longitudinal perspective, have focused on the relation between social background and educational opportunities. We shall briefly summarize how this work was done and present some of the outcomes of the analyses of the relationship between achievement at the primary and secondary stages and social background.

It was the Population Investigation Committee in England that initiated this study which focused initially on the maternal care provided to infants. Data collection began in 1946 and in order to secure a representative sample of newborn children it was decided to include all those born during the first week of March that year. To obtain sub-groups of adequate size, all the children of non-manual workers and farm labourers and only a quarter of the children whose parents were manual workers or self-employed were included. After the initial data had been collected, among other means by home interviews with the mothers, a follow-up study was undertaken of the influence of pre-school conditions on subsequent school achievement.

Most of the information needed for the first follow-up investigation (Douglas, 1964) was collected with the help of teachers in the primary and preparatory schools. They provided information relating to:

a) absences from school and reasons for them;
b) children's behaviour in school and attitudes to work;
c) intelligence and achievement test scores at the age of 8 and 11 (82 per cent of the sample had complete records of these); the performances on the tests were expressed as T-scores with 50 as the mean and 10 as the standard deviation;

and

d) parental interest in the child's progress in school work.

Health information was provided by the school doctors and the visitors who paid yearly visits to the homes of the children concerned. The latter also collected information on family and home circumstances and on parental educational aspirations. The Local Educational Authorities provided data about the 11 plus examinations.

Independent schools were left out of the enquiry into selection for secondary education simply because their students did not compete for places in the state secondary schools.

Perhaps the most outstanding feature of this project was the opportunity it gave to investigate the influence of parental attitudes and encouragement during very early childhood on subsequent school careers and, indeed, a series of psychological variables measuring this were included in the survey. Douglas (*op. cit.*, p. 39), with ample justification, concludes that there is " much evidence to show that the care of intelligent and understanding parents in the early years gives background and meaning to what is learned " later at school.

As we have said, the mothers' aspirations were assessed by health visitors. The children with mothers who wanted them to go to grammar school got 11 per cent more places than would be predicted from test scores alone. On the other hand, children whose mothers wanted them to go to a secondary modern school had no less than 60 per cent fewer places in grammar school than could be predicted from test scores. Another indicator of parental interest in the child's education was whether or not the father visited the school to discuss his progress with his teacher — as, in fact, 32 per cent of the middle class and 12 per cent of the working class fathers did. 40 per cent of the working class children whose fathers evinced such interest went on to grammar school, as compared with only 10 per cent of those whose fathers did not discuss their progress with their teachers.

In the Douglas report, classification by social status was based on parental occupation and education. The dividing line lay between non-manual (middle class) workers and manual workers. This line proved to be " permeable " to a small extent only: 5 per cent moved up and 3 per cent moved down during the long period covered by the follow-up. " Upper middle class " children were those whose parents had a middle class background and had gone to a secondary school. A " lower middle class " background meant that the parents had either a middle class background or a secondary education. " Upper manual working class " was defined as a milieu where at least one of the parents had a middle class background *or* went to secondary school. "Lower manual working class " comprised those cases where both parents had a working class background and had not gone to a secondary school. As can be seen from Table 6.2, social class turned out to be closely related to psychological variables conducive to grammar school entrance.

Leaving aside the children who went on to independent schools, 54 per cent of the children from the upper middle class and 11 per cent from the lower working class were admitted to grammar schools. Had the independent schools been included, this inequality would have been even more marked. As has been shown in other surveys (see, e.g., Husén and Boalt,

Table 6.2 TRANSFER TO GRAMMAR SCHOOL BY SOCIAL CLASS, PARENTAL INTEREST AND ASPIRATIONS

In percentage

	Middle class		Manual worker	
	Upper	Lower	Upper	Lower
Interest in child's progress	42	25	11	5
Desires grammar school place	73	73	58	49
Late school leaving wished	78	41	22	13

Source: J.W.B. Douglas, 1964.

1968), social background is of little importance among children who score intellectually at the very top; but in the IQ range 110-120 social class strongly affects the chances of transferring to or being selected for an academic type of secondary education. The more selective the system, the slimmer the chances for lower class students. Douglas showed that when grammar school places were in short supply, the chances of middle class children being selected were not greatly affected. Such competition, however, weighed strongly against working class children. Those who lived in areas with a poor supply of grammar school places got 48 per cent fewer than an equivalent group (in ability) of upper middle class children.

Whereas most previous studies of social bias in the school system had focused on selection for, and achievement in, secondary education, Douglas was able to show how such bias already operates in primary education. When the children he was studying were 10 years old, their teachers were asked to rate them on a five-point scale from "very hard-working" to "lazy". The top rating was given to 26 per cent of the children of the upper middle class, 17 per cent of the lower middle, 11 per cent of the upper working class, and 7 per cent of the lower working class. The interesting thing here is not whether, or the extent to which, these ratings were "objective", but the very fact that the teachers perceived the children of various social statues differently. Since teachers' judgments are the basis for promotion, grouping practices such as "streaming", and transfer to further education, they become of great importance in the child's educational career.

Middle class children tended to go to primary schools that had a good record *vis-à-vis* grammar school admission. Thus, 44 per cent of upper middle class children went to primary schools from which 31 per cent or more traditionally went on to grammar schools. The corresponding figure for the lower class was only 16 per cent. Interestingly enough, the test scores from ages 8 to 11 improved for children who went to primary schools having a good record for grammar school admission; but they deteriorated for those who went to primary schools with a poor record in this respect. What is even more noteworthy is that those attending primary schools with a good record (31 per cent or more admitted to grammar school) obtained 20 per cent more places in grammar schools than could be predicted from their test scores. The reverse happened for those who went to poor record schools (10 per cent or less admitted); they got 37 per cent fewer places than predicted from their test scores.

144

The quality of maternal care was also related to streaming, and the report shows that conditions of upbringing during pre-school age are highly correlated with the early school career (Table 6.3).

Table 6.3 NUMBER OF CHILDREN
WITH POOR MATERNAL CARE BY STREAM
AND TEST SCORE

In percentage

Intelligence at 8 (T-score)	Upper stream	Lower stream
41–45	–	42
46–48	12	20
49–51	15	36
52–	10	13

Source: Douglas, 1964.

The secondary school traditionally tends to serve as a social class stratifier by the way it allocates students to different programmes or tracks. The same effect is brought about by place allocations for students who compete for entry to grammar and technical schools. From the upper middle class, 14 times as many went to grammar schools as to technical schools, whereas the ratio for the lower manual working class was 2.1.

Douglas sums up his findings on selection for secondary education in the following statement thus: " Comparing children of equal measured ability at eleven, those from upper middle classes get three times as many selective school places as those from the lower manual, more than twice as many as those from upper manual, and one and a half times as many as those from lower middle class " (*op. cit.,* p. 122).

Information on secondary school careers up to the beginning of the sixth form was available for 98 per cent of the original 1946 sample (Douglas, *et al.,* 1968). The following sets of data were collected from school principals, teachers, school doctors and nurses, health visitors to the homes, parents, and the young people themselves. At the age of 15, verbal and non-verbal intelligence tests as well as achievement tests in reading and mathematics were administered. (As pointed out above, the pupils had been tested twice earlier, at the ages of 8 and 11). The teachers rated the pupils twice, at 13 and 15; and they were asked, among other things, to indicate those who they expected would profit from higher education. The pupils themselves filled in self-rating inventories at 15 and completed a questionnaire about their aspirations for further education and future jobs. The health visitors obtained information from the parents, including their aspirations for their children. Complete test information was available for 77 per cent of the sample. This sub-group, referred to as the " educational sample ", was not significantly biased in terms of tested intelligence by missing cases.

As Douglas and his associates pointed out, the 1964 report, which covered school careers through entry to secondary education, raised " serious questions about how far children from economically and culturally deprived homes were being given the educational support they needed; they seemed to be saddled with a cumulative series of handicaps. Not only did they come from homes where education itself is little valued, but they were also at a disadvantage at school." (Douglas *et al.,* 1968, p. 3). The follow-up through secondary school can therefore be regarded as an examination of the extent to which the "gloomy prediction" based on the experiences from primary school is justified. Have the environmental influences on scholastic performance been reinforced or attenuated? The study of the age span 11 through 16 can also be regarded in a way as an evaluation of the 1944 Education Act. When this Act, which provided free secondary education for everybody, was passed, those who promoted it found it "reasonable to anticipate that the children of manual working class parents would benefit most from the increased opportunities, since previously there had been relatively few free or scholarship grammar school places available. The intention of the Act was to give each child, irrespective of his family circumstances and social origins, the type of secondary education that was best suited to his abilities. Entry to any type of secondary school was not meant to be competitive – each pupil was to be allocated to the school that provided the course most appropriate to his ability " (Douglas *et al.,* 1968, p. XI). The overall outcome of the follow-up of the pupils in the secondary school was that " the middle class pupils have retained, almost intact, their historic advantage over the manual working class (*ibid.,* p. xii). The proportions between the two strata in terms of their representation in the grammar school were by and large the same as before the 1944 reform.

A comparison between social classes in tested intelligence and achievement at the ages of 8, 11 and 15, was somewhat complicated by the regression effect, but the results seem to indicate a fairly stable pattern. Middle class pupils tended to do better in achievement tests than in non-verbal intelligence which was not the case among those with manual working class background. This would indicate that the middle class pupils not only "over-achieved" but in doing so also widened the achievement gap between themselves and the working class students.

About half the pupils left school as soon as they had reached the statutory leaving age at 15, which meant they left before the end of the school year. An additional 10 per cent stayed on until the end of that year. The proportion leaving school at the earliest opportunity was much higher among the lower class pupils; after the age of 15 the upper middle class proportion of the total enrolment increased from 5 to 15 per cent.

Pupils of high ability (according to the test) had equal chances of entering secondary grammar school whatever their background. But the high percentage of pupils from lower class families leaving school at the end of the statutory period. meant, as Douglas puts it, a "heavy loss" in talent. About 50 per cent of pupils from manual working class homes who scored more than one standard deviation above the mean on the tests left school as soon as they could, as compared with only 22 per cent from the lower middle class and 10 per cent from the upper middle class. The same tendency could be observed when it came to taking a school-leaving certificate examination. Those who obtained a good certificate and scored better than one standard deviation above the mean were, by social class:

upper middle	77 per cent
lower middle	60 per cent
upper working class	53 per cent
lower working class	37 per cent

Teachers in the secondary school were asked to indicate those among their students who were considered to be able to "profit from higher education". Of those who had scored in the high-ability group, i.e. more than one standard deviation above the mean, 91 per cent of the upper middle class pupils were rated as suitable as compared to 69 per cent of those from lower manual working class homes.

About one fourth of the primary school leavers entered selective secondary schools, i.e., schools that selected their pupils on the basis of some ability criterion. The remainder (with few exceptions, such as those in comprehensive schools) entered secondary modern schools. It was found that those who went to selective schools improved their relative standard as measured by the tests, whereas those who went to secondary modern schools tended to fall somewhat behind. Another way of stating this phenomenon is to say that during the age span 11 to 15 the social classes "grow further apart" in terms of educational achievement.

So far there have been very few studies of how parental aspirations pertaining to their children's education are related to their own education and social background. Douglas and his associates present quite a lot of evidence as to the strength of the "social heritage" in this respect. Forty per cent of the middle class parents wanted their children to have higher education as compared to 21 per cent of the manual workers. But within the social classes the amount of education the parents had obtained either before entering the labour market or afterwards (through evening classes and suchlike) made a lot of difference, as can be seen from Table 6.4.

Table 6.4 PARENTAL INTEREST IN HAVING CHILDREN
OF HIGH SCHOLASTIC ABILITY GO ON TO HIGHER EDUCATION:
BY PARENTAL EDUCATION

In percentage

	Parental education			
	Both parents elementary education only	Both elementary but some further education (adult)	one or both secondary education	Both secondary education plus some further education
	Percentage with highly interested parents			
Middle class	41	60	72	84
Manual workers	21	40	37	69
	Percentage with mother favourable to higher education			
Middle class	69	81	87	93
Manual workers	53	71	78	100

Source: Douglas *et al.,* 1968.

Thus 71 per cent of parents who were manual workers with only elementary school but also with some adult education wanted their children with high ability to go on to higher education, as compared with only 53 per cent of those who had had no adult education. Douglas pointed out that men who marry women with superior education or who come from the middle class get in the bargain an insurance against downward social mobility, and their children's chances of getting further education are considerably enhanced. His conclusion on the secondary school follow-up is:

> The social class inequalities in opportunity observed in the primary schools have increased in the secondary and extend, in a way that was not evident at the time of secondary selection, even to the highest ability. It seems that the able boys and girls from manual working class families, although encountering no obstacles at entry to the selective secondary schools, have been heavily handicapped in their later secondary school careers through relatively early leaving and poor examinations results (*op. cit.,* pp. 27-8).

B. *The Plowden National Survey (England)*

The Plowden Commission in England in a separate volume *Children and their Primary Schools* (HMSO, 1967) reported an impressive body of research and surveys. Of particular interest here is a national survey which comprised a random sample of children at the top infant level, and the first and the fourth years of the junior school. The total number of children sampled at these three levels were 3,300 from 173 schools. Information on home conditions and parental attitudes toward school work done at home, the education of children there and other interest taken in them was collected by means of interviews, as a rule with the mothers.

The results were presented in two parts. The first is simply a description of how various home circumstances, parental attitudes and aspirations were distributed by social class. The second consists of an attempt by means of stepwise multiple regression analysis to link the evidence collected from the parents (about home circumstances and attitudes) to the evidence collected from the schools the pupils were attending. Performance on a reading comprehension test was used as a criterion of pupil achievement. On the basis of father's occupation, a grouping into social classes was made according to the classification used by the Registrar General in England: (1) Professionals (4 per cent), (2) Managerial (14 per cent), (3a) Clerical (11 per cent) (3b) Skilled manual (48 per cent), (4) Semi-skilled manual (16 per cent), (5) Unskilled labourers (6 per cent) and (6) Unclassified (1 per cent).

Since the mothers were interviewed on average for more than an hour, quite a lot of information could be collected about the attitudes, interests and aspirations the parents had with regard to their children's schooling. The upper stratum parents were less alienated from the school than were those from the lower stratum. Very few parents in classes 1 to 3a indicated willingness for their children to leave school as soon as they reached statutory leaving age, whereas 8 per cent in class 3b and 15 per cent in class 5 were agreeable to their children leaving as soon as they were allowed.

The level of aspiration and the extent to which this was realized both showed large social class differences. As can be seen from Table 6.5, parents from the upper strata were able to achieve their ambitions to a much larger extent than those in the lower strata. More than two thirds of

148

professional parents hoped that their children would get into grammar school as compared with between half and one third of those from manual occupations. But more than half of the professional category were able to get their children into grammar school, as compared with about one out of six among skilled and semi-skilled workers and only one out of 15 among unskilled workers. Moreover, it should be noted that very few parents in the two top strata wanted their children to enter secondary modern schools and most of those in the top stratum succeeded in avoiding it. The expressed preference for a secondary modern school education goes up as we move down the social ladder but it never applies to more than half the parents. Nevertheless, the great majority of the children with manual working class background are allocated to secondary modern schools.

Table 6.5 PARENTAL HOPE FOR AND ACTUAL ALLOCATION
TO SECONDARY SCHOOL: BY SOCIAL CLASS
(In per cent of parents within each social class)

	Social class						
	1	2	3a	3b	4	5	Un-class.
Grammar school:							
Hope	69	66	68	48	42	30	43
Actual allocation	52	33	39	18	18	7	22
Secondary modern:							
Hope	14	15	10	25	30	45	7
Actual allocation	21	50	42	66	68	81	64

Source: Children and Their Primary Schools. Vol. 2: Research and Surveys. London: HMSO, 1967.

The reasons given for preferring grammar school education were most frequently that this type of school "will lead to a better job" or provide "good future prospects". Aversion to the secondary modern school was voiced mostly in the two top strata where this type of school was considered to have too many "bad-mannered" pupils, "bad discipline" and a "low standard" of teaching.

The parents were asked about the methods of allocating pupils to the junior classes in the schools their children were going to (e.g., whether by age or ability) and which they would prefer. As can be seen in Table 6.6, there are very small differences between social strata with regard to such a choice. The majority in all strata wanted the "quicker" and "slower" children to be taught in separate classes.

Parental attitudes and interest, home circumstances, and learning conditions at school were weighed against what was regarded as a key outcome of learning, namely reading skills as measured by a test of reading comprehension. This was one of the first two large-scale attempts (the other being the Coleman (1966) survey in the United States) to employ multivariate analysis in order to find out what factors account for the major variance in differences between schools and between students within schools. In this second part of the report, 104 independent variables were "candidates" for the between-schools analyses and 73 for the analyses between students within schools. About a dozen variables in each type of analysis emerged

Table 6.6 ACTUAL GROUPING PRACTICES
IN THE JUNIOR SCHOOLS PUPILS WERE ATTENDING
AND THE GROUPING PRACTICE PARENTS SAID THEY WOULD PREFER

(In per cent within social class)

	Social class					
	1	2	3a	3b	4	5
Actual practice:						
Grouping in classes by age	56	57	53	52	54	47
Grouping in classes by ability	34	35	36	35	32	40
Preference:						
Grouping in classes by age	30	27	28	28	27	30
Grouping in classes by ability	64	67	67	65	60	63

Source: Douglas *et al.*, 1968.

as making significant contributions to the criterion variation. The complex technicalities involved, to say nothing of the conceptual problems connected with multivariate analyses of cross-sectional survey data, by now make up an impressive body of literature and will have to be left aside here, apart from the observation that about one third of the variation between schools and about one half of the variation between pupils within schools was left unaccounted for. The unexplained variance is due to some extent, of course, to errors of measurement but in all likelihood it should primarily be attributed to individual differences that are not related either to parental attitudes or to material circumstances in the home. Since the pupils in the between-schools analyses are aggregated, this latter type of difference tends to be averaged out, and this explains why a higher portion of the variance in the criterion is accounted for in the between-schools analyses (cf., the critique of the IEA strategy by Härnquist (1974) cited below).

Table 6.7 PERCENTAGES OF THE CRITERION VARIATION
ACCOUNTED FOR BY THE THREE MAIN CLASSES
OF INDEPENDENT VARIABLES IN THE PLOWDEN SURVEY

	All students in junior schools	Top grade students	First grade students
Between-school analyses			
Parental attitudes	28	39	20
Home circumstances	20	17	25
School variables	17	12	22
Total	65	68	67
Between-pupils-within-schools analyses			
Parental attitudes	20	29	15
Home circumstances	9	7	9
School variables	17	22	15
Total	46	58	39

Source: Children and Their Primary School, Vol. 2, App. 4. London: HMSO, 1967.

The findings, in terms of the percentages of variation in the criterion explained, are summed up in Table 6.7. We note that the specific contributions by variations in parental attitudes, interests and aspirations are greater than the material circumstances at home, which in their turn account for more than the school and instructional variables. Furthermore, the relative importance of parental attitudes increases as the children approach the end of primary school.

Gilbert F. Peaker, who was responsible for the multivariate analyses and the reporting of the outcomes, points out that in a way this survey is an extension of earlier surveys that focused mainly on rough indices of social background: *Early Leaving* (HMSO, 1954), *Fifteen to Eighteen* (HMSO, 1959) and *Half Our Future* (HMSO, 1963). As could already be seen from the descriptive part of the report, parents in the upper strata have higher aspirations and hopes, and take more elaborate steps to promote their children's educational career, than do those in the lower social strata. Attitudes are malleable, and the report points out that only a minor portion of the variations in attitudes are accounted for by material circumstances in the home. This leaves quite a lot of scope for "communication and persuasion" (*op. cit.*, p. 189).

C. *The IEA Surveys*

The International Association for the Evaluation of Educational Achievements (IEA) has conducted two major surveys. The first, comprising mathematics only (Husén, 1967), was conducted in 12 countries, all of them highly industrialized. The second, the so-called, Six-Subject Survey, (Comber and Keeves, 1973; Purves, 1973; Thorndike, 1973) was administered in 22 countries, four of them less developed, in two stages — that is, field testing took place in two consecutive years, with Science, Literature and Reading Comprehension in the first and English and French as foreign languages and Civics in the second. Student achievement in these subject areas was related to certain background factors, such as area of residence (rural-urban), father's and mother's education (number of school years), father's occupation, availability of newspaper, radio, television, and encyclopedia at home, number of books at home, and size of family.

The correlations between achievement scores and background variables were scrutinized over countries and in separate populations within countries (10-year-olds, 14-year olds, pre-university students). On the basis of the partial regression on the achievement variables the following background variables were selected to form a composite called "school handicap score" (SHS): father's occupation, father's education, mother's education, number of books at home and size of family.

Two major types of analysis were used to explain the variation in the criterion variables (Science, Reading and Literature): between-school and between-student multiple regression analyses. The explanatory variables were structured into four major "blocks":

(1) Student background — consisting of SHS, age and sex of student — which by implication, included one unmeasured background variable, namely student intelligence or "native wit".
(2) Type of school and type of programme within school.

(3) Learning conditions in the school.

(4) "Kindred variables", such as attitudes toward school learning or motivation for school work, which can be conceived of both as outcomes of school teaching and as inputs that explain differences in achievements.

It would take us too far afield in this context to go into the detailed rationale for the analytic strategy employed, but, in short, the "blocks" were ordered according to what seemed to be a reasonable temporal sequence with background variables first, type of school next, and learning conditions that affect the student, once he has entered a particular school or programme, third. Apart from misgivings that could be expressed about the temporal ordering of the variables, there are other methodological snags and these have by and large been the same as were the subject of much of the debate that followed on both the Coleman 1966 survey and the re-analyses conducted by Jencks (1972) and his associates as well as on the IEA surveys (Härnqvist, 1974). The rationale for the analygical strategy has briefly been spelled out in the subject matter volumes (see, Comber and Keeves, 1973; Purves, 1973; Thorndike, 1973), and a detailed technical account has been given by Peaker (in press). It should be mentioned that the IEA strategy has been critically reviewed by Coleman (1974) and Härnqvist (1974). The latter, for instance, points out that the level of aggregation of data determines to a large extent the amount of variance accounted for in the dependent variables. This explains why much more of the between-school than the between-student variance is attributable to the independent variables. He further points out the difficulty of interpreting simultaneously introduced variables because they are given weights in relation to their strength. Common variance between several variables is attributed to the one which is strongest.

Both Coleman (1974) and Härnqvist (1974) have collated the outcomes of the multivariate analyses conducted by IEA. In his paper to the Harvard conference on the IEA project in 1973, Coleman criticized the use of increments in squared multiple correlations as measures of the effects of the respective blocks and variables within blocks. He suggested instead the use of standardized partial regression coefficients. Härnqvist, however, has averaged the contributions of the various blocks over countries and age levels. He finds a fairly consistent pattern from one subject area to another, as well as from one age level to another. In the between-school analyses 67-70 per cent of the variance is explained by the independent variables at hand. Of the total explained variance, between 41 and 42 per cent is accounted for by background, while about 20 per cent is accounted for by school type, school programme and instructional variables together. Between 5 and 10 per cent is explained by the kindred variables. Härnqvist (1974) finds that there is a clear-cut tendency for the background block to become more important as one moves up to higher levels of the system.

In the between-student analysis only about one third of the variance is explained. This could be expected, because the between-school variance is only about 25 per cent of the between-student variance and the correlations between the variables at the level of the school are much higher than at the level of the individual student. The following averages emerged from the between-student analysis:

	Science	Reading	Literature
1. Background	14	13	12
2. School type and programme	5	6	5
3. Learning conditions	11	6	5
4. Kindred variables	5	7	6
Total explained	35	32	28

With a different method Coleman attempted to separate total home background effects from the total *direct* school effects, and after having looked at six countries (Chile, England, Finland, Italy, Sweden and the United States) he arrived at the following proportions which, leaving out the indirect effects, add up to 100 per cent:

	Age level	
	10 years	14 years
Total home background effects		
Science	0.34	0.42
Reading	0.35	0.44
Literature	n.a.	0.42
Total direct school effects		
Science	0.24	0.29
Reading	0.20	0.22
Literature	n.a.	0.26

The relative explanatory power of the school factors tends to be larger in the IEA survey than in, for instance, the Coleman 1966 survey; nevertheless it turns out that here, as in previous investigations, background factors tend to account for considerably more of the variation in performance than do the factors constituting the learning conditions in the school itself. But in as much as certain conditions vary between countries, one readily realizes that the less the spread in a variable, the less is accounted for by that particular variable.

D. *A Canadian Survey*

An extensive national survey to elucidate the school's role in career decisions was conducted by Breton (1970 a-b) under the auspices of the Canadian Department of Labor and the Provincial Departments of Education. The general theory behind the study was briefly this (Breton, 1970b): career decisions taken by students are determined by internalised opportunities, socio-economic circumstances and, not least, by subjective circumstances related to their own values, attitudes and identity feeling. Among the latter factors the most important are those related to the student's having decided whether the course of events is under his own control or under that of someone else, or is determined by quite impersonal influences. The "conceptual self-system" is the tool the youngster applies in his career decisions which can be regarded as testings of self-hypotheses.

153

Attitudes towards the self and the future which contribute to moulding career goals are: (1) attitudes towards one's own identity; (2) sense of personal control over future events; (3) anxiety about finding a job; (4) independence in decision-making; (5) vocational competence or preparation for vocational decision-making; and (6) attitudes towards work and achievement.

The general approach in the Breton survey, therefore, was to relate career decision-making both to objective background factors and to subjective ones. The background factors were: parental occupational status, parental education, size of community of residence, region of the country, linguistic affiliation, size of family, birth order and problems of authority in family. Ethnic and religious affiliations were excluded.

As has already been said, the survey focused mainly on the school's role in career decision-making. The school as a social system was regarded as probably the "single most important influence on the career developments of adolescents" (*op. cit.,* p. 7) – indeed, as Breton points out, one of its primary functions is "to serve as an agency of allocation with respect to the socio-economic structure" (*op. cit.,* p. 5). The survey takes into particular account the effects on students' career decisions caused by school organisation (the structure of the curriculum, the number and nature of programmes), the evaluation of students and diversity of opportunity.

A random national sample of 145,817 high-school students was drawn from all four grades. The full sample was used for measures of school characteristics based on aggregate student responses. A weighted sub-sample was used for most of the analyses. All the relationships established between independent and dependent variables were controlled for ability, socio-economic background and language. In studying the effect of background factors and subjective factors on career decisions, Breton used Coleman's Multivariate Index (Coleman, 1966).

The school affects the career decisions through programmes such as "practical" versus "academic", or by designing some programmes as "preparation for post-secondary education" whereas others are "terminal". Since the structure of programmes in the school serves as a means of stratification that, by and large, corresponds to the prestige stratification in society at large, the mobility between programmes, the number of programmes, and thereby the flexibility of offerings, are of great importance.

As could be expected, socio-economic origin was closely related to the aspiration for education. Thus, plans to stay on at high school until graduation were more frequent among students from higher than from lower socio-economic strata. As concerns the desire to go on to post-secondary education, social class tends to have a stronger effect on the more able students and on those less gifted. Educational plans are strongly associated with parental education. This is more marked in students' plans to enter post-secondary education than in intentions simply to complete high school. Even when parental occupation status and ability were controlled for, this association remained relatively strong.

A very important factor in student career planning is that some programmes are terminal whereas others are structured to prepare for education beyond secondary school. Breton shows that programmes of study are ranked by the students in terms of their attractiveness – for example, the prestige attached to them or the ability they are said to require. The

154

student self-concept, which is determined partly by his social background, is therefore acting as an intermediate variable in making the curriculum or individual programmes part of the stratification system of the school. Another contribution to this stratification is teacher expectation as to the kind of student best suited to these more highly-regarded programmes. Finally, multiprogramme schools tended to attract more students from the lower socio-economic class than those offering only a single academic programme.

4. EDUCATIONAL ASPIRATIONS AND ATTAINMENTS AS RELATED TO PARENTAL BACKGROUND IN SOME SOCIALIST COUNTRIES

Increased opportunity for the previously underprivileged groups has been a major target for policy in the Socialist countries. In the Soviet Union, for example, the introduction of universal primary schooling had in its wake highly increased participation in secondary schooling and higher education. The broadening of opportunities which in principle were equal for all strongly affected the aspirations of young people. One of the notable features of Soviet higher education has been its highly selective character. Whereas secondary schooling has been opened up to more and more students, the expansion of university education has been kept rather restrained, increase in enrolment being no more than modest during a period when it was almost explosive in some Western countries. Only 25 % of those who graduate from the general secondary school are admitted to a university.

At the beginning of the 1960s surveys began to be published as to the career plans of secondary school students and the social background of students at the senior stage of the secondary school and at the university. In introducing the new education act to the Supreme Soviet in 1958, Premier Khrushchev made reference to the fact that the overwhelming majority of students at Moscow University came from families of the intelligentsia and the functionaries. It was later made known that about 75 per cent belonged to those categories as compared with only 20 per cent with working class and 5 per cent with peasant background (Sauvy, 1973, p. 28).

The aspirations of Soviet pupils at the end of grade 8, i.e., after completion of the basic school period, have been the subject of several surveys reviewed by Yanowitch and Dodge (1968) and Lagneau-Markiewicz (in Sauvy, 1973). The three routes which offer themselves after completion of grade 8 are: the general secondary school (two or three grades) preparing for university, a semi-vocational or entirely vocational secondary school, or work. In Sverdlovsk, for example, 39 per cent of those from homes of manual workers planned to proceed with general education as compared to 63 per cent of those whose parents were "specialists", i.e., professionals and managers with advanced education. The Soviet sociologists who have studied the phenomenon indicate the impact of the "cultural level" and the "family tradition" in moulding the aspirations. Thus, only 25 per cent of the pupils whose parents had had no more than four years of elementary schooling planned to take upper secondary education, as compared with 72 per cent among those whose parents had themselves had higher education.

"The children of the *intelligentsia* typically plan to follow an educational path which will permit them to duplicate (in broad terms) the occupational status of their parents. " (Yanowitch and Dodge, 1968, p. 253).

It is not surprising therefore, to find that the distribution of parental background of the pupils in grade 11 differs from that in grade 8 or from the one in the vocational schools that follow after grade 8 (Yanowitch and Dodge, 1968, p. 254). The following figures refer to the city of Sverdlovsk:

	In percentage	
	Grade 8	Grade 11
Manual workers	62	39
Employees (white collar workers) ...	11	19
Specialists	22	33
Others	5	9
Total	100	100

There was some disparity (as might be expected) between planned entry into the university-preparing general secondary school and actual entry when it came to university entrance, but the gap between aspiration and achievement had grown considerably. Selection for entry is severe and only a small proportion of those who want to enter are admitted. Surveys cited by Yanowitch and Dodge (1968) record that in Moscow in the mid-1960s as many as 90 per cent of secondary school graduates planned to go on to a university, but only 36 per cent actually got there. Similar discrepancies between plans and actual status have been reported from other cities. The desire to go to a university is not apparently closely related to home background, which indicates that entering upper secondary education is connected with the expectation of joining the intelligentsia; but background plays a role in one's actually being granted entry to a university. Students from the homes of specialists get in more frequently than those from other categories. A study of how university entry was related to background arose from the finding that the chance of being accepted by a university among those who had completed secondary school was 82 per cent for those whose parents had had higher education, whereas it was only 31 per cent for those whose parents' education had been less than 7 years (Yanowitch and Dodge, 1968).

Trends similar to those that are reported from the Soviet Union are found also in other European Socialist countries (see, e.g., Szczepanski, 1963).

Particular attention should be given in this context to university entrance. Because of planning quotas and resource restraints, the number of openings at the university, and thereby access to the intelligentsia, is rather limited. Thus in the first place there is a conflict between student aspirations and the set quota of intakes. Furthermore, there is also a conflict between attempts on the part of the universities to maintain high standards and the policy of broadening the opportunities for students from all walks of life. "True socialism" means that the doors to institutions that are instrumental in social promotion should be open for young people whose parents are workers and peasants. On the other hand, the demand for high standards at the university and for good "products" to man the managerial and technical jobs needs to be emphasized. Furthermore, the new intelligentsia has a vested interest in seeing to it that formal justice in the selection is maintained, so that social origin does not formally enter into the selection procedure. In Poland, extra credits are given for social origin – i.e., to children of parents of particular "merit in reinforcing the power of the people" (Sauvy *et al., op. cit.,* p. 42). But since the number of applicants having a manual work or peasant background is relatively small, such regressive-credit giving does not seem to have any decisive effect towards altering the differential social class representation in higher education.

Chapter 7

POLICY IMPLICATIONS OF RESEARCH ON SOCIAL BACKGROUND AND EDUCATIONAL ATTAINMENT

1. AN INTRODUCTORY CAVEAT

Policy can be defined as an institutionalized manifestation in planning and decision-making of ideologically imbedded, vested interests. Policy makers, therefore, cannot be expected to behave like Plato's philosopher-kings, and this should be kept in mind when attempting to divine the "policy implications" of research that has borne upon equality of educational opportunity. There are no clear-cut relationships between "research findings" and policy-making that would make it just a matter of "applying" the results of "pure" research in order to arrive at the "right" decisions. In another connection (Husén, 1968c) I have already spelled out what I consider to be a proper and realistic role for the researcher *vis-à-vis* the policy-maker. It is perhaps enough here to repeat that he can provide some assistance in posing problems that are conceptually and methodologically accessible to research, and he can also assist in providing more enlightened interpretation of findings, not least by bringing out the value-determined implications of alternative interpretations. In general terms, then, the researcher can contribute to a broadening of the facts, perspectives and viewpoints on which the policy-maker has to base his decisions.

We must in this context leave aside how ideologically anchored values enter into the process of research by means of the ways in which research problems are posed and tackled (Myrdal, 1969). The fierce criticism of both the data base and the procedural details of studies from which estimates of so-called heritability have been calculated can be cited as an example of value-loaded involvement in what on the surface would seem to be a purely academic problem that should be dealt with in the serene and aloof atmosphere of an ivory tower. The impact of strongly held implicit values becomes particularly obvious when it comes to the interpretation of findings. Henry Levin (1972), in reviewing Jencks's *Inequality,* refers to this phenomenon as the "social science objectivity gap". Even more striking are examples from recent policy-oriented research (like that reported in *Inequality*) in which investigators who have drawn upon the same sets of data have arrived at highly divergent conclusions.

159

The same caveat should be kept in mind in interpreting the research that has been reviewed in this book and in interpreting the author's review of it. I am myself not exempted, of course, from the bias I have just described, which means that the selection of studies that have been reviewed, the evaluative judgments that have been passed, and the interpretation of the findings from these studies are all affected by my own value frame of reference.

The "objectivity gap" is obvious to anybody who has ever tried to cover the relevant literature on the heredity-environment issue. The significance of given statistical results — be they regression coefficients, correlation coefficients or just simple means — are often looked upon quite differently as either supporting or refuting a hereditarian or an environmentalist interpretation of individual and, particularly, of group differences.

We can, somewhat schematically, distinguish two opposing interpretative ideologies. On the one hand there is the conservative (and as a rule meritocratic) conception, according to which human abilities are mainly inherited and differences in educational and particularly in occupational careers are largely accounted for by differences in ability. The educational system that does not take such inherited differences into account is considered to fight against nature. Selective provisions have to be made for the élite. A broadening of educational opportunities could easily lead to an exhaustion of the resources of talent.

On the other hand we have the more radical conception, according to which education and interventions into environmental conditions by means of social and economic policy have a strong impact and play an important role in improving human ability. Policy measures in these domains can, in Faris's words (1961), "lift a nation by its bootstraps". I myself, leaning towards such an ideology, have taken the position that one should not begin by investigating the genetic limitations of ability (if any), but by attempting to assess the extent of the limits within which socio-economic and educational influences can operate. This view is wedded to the belief that the pool of talent can be expanded by means of an adequate social policy, and that a broadening of opportunities for advanced education will not easily exhaust the "reserve", because it is expandable.

2.   DILEMMAS OF A POLICY OF EQUALITY

The caveats implied in these observations will hopefully prove useful to the reader, not least when he is confronted with the incompatibilities or, rather, dilemmas that are inherent in attempts to achieve not only greater equality of opportunity but equality of results also.

Perhaps the most pervasive dilemma, which faces all highly industrialized societies of today and with which no doubt they will have to come to grips in the post-industrial stage, is the one of self-realization versus social and economic efficiency. If we want to label it differently, we could call it the equality-meritocracy dilemma which, as we have seen earlier, cuts across widely different social orders, be they formally capitalist or socialist.

At the root of this dilemma lies the problem of economic growth and its compatibility with a social and educational system of equality of *results*.

If criteria of efficiency are those of growth within a national economy and the extent to which the growth is accruing to the material standard of living of the ordinary man, then the massive redistribution of resources required to achieve what even remotely could be considered equality of results might be so costly that it could well affect the average standard of living adversely. It seems extremely difficult to envision even a "zero-growth" society, with the complexity of the present highly industrialized service society, in which the great demand for highly trained scientists, engineers and administrators would not reinforce the meritocratic element that is already beginning to become prevalent in both East and West.

In the pre-industrial, and particularly in the industrial, society those who have mastered the operation of verbal and numerical symbols have tended to come to the forefront and have moved into higher status, influence and power. This has been the passport to the (relatively few) white-collar jobs on both professional and sub-professional level, a certain amount of formal schooling over and above the compulsory, elementary school being the qualification required. Those from the blue-collar group who have become equipped with such proper certification can now, therefore, advance to higher social status.

But in a society approaching the post-industrial stage the expansion of institutionalized education beyond the point of compulsory attendance means a democratization of the verbal and similar skills which are no longer required by a few individuals but by everybody. In so far as this has already occurred, it has tended to make the "white-collar line" disappear. Furthermore, modern technology, not least the computer, has taken over the execution of routine skills which previously required some additional formal schooling and special qualifying skills for white-collar jobs. We need only think about what has happened to office work, such as bookkeeping, during the last 20 years. What is now important in terms of creating distinctions are skills at a more abstract level, which draw upon higher mental abilities than the ones involved in previous, more routinely performed work such as finding new solutions to new problems and devising appropriate programmes. This means that the "meritocracy line" has been moved up to the level where advanced university training is given.

3. STRATEGIES ENSUING FROM ALTERNATIVE RESOLUTIONS OF THE HEREDITY-ENVIRONMENT ISSUE

Cognitive differences at any given time between individuals belonging to a particular sub-group in a particular society are attributable to three types of factor: differences in genetic disposition, differences in the environment, and differences due to the interaction between genetic disposition and environmental factors. In the debate so far on the heredity-environment issue there has been a tendency to disregard the third type in the attempt to separate "influences" which can be regarded as "purely" genetic and "purely" environmental. But since policy interventions can affect all three sources of differentiation as well as the relative weights they carry, one has to take all of them into account.

Some 25 or more years ago many leading researchers with a hereditarian view on what caused differences in ability were more or less explicitly advocating eugenic measures in order to reduce dysgenic influences that seemed to be conducive to a deterioration of the gene pool. This was the case in England in the Darwinian-Galtonian tradition under the auspices of the Eugenics Society, which sponsored several surveys aimed at assessing the relationship between fertility and IQ. In the United States during the 1920s eugenic views were influential in determining immigration policy (Cronbach, 1973). Recently a heated debate on the justification for eugenic intervention has emerged in the wake of the studies of educability and group differences published by Jensen (see, e.g., Jensen, 1973). Jensen himself has been rather cautious about bringing out the eugenic implications of his conclusions, whereas Shockley has been much more outspoken.

Policy intervention aimed at enhancing equality in terms of environmental conditions has been advocated much more frequently. Social reforms which constitute a welfare society as well as attempts to broaden access to education and to equalize the resources between areas, school districts, etc., are moves in this direction. The core idea in the philosophy behind attempts to bring about "equality of educational opportunity" has been, as repeatedly noted here, to help the individual make the best possible use of his "native wit" – to realize his potential. As pointed out by Kencks and his associates (1972, p. 73), the genes an individual has been born with are in some way regarded as his "property", which he is expected to make the best possible and profitable use of, whereas the milieu in which he is born is regarded as accidental. Therefore environmental differences have to be corrected. This is the philosophy behind what Frankel (1973) calls "corrective egalitarianism".

But inequality determined by biological accident might in principle be regarded as not much different from inequality determined by social accident and could therefore be the object of justified intervention. Eckland (1967) points out that the distinction made between ascriptive and achieved status is basically not tenable. According to this distinction, ascription is status allocation based on properties assigned by birth, such as social class, race and ethnicity, whereas achievement refers to factors over which the individual is supposed to have control and hence the achievement is merited. These factors, such as inherited intellectual capacity, are regarded as the individual's "private property". "But do not the individual's capacities depend to more than a trivial degree upon the genetic material with which he enters the social contest, and over which he has no more control than his race or his sex?" Thus status allocation according to ability could be just as much "ascribed" as the allocation that traditionally was made on the basis of social origin. Jencks and his associates have depicted the consequences of a philosophy according to which it is no more a moral asset to be born with good genes than in a good parental milieu: "for a thorough-going egalitarian, inequality that derives from biology ought to be as repulsive as inequality that derives from early socialization" (*op. cit.,* p. 73). This is the moral justification for John Rawls' suggestion that the "natural lottery" or the "arbitrariness found in nature" should be corrected. In his book *A Theory of Justice* he builds up a case for a "redemptive" egalitarianism by asserting that the voluntarism of the traditional liberal egalitarianism has no more moral justification than the old ascriptive allocation according to some divine force. One does not "deserve" the genetically inherited assets any more than the socially inherited ones: " ... no one deserves his place in the distribution of native endowments, any more than one deserves one's initial starting place in society. " We shall not in this context discuss the deeper social-philosophical implications of Rawls' redemptive egalitarianism. Suffice it to note that he regards the individual as a passive recipient of whatever benefits life more or less randomly bestows upon him, whereas Frankel as a spokesman of the liberal and voluntaristic philosophy of equal opportunity sees the individual as an active player who takes responsibility for what he is doing with his assets.

It is hardly deniable that systematic attempts to equalize the environmental conditions are conducive to an increased correlation between the genotype and the phenotype. The greater the equality of educational opportunity, the larger the proportion of the individual differences in attainment that, over the generations, would be accounted for by inherited ability. Thus, equalization in opportunities would contribute to allocating each individual to the position in society where he "belongs" according to his inherited endowment. Herrnstein (1973) and Eysenck (1973) have taken this argument to its extreme and tried to make a consistent case for a liberal meritocracy. If society tries to minimize the role of social inheritance − and that is the explicit aim of social policy in many countries − it will at the same time maximize the role of genetic inheritance. Thereby one can avoid a caste society in which there will be a class of dull and unemployable persons on the one extreme and a class of intelligent and wealthy persons on the other, each passing on its disadvantages and privileges to the next generation. A system of mobility based on optimizing the opportunity for talent to find its proper place is, therefore, a socially just one.

Another way of manipulating the relationship between the phenotype and the genotype would be to introduce a principle of reversed equality of opportunity whereby those who are most needy are awarded the greatest benefits (at least during the time they are growing up). This is the strategy of compensatory education. Thus, in several countries more resources in terms of money per pupil are allocated to handicapped children than to those who are able to follow normal school instruction.

On the basis of their review of the existing research literature and re-analyses of existing sets of data, Jencks and his associates conclude that environmental intervention can substantially reduce cognitive differences in spite of the estimation that in present-day society genetic differences account for between one third and one half of the variance in IQ.

4. PRINCIPLES FOR FORMULATING STRATEGIES

Before attempting to formulate specific strategies we should briefly review two principles that have been of pervasive importance in our analysis of the concepts of "talent" and "equality of educational opportunity" and are fundamental to the policy recommendations to be spelled out below.

1. In dealing with the concept of "talent" in Chapter 3 and the utilization of talent in Chapter 4, it was impossible to neglect the heredity-environment controversy. A dogmatic hereditarian view runs counter to the

optimistic philosophy that ought to guide every educational endeavour, namely that planned and/or systematic actions under the label of up-bringing and/or of teaching can produce significant worthwhile changes in children. Accordingly, the researcher who wants to find out the extent to which scholastic attainments can be modified by planned action must begin by investigating how modifications can be brought about by environmental influences in general and scholastic ones in particular.

There is yet another special reason why the educational researcher should adopt his strategy. Attempts in both surveys and experimental research to study relevant environmental influences, such as home background, on cognitive development during pre-school and school age have for a long time concentrated mainly on what are now called "frame variables" (the over-all, static socio-economic structure), whereas "process variables", such as the mother-child relationship and language training at home, have been neglected or completely avoided because of a lack of appropriate means to measure them. The yardsticks that have been employed to assess environmental conditions have, indeed, been very crude ones; in most cases they have been socio-economic indices, such as parental education or occupational status. By measuring parent-child interaction, language training, etc., a better coverage has been achieved.

The more successfully one can measure relevant environmental variables that account for individual differences in school achievement, the greater the proportion of observed scholastic differences that can be attributed to environmental variations. This means that what is left unaccounted for after we have covered as much as possible of what is tangible can be said, at least for the time being, to be possibly due to "heredity". An educational researcher who sets out to make a case for heredity begins at the wrong end of the problem.

2. Recent large-scale survey research has accumulated an overwhelming body of evidence showing that both between-student and between-school differences in achievements have to be accounted for by factors that are endemic in the over-all socio-economic structure of the society. Thus, in trying to evaluate what is achieved by individual students, schools or school systems, one consistently finds that a large proportion of the differences among them is attributable to out-of-school factors. For a long time it has been almost a professional disease among educators to regard school education as though it operated in a social vacuum and to disregard incompatibilities between school and society. This attitude provides a very efficient defence mechanism against demands for educational change that would bring the educational system into line with changes in society at large.

Now, however, there is a growing realization that educational reforms must be co-ordinated with social and economic reforms. Indeed, it is impossible to establish better equality of opportunity in the educational system without its being established previously or simultaneously in the over-all prevailing social system. To give only one, albeit a pretty substantial, quotation in support of this assertion, let me recall a statement made in the working document for the 33rd session of the International Conference on Education in 1971, where the main topic was "The Social Background of Students and Their Chance of Success at School". In spelling out the general principles for educational policy, the document said (p. 35): *With the best will in the world, the education authorities cannot tackle the problems at the root. Unemployment, inadequate pay, housing conditions, malnutrition and lamentable standards of health call for economic and social measures.*

5. SPECIFIC STRATEGIES

Strategies for bringing about greater equality of educational opportunity can be brought to bear at three distinct levels: (*a*) at pre-school age; (*b*) in the school as an institution; and (*c*) during the post-school period, for example through recurrent education. Strategies for all levels were discussed at length by the CERI/OECD Strategy Group in its 1970 and 1971 meetings.* We shall here examine some of their more specific policy implications.

A. *Pre-school Education*

It follows from our reasoning at the beginning of this chapter that pre-school education needs to be moved up on the list of priorities. Steps taken to establish formal equality of opportunity within the school system are futile if, as an outcome of substantial differences in home background, students enter a standard school with widely different capacities to profit from the teaching which, by and large, takes place in a collective setting that permits only a modest amount of individualization. Studies of early childhood experiences and the socialization of cognitive modes in children, as well as longitudinal studies of intellectual development, have consistently confirmed the importance of home background in the child's ability to succeed in a normal school. Previously, the emphasis was on how cultural deprivation suffered by children from minority or lower-class homes was related to their chances of getting into the formal educational system and succeeding there. More recently the focus of attention has shifted to the processes that mediate between the individual and his environment, particularly during pre-school age. Relevant illustrations of this are given, for example, by Bernstein's research on language development, by Hess and his associates' work on cultural deprivation, and Bloom and his associates' studies of the stability of individual differences over various time-spans up to the age of 18.

Realization of the importance of language development and the communication style at home (i.e. whether it is verbally "restricted" or "elaborated") and its impact on the development of adequate cognitive styles of problem-solving, as well as the coping behaviour that is fostered there, has inspired a demand for nationwide, institutionalized pre-school education in several OECD countries, notably in the Federal Republic of Germany and in Sweden. Limitations of cost and time, however, would restrict the availability of such institutions to two years at most prior to

* The CERI/OECD Strategy Group consisted of policy-makers and experts from the OECD Member countries. Its discussions were focused on educational policies and structures that promote equality of educational opportunity.

165

the children's entering a normal school; hence, in the majority of cases, the first three or four years would still have to be spent at home or partly in day nurseries. By the age of 4, however, a considerable proportion (perhaps 50 per cent) of the differences in language skills among school children have already developed.

Closely related to systematic provision for pre-school instruction, with or without built-in special activities that aim particularly at stimulating culturally deprived children, are attempts by various institutions to broaden out-of-school experiences that the child has no other opportunity to acquire. It has repeatedly been found that children who grow up in big cities, and particularly in slum areas, are confined to a surprising extent to the block or the neighbourhood where their families live. This limits the range of cultural experience and depresses the level of ambition. A child who has never seen the physical plant of an institution of higher learning, who has never visited a library and has not even a vague idea of what a theatre or a concert hall might look like, cannot later be expected to want to participate in whatever is going on in such institutions.

There is, however, a dilemma which should not be overlooked in this context. As has been pointed out by Eckland (1967) and Lipset (1972), a consistent policy of equality of results implies severing the ties between the child and his family almost completely. If we want totally to remove the socio-economic background effects on a child's opportunity to benefit from regular school teaching, some kind of boarding school system for children born into less favourable circumstances, with a minimum of contact with the parents, will have to be established. Lipset points out that if one is to bring about a society where success is entirely unrelated to social class background, the price would appear to "include the practical abolition of the family, the suppression of varying cultural and ethnic influences, and a vigorously imposed uniformity in the education of the young". The introduction of a new economic order does not in itself help (p. 108).

B. *Strategies Pertaining to the School as an Institution*

Coleman, in a working paper for the CERI/OECD Strategy Group,* has made a useful analysis of the strategies for achieving improved quality of opportunity that relate to the formal school system as such. This challenges certain institutionalized features of the school. He considered three main strategies, outlined as follows:

i) *Lessening or removal of selective admission procedures:* Increased access can be achieved by opening up the courses of study to an increased student population without competitive and/or selective procedures of admission. By increasing the number of places and by removing hurdles such as entrance examinations or admission requirements in terms of marks obtained, social bias at the time of admission can be considerably reduced.

ii) *Organisational measures aimed at alleviating and eventually removing rigidities in the structure of the school system:* Steps taken to abolish and/or postpone an organisational differentiation in the

* Document CERI/SG/71.01.

system contribute to improved equality. Practices such as streaming and tracking during early stages tend to be biased against lower-class children — in the first place because the educational aspiration in their homes rarely aims as high as the academic track, and secondly because teachers tend to expect less from these children. There is ample evidence to show that the earlier organisational differentiation takes place the stronger is the social bias that goes into the procedure for allocating students to the various tracks. More specifically, the following strategies pertain to the structure of the educational system :

a) The more flexible the system, i.e. the longer the options are kept open, the higher the degree of equity of access to more advanced stages in the system. By avoiding decisive selection or a forced choice at an early stage in the school career (for instance, by abolishing the selection to the lower academic secondary school after a few years in the elementary school), a higher degree of participation from less privileged children is secured. The ideal would be to grant entry to a more demanding or "academic" programme at almost any stage. Blind alleys, which are results of early, definitive selection or forced choice in the educational career could thereby be avoided.

b) No sharp distinction at the secondary stage should be made between a general academic and a vocational programme. Such a distinction is no longer justified by pedagogical and/or economic reasons. In a rapidly changing society, the trend is to merge the two types of programme. In such a society it has become increasingly important to widen the range of cognitive social skills, interests and attitudes that constitute general education. The continuous demand for new learning and relearning of specific vocational competencies would have to draw upon the resources that a good general education has laid down. In a paradoxical way, general education in our times is, due to the skills it can provide for a broad repertoire of unforeseen vocational competencies, the best vocational education an individual can obtain.

c) The programme at the upper secondary, and particularly at the post-secondary level, should allow for increased flexibility by being divided into "modules" or "packages" that could readily be combines into different career-preparing programmes. The modules or packages could thereby be assigned different points in a vocational career and thus become an integral part of recurrent education.

The introduction of rigid, full-scale programmes offered in different tracks early in the school career is beset with one important drawback. Selection and/or allocation to such programmes or tracks always tends to anticipate future careers, which is to the disadvantage of students whose parents have low educational aspirations.

iii) *Teaching-learning strategies to improve instruction for the disadvantaged*: Since equality is not now seen as being confined to access to education and its resources but means also greater opportunity to achieve, the teacher's problem is to designate certain groups who need special, and often compensatory, treatment. The common denominator for such treatment is individualized teaching within such socio-economic groups as have low participation rates and educational attainments in common. We often forget, however, that as educators we are concerned with individual children and that differences within socio-economic groups are usually greater than between the groups themselves. If the goal is increased equality in terms of attainments and performance, and not only in terms of starting opportunities, certain additional measures have to be taken with those who lag behind. These measures mostly mean modification of conventional instruction (such as individual tutoring, small group instruction, continuity of adult contact, modified curriculum content) and better teaching aids.

As Coleman indicates, the sorting and stratification feature of the school system, at both primary and secondary levels, should be de-emphasized. This means that teaching and certification-examination functions of the school should be separated. The school should teach while society should examine. It is not up to the school to serve as a gate-keeper to vocational careers. It is not a primary function of the school to find out whether the student has reached the competence needed for any particular vocation. The prime requirement for the school, then, is evaluation of its teaching, not of its students.

The school as an institution is in Coleman's words "information-rich but action-poor" (cf. Coleman *et al.*, 1974). One pedagogical implication of this is that docility easily becomes a goal in itself. Another is that premium is put on the ability passively to absorb abstract, verbalized knowledge, while less importance is attached to the ability to be active and to apply received knowledge. In former days, young people were integrated early into the adult world and had to learn early to assume responsibility. They had to begin supporting themselves after a few years at school and they began to work early with adults at home. Now they are kept outside the adult world in these and other respects, mainly because the adult world and the young world in our complex society are kept separate by generally accepted institutional arrangements. Much of adult life is something that contemporary youth experiences only at second remove through the mass media. These observations apply also to the school. The reality for which the school allegedly prepares is presented through the printed and spoken word. In spite of fancy talk about " self-activity " and " independent work ", it is difficult to avoid the conclusion that the dominant attribute of the school is to communicate reality through abstract-verbal tools. The mastering of these instruments readily becomes an end unto itself. The pupil who masters the forms is rewarded, while the one who can master the practical real-life problems but not the verbal images through which they are seen at school is not.

The verbalistic feature of the school constitutes a handicap for pupils from homes where the mode of communication is "restricted" instead of "elaborated". The more a verbally-mediated docility is required, the greater the handicap. Conversely, the more "action-rich" a school is, the greater its chances of bringing its culturally impoverished pupils into the "mainstream".

What can be done to make what goes on in the school more "functional"? The following two measures are proposed, but they would mean a reshaping of the school as an institution (the reasoning has been spelled out more fully out in Husén, 1974a).

  i) The school must give, particularly to teenagers, an opportunity to partake in meaningful tasks where they have the chance to feel genuinely productive. This can be achieved by giving them responsibility for work that affects the welfare of their fellow human beings. It is only by making contributions to the adult community and by being treated as adults that they will learn adult roles. One could let all young people after the age of 14-15 experience what it means to accept the discipline inherent in sharing with others the responsibility for carrying out major tasks. One should consider letting young people of school age get work practice in labour-intensive service sectors, such as child welfare or care of the sick and the old.

  ii) The school should try to exploit the wealth of competence that exists in other public agencies and institutions and in certain private enterprises by bringing it to bear on its instruction. Politicians, writers, administrators in local government, and outstanding professionals all comprise an untapped reservoir of experience and talent that could be put to use intermittently in school. Furthermore, teachers could alternate between classrooms and other places of work and thereby become better educators. Theirs is an occupation that is much more conducive than others to isolation and inbreeding.

C. *Recurrent Education*

A system for multiple re-entry into formal education for those who have left it early, as well as for those with a broad basic education, is already being considered, at least in principle, by several European countries. "Recurrent education" offers greater possibilities for attaining a high level of competence for the majority of students than does the dual or parallel system with its fateful finality of early choice or selection. The launching of the idea of "recurrent education" is therefore a major response to the quest for more equality as well as for increased flexibility of structures and programmes.

D. *Reform of Teacher Education*

Several of the policy recommendations put forward in this chapter imply a reshaping of the conventional role of the teacher and hence of teacher training. One of the most drastic of the changes that have been brought about by the " learning society " is in the social role of the teacher — particularly of the secondary school teacher who has to deal with teenagers. The role of the teacher should no longer be confined to imparting a certain amount of pre-packed knowledge that the pupil is supposed to receive and retain. It should now embrace many educative tasks, effective as well as intellectual, wherein the teacher's main job is to guide each individual pupil towards a differentiated set of goals, not to " drop " those who cannot meet uniform demands. Individualization requires not only other teaching strategies but also another basic attitude towards teaching. It entails the teacher serving not only as an instructor but as a guide and counsellor as well. Thus, the teacher in a highly mobile society has a great responsibility in helping the pupil to approach his or her first choice of occupation through a series of choices as to courses of study.

There are three aspects of reform of teacher education that are conducive to greater equality of educational opportunity:

i) It has repeatedly been emphasized, not least by educational sociologists, that school education is characterized by a middle class orientation prevalent among teachers. This is attributable largely to the fact that in many industrialized countries teachers, particularly elementary school teachers, come from lower middle class and upper working class homes characterized by upward social mobility. The choice of the teaching profession is a symptom of such mobility. But this middle class orientation also reflects the traditional character of the school as an institution where pupils are sorted, examined, certified and helped along to various careers, for this "helping along" tends to be influenced by the expectation of the teacher as to what pupils with different social backgrounds can attain.

ii) Teacher training should give more emphasis to the sociological and less to the didactic aspects of school education. As far as the didactic aspects are concerned, greater importance should be attached to individualized methods of instruction that make allowance for individual differences in social background. Part of an individualized attitude towards the teaching task is a "diagnostic" orientation. Instead of spending a considerable time on checking the progress of individual pupils in relation to the rest of the class, the teacher should use this time for following the individual pupils' progress in relation to some absolute standard. Evaluation should therefore focus on the efficiency of the teaching and not so much on the relative competence attained by the pupils. Whereas a system that adopts a "frontal approach" (all pupils being required to move at the same pace towards a uniform standard of attainment) tends to be biased against those who have a less privileged background, and individualized approach should lead to more equality in results. Educators are beginning to realize that it is not the task of the school to contribute to increased individual differences in attainment by using various selective measures, but to bring out the potential of each individual pupil. The very fact that the school is there to impart certain competences unavoidably entails a differentiating function which can be either more or less emphasized.

iii) The teaching cadre should be diversified in the sense that people other than certified teachers should be enlisted for classroom work. It would be advantageous if students while still in their teacher training colleges could learn to collaborate with parents (e.g. housewives), asking them to come in and do part-time work — not only clerical and administrative chores but also actual teaching in small groups or by tutoring individual students. In addition to calling in such assistance, people of some achievement in the surrounding community should also be recruited to come to the

170

teacher training colleges from time to time and give expression to their experiences in their various chosen fields. This would counteract the isolation and the one-sided orientation towards didactic problems that has characterized teacher training for so long.

6. THE NEED FOR A "SYSTEMS APPROACH"

The objective of increased equality of opportunity, and of performance, cannot be achieved by educational policy alone. It requires concerted efforts on the part of those formulating social and economic policies for the society in its entirety.

Quite a lot of the technology stemming from recent advances in the natural sciences has been applied to social and environmental problems in a "fragmented" form without consideration of the total situation. This is why many short-range productive gains and improvements of standards of living have been bought at the price of seriously upsetting the equilibrium of the ecological system. The same problem is now being encountered with "social technology" based upon the progressively specialized social sciences. The majority of major public issues cut across disciplinary and administrative borderlines. However, because of the general inability, or even refusal, to realize that big social issues are, therefore, "systems problems" whose solutions require the co-ordinated efforts of many experts and several administrative agencies, essentials of "major reforms" sometimes never get further than the paper they are written on.

Thus, compensatory education alone does not work. Resources spent on programmes that give children from underprivileged homes stimulating and individualized experiences before entering regular school is one example of a non-systems approach. A few hours per day of stimulating adult contact has little or no effect for slum children unless large-scale and vigorous action is simultaneously taken to deal with other causes of cultural poverty, such as unemployment and substanding housing.

What is needed at the policy-making level is a group of broadly-oriented social scientists who are willing and able to take a cross-disciplinary look at issues. Such a group should take the systems approach that must precede any measures to produce suitable strategies for the treatment of the identified problems. So far, only the military has run central co-ordinating bodies of this type.

REFERENCES

Aebli, H. (1968). "Die geistige Entwicklung als Funktion von Anlage, Reifung, Umwelt- und Erziehungsbedingungen", in H. Roth (Ed.) *Begabung und Lernen*. Stuttgart: Klett, 151-191.

Allen, G., and K.D. Pettigrew, L. Ehrlenmeyer-Kimling, and S.E. Stern (1973). "Heritability and Social Class: Evidence Inconclusive", *Science, 182,* 7 December, 1042-1045.

Anastasi, Anne (1948). "The Nature of Psychological 'Traits'", *Psychological Review, 55,* 127-138.

Anastasi, Anne (1956). "Intelligence and Family Size", *Psychological Bulletin, 53,* No.3, 187-209.

Anastasi, Anne (1958). " Heredity, Environment, and the Question 'How?'", *Psychological Review, 65,* 197-208.

Anastasi, Anne (1958a). *Differential Psychology: Individual and Group Difference in Behavior,* 3rd ed. New York: Macmillan.

Anastasi, Anne (1959). "Differentiating Effect of Intelligence and Social Status", *Eugenics Quarterly, 6,* No. 2, 84-91.

Anderson, C. Arnold (1974). *Expanding Educational Opportunities: Conceptualisation and Measurement.* Institute for the Study of International Problems in Education, University of Stockholm (Mimeo).

Anderson, C. Arnold, and Mary Jean Bowman (1952). "Intelligence and Occupational Mobility", *Journal of Political Economy, 60,* 218-239.

Anderson, C. Arnold, and Philip J. Foster (1964). "Discrimination and Inequality in Education", *Sociology of Education, 38,* No. 1, Fall 1964, 1-18.

Arnold, W. (1968). " Bildungswilligkeit der Eltern im Hinblick auf ihre Kinder", in H. Roth (Ed.) *Begabung und Lernen.* Stuttgart: Klett, 357-375.

Bajema, Carl Jay (1962). "Estimation of the Direction and Intensity of Natural Selection in Relation to Human Intelligence by Means of the Intrinsic Rate of Natural Increase", *Eugenics Quarterly, 9,* No. 4, December, 1962, 175-187.

Bajema, Carl Jay (1968). "A Note on the Interrelations among Intellectual Ability, Educational Attainment, and Occupational Achievement: A Follow-up Study of a Male Kalamazoo Public School Population", *Sociology of Education, 41,* No.3, Summer 1968, 317-319.

Banks, O. (1955). *Parity and Prestige in English Education.* Routledge and Kegan Paul, London.

Becker, Gary S. (1964). *Human Capital.* New York: National Bureau of Economic Research, Columbia University Press.

Begemann, Ernst (1970). *Die Erziehung der Socio-Kulturell Benachteiligten Schüler.* Hannover: Schrödel.

Bell, Daniel (1973). *Coming of Post-Industrial Society: A Venture in Social Forecasting.* New York: Basic Books.

Belmont, Lillian and Francis A. Marolla (1973). " Birth Order, Family Size, and Intelligence ", *Science, 182*, December 14, 1973, 1096-1101.

Bengtsson, Jarl (1972). *Utbildningsval, utbildningsforskning och utbildningsplanering.* Lund: Studentlitteratur.

Bengtsson, Jarl and Kjell Härnqvist (1973). " Utbildningsreformer och jämlikhat ", in Värde, Välfärd och Jämlikhet.

Benjamin, B. (1966). " Social and Economic Differences in Ability ", in J.E. Meade and A.S. Parkes (Eds.), *Genetic and Environmental Factors in Human Ability.* Edinburgh: Oliver and Boyd.

Bereday, George Z.F. and Lauwerys, Joseph A. (Eds.) (1962). " The Gifted Child ", *Year Book of Education, 24,* 1962.

Bereiter, Carl (1970). " Genetics and Educability: Educational Implications of the Jensen debate ", in Jerome Hellmuth (Ed.) *Disadvantaged Child.* Vol. 3. New York: Brunner/Mazel.

Berg, Ivar (1971). *Education and Jobs: The Great Training Robbery.* Boston: Beacon Press.

Bernstein, Basil (1961). " Social Structure and Learning ", *Educational Research, 3,* No. 3, June 1961, 163-176.

Blackburn, Julian (1947). " Family Size, Intelligence Score and Social Class ", *Population Studies, 1,* No. 2, Sept. 1947, 165-176.

Blau, Peter M. and Otis Dudley Ducan (1967). *The American Occupational Structure.* New York: Wiley.

Block, J.H. (Ed.) (1971). *Mastery Learning: Theory and Practice.* New York: Holt, Rinehart and Winston.

Bloom, Benjamin S. (1964). *Stability and Change in Human Characteristics.* New York: Wiley.

Bloom, Benjamin S. *et al.* (1965). *Compensatory Education for Cultural Deprivation.* Based on working papers contributed by participants in the Research Conference on Educational and Cultural Deprivation, Chicago, 1964. New York: Holt.

Bloom, Benjamin S. (1971). " Mastery Learning " in J.H. Block: *Mastery Learning: Theory and Practice.* New York: Holt, Rinehart and Winston, 47-63.

Bloom, Benjamin S. *et al.* (1971). *Handbook on Formative and Summative Evaluation of Student Learning.* New York: McGraw-Hill.

Boalt, Gunnar (1947). *Skolutbildning och skolresultat för barn ur olika samhallsgrupper i Stockholm.* Stockholm: Norstedt.

Borg, W.R. (1965). " Ability Grouping in the Public Schools ", *Journal of Experimental Education, 34,* No. 2, 1-97.

Boudon, Raymond (1973). " Education et mobilité ", *Sociologie et Sociétés, 5,* 111-125.

Boudon, Raymond (1974). *L'inégalité des chances.* Paris: Armand Colin, " U ".

Boudon, Raymond (1973). *Education, Opportunity and Social Inequality.* New York: Wiley and Sons.

Boudon, Raymond (1974). *Education, Opportunity and Social Inequality* (in press).

Bourdieu, Pierre (1964). *Les Héritiers: Les Etudiants et la Culture.* Paris: Editions de Minuit.

Bourdieu, Pierre (1967). " Systèmes d'enseignement et systèmes de pensée ", *Revue internationale des sciences sociales, 19,* No. 3, 367-388.

Bourdieu, Pierre et J.C. Passeron (1971). *Die Illusion der Chancengleichheit.* Stuttgart: Klett.

Bowles, Samuel (1971). " Cuban Education and the Revolutionary Ideology ", *Harvard Educational Review, 41,* Nov. 1971, 472-500.

Bowles, Samuel (1972). " Schooling and Inequality from Generation to Generation ", *Journal of Political Economy, 80:2,* No. 3, May-June 1972, 219-251.

Bowles, Samuel, and Herbert Gintis (1972-1973). " IQ in the U.S. Class Structure ", *Social Policy, 3,* No. 4-5, 65-96.

174

Bowles, Samuel, and Henry M. Levin (1968). "The Determinants of Scholastic Achievement — An Appraisal of Some Recent Evidence", *Journal of Human Resources, 3*, No. 1, Winter 1968, 3-24.

Bressler, Marvin (1968). "Sociology, Biology, and Ideology", in *Genetics: Biology and Behavior*. Proceedings of a conference under the auspices of Russell Sage Foundation, The Social Science Research Council, and the Rockfeller University. Ed. by David V. Glass. New York: The Rockefeller University Press, 178-210.

Breton, R., and J.C. McDonald (1967). *Career Decisions of Canadian Youth. A Compilation of Basic Data*. Ottawa: Department of Manpower and Immigration.

Breton, R. (1970). *Social and Academic Factors in the Career Decisions of Canadian Youth.* Part I and II. Ottawa: Department of Manpower and Immigration.

Breton, R. (1970a). *Social and Academic Factors in the Career Decisions of Canadian Youth.* Part III, IV and V. Ottawa: Department of Manpower and Immigration.

Breton, R. (1970b). "Academic Stratification in Secondary Schools and the Educational Plans of Students", *Review of Canadian Sociology and Anthropology Association, 7*, No. 1, 17-34.

Buckingham, B.R. (1921). "Intelligence and its Measurement: A Symposium", *Journal of Educational Psychology, 12*, May 1921, 271-275.

Bulcock, Jeffrey W., Ingemar Fagerlind, and Ingemar Emanuelsson (1974). *Education and the Socioeconomic Career: U.S.-Swedish Comparisons*. Stockholm: Institute for the Study of International Problems in Education, University of Stockholm (mimeo).

Bungarth, Karl *et al.* (1970). *Begabung und Begabtenförderung, 2,* Ed. Hannover: Schrödel.

Burks, Barbara S. (1928). "The Relative Influence of Nature and Nurture upon Mental Development", *Yearbook of the National Society for the Study of Education, 27*, Part I, Chicago: Univ. of Chicago Press, 219-316.

Burt, Cyril (1943). "Ability and Income", *British Journal of Educational Psychology, 13*, 1943, 83-98.

Burt, Cyril (1946). *Intelligence and Fertility*. Occasional Papers on Eugenics No. 2. London: Hamilton.

Burt, Cyril (1947). "Family Size, Intelligence and Social Class", *Population Studies, 1*, No. 2, Sept. 1947, 177-186.

Burt, Cyril (1958). "The Inheritance of Mental Ability", *American Psychologist, 13*, Jan. 1958, 1-15.

Burt, Cyril (1966). "The Genetic Determination of Differences in Intelligence: A Study of Monozygotic Twins Reared Together and Apart", *British Journal of Psychology, 57*, 1966, 137-153.

Burt, Cyril (1969). "What is intelligence?", *British Journal of Educational Psychology, 39*, 1969, 198-201.

Burt, Cyril (1970). "The Mental Differences between Children", in Cox, C.B . and Dyson, A.E. (Eds.) 1970, *Black Paper Two: The Crisis in Ed.* London: The Critical Quarterly Society, 16-25.

Burt, Cyril (1972). "Inheritance of General Intelligence", *American Psychologist, 27*, No. 3, March 1972, 175-190.

Butcher, H.J. (1968). *Human Intelligence: Its Nature and Assessment*. London: Methuen.

Carlson, Kenneth (1972). "Equalizing Educational Opportunity", *Review of Educational Research, 42*, No. 4, Fall 1972, 453-72.

Cattell, Raymond B. (1937). *The Fight for Our National Intelligence*. London: King.

Cattell, Raymond B. (1950). "The Fate of National Intelligence: Test of a Thirteen-Year Prediction", *Eugenics Review, 42*, No. 3, Oct. 1950, 136-148.

Cattell, Raymond B. (1971). "The Structure of Intelligence in Relation to the Nature-Nurture Controversy", in: Robert Cancro (Ed.), *Intelligence: Genetic and Environmental Influences*. New York and London: Grune and Stratton.

CEEB (College Entrance Examination Board (1960). *The Search for Talent*. College Admission No. 7. New York: College Entrance Examination Board.

Charters, W.W.Jr. (1963). "The Social Background of Teaching", in N.L. Gage (Ed.), *Handbook of Research on Teaching*. Chicago: Rand McNally and Co., 715-813.

Cohen, David K. (1972). "Does IQ Matter?", *Commentary, 53*, No. 4, April 1972, 51-59.

Coleman, James S. (1961). *The adolescent Society: The Social Life of the Teenage and Its Impact on Education*. Glencoe: The Free Press.

Coleman, James S. (1966). "Equal Schools or Equal Students?", *Public Interest*. Summer 1966, No. 4, 70-75.

Coleman, James S. (1967). "Toward Open Schools", *Public Interest*. Summer 1967, No. 4, 20-27.

Coleman, James S. (1968a). "The Concept of Equality of Educational Opportunity", *Harvard Educational Review*, Winter 1968, *38*, No. 1, 7-37.

Coleman, James S. (1968b). "Equality of Educational Opportunity: Reply to Bowles and Levin", *Journal of Human Resources, 3*, No. 2, 237-46.

Coleman, James S. (1973a). "Equality of Opportunity and Equality of Results", *Harvard Educational Review, 43*, No. 1, February 1973, 129-137.

Coleman, James S. (1973b). "*Effects of School on Learning: The IEA Findings*", Paper presented at the IEA–Harvard Conference on Educational Achievement, November 1973. Cambridge, Mass: Harvard Graduate School of Education (mimeo).

Coleman, James S., *et al.* (1966). *Equality of Educational Opportunity*. Washington, D.C.: U.S. Department of Health, Education and Welfare, Office of Education.

Coleman, James S., Thomas F. Pettigrew, and William H. Sewell (1973). "Review Symposium", (Rev. of Ch. Jencks *et al.*, Inequality: A Reassessment of the Effect of Family and Schooling in America). *American Journal of Sociology, 78*, No. 6, May 1973, 1523-44.

Coleman, James S. *et al.* (1974). *Youth: Transition to Adulthood*. Report of the Panel on Youth of the President's Science Advisory Committee. Chicago: University of Chicago Press.

Comber, L.C., and John P. Keeves (1973). *Science Education in Nineteen Countries: An Empirical Study*. With a Foreword by Torsten Husén. Stockholm: Almqvist and Wiksell; New York: Wiley, Halsted Press.

Conant, James B. (1959). *The American High School Today*. New York: McGraw-Hill.

Cook, Robert C. (1951). *Human Fertility: The Modern Dilemma*. New York: Sloane.

Cox, C.B., and A.E. Dyson (Eds.) (1969). *Fight for Education: A Black Paper*. London: The Critical Quarterly Society, March 1969.

Cox, C.B., and A.E. Dyson (Eds.) (1970). *Black Paper Two: The Crisis in Education*. London: The Critical Quarterly Society, Oct. 1970.

Cremin, Lawrence (1970). *American Education. The Colonial Experience 1607-1783*. New York: Harper and Row.

Cronbach, Lee J. (1973). "Five Decades of Controversy over Mental Testing", in Charles Frankel (Ed.) *Social Science Controversies and Public Policy Decisions*. Paper presented at a conference sponsored by the American Academy of Arts and Sciences, February 16-17, 1973.

Dahllöf, Urban (1971). *Ability Grouping, Content Validity and Curriculum Process Analysis*. New York: Teachers College Press.

Dahrendorf, Ralf (1965). *Arbeiterkinder an deutschen Universitäten*, in: Recht und Staat, Heft 302-303. Tübingen: C.B. Mohr (Paul Siebeck).

Daniëls, M.J.M., and M. Albinski (1958). "Vrang en Aanbod van Intellect", *Universiteit en Hogeschool, 4*, 168-177.

Daniels, Norman (1973). "The Smart White Man's Burden", *Harper's Magazine*, Oct. 1973, 24-40.

Dave, R.H. (1963). *The identification and Measurement of Environmental Process Variables Related to Educational Achievement*. University of Chicago: Unpublished Doctoral Dissertation.

Denison, Edward F. (1962). *The Sources of Economic Growth in the United States and the Alternatives before Us.* New York: Committee for Economic Development.

Deutscher Bildungsrat (1970). *Strukturplan für das Bildungswesen. Empfehlungen der Bildungskommission.* Bonn: Bundesdruckerei.

Dobzhansky, Theodosius (1967). *The Biology of Ultimate Concern.* New York: The New American Library.

Dobzhansky, Theodosius (1968). "On Genetics, Sociology, and Politics", in *Perspectives in Biology and Medicine,* Summer 1968, 544-554.

Dobzhansky, Theodosius (1973a). *Genetic Diversity and Human Equality.* New York: Basic Books.

Dobzhansky, Theodosius (1973b). "Race, Intelligence, and Genetics: Differences are not Deficits", *Psychology Today,* No. 7, 96-102.

Douglas, J.W.B. (1964). *The Home and the School.* London: MacGibbon and Kee.

Douglas, J.W.B., J.M. Ross, and H.R. Simpson (1968). *All Our Future.* London: P. Davies.

Duncan, Beverley (1967). "Education and Social Background", *American Journal of Sociology,* 72, 363-372.

Duncan, Otis Dudley (1952). "Is the Intelligence of the General Population Declining?", *American Sociological Review,* 17, No. 4, 401-407.

Duncan, Otis Dudley (1961). "A Socioeconomic Index for All Occupations", in A.J. Reiss, *et al.* (Eds.), *Occupations and Social Status.* Glencoe: Free Press.

Ducan, Otis Dudley (1968). "Ability and Achievement", *Eugenics Quarterly,* 15, March 1968, 1-11.

Ducan, Otis Dudley (1968) *et al., Socio-economic Background and Occupational Achievements.* Project No. 5-0074 (EO-191). U.S. Dept. of Health, Education and Welfare, Office of Education, Bureau of Research.

Dunn, L.C. and Theodosius Dobzhansky (1956). *Heredity, Race and Society.* New York: The New American Library, a Mento Book.

Dyer, Henry S. (1968). "School Factors and Equal Educational Opportunity", *Harvard Educational Review,* 38, No. 1, Winter 1968, 38-56.

Eckland, Bruce K. (1967). "Genetics and Sociology: A Reconsideration", *American Sociological Review,* 32, No. 3, April 1967, 173-194.

Edding, Friedrich and Roderich von Carnap (1962). *Der relative Schulbesuch in den Ländern der Bundesrepublik 1952-1960.* Frankfurt a.m.: Hochschule für Internationale Pädagogische Forschung.

Edlund, Sven (1947). *Diskussionen am Begåvningsurvalet under reformations- och stormaktstiden.* Lund: Gleerups.

Edmonds, Ronald (Ed.) (1973). "A Black Response to Christopher Jencks's Inequality and Certain Other Issues", *Harvard Educational Review,* 43, No. 1, Feb. 1973, 76-91.

Edmonds, Ronald and Evelyn K. Moore (1973). "IQ, Social Class and Educational Policy", *Change,* 5, No. 8, Oct. 1973, 12, 64.

Ekman, Gösta (1949). "Om uppskattningen av begåvningsreservens storlek", *Pedagogisk Tidskrift,* No. 7-8, 125-150.

Ekman, Gösta (1951). "Skolformer och begåvningsfördelning", *Pedagogisk Tidskrift,* No. 1, 15-37.

Ekstrom, Ruth B. (1959). *Experimental Studies of Homogeneous Grouping.* A Review of the Literature. Princeton: Educational Testing Service.

Eliasson, Torsten, and Bengt Höglund (1971). *Vuxenutbildning i Sverige: En strukturell översikt.* Report No. 54, Stockholm School of Education. Stockholm: Utbildningsdepartementet (Ministry of Education).

Elmgren, John (1952). *School and Psychology.* A Report on the Research Work of the 1946 School Commission, 1948:27, Stockholm: Utbildningsdepartementet (Government Printing Office).

Emmerij, Louis (1974). *Can the School Build a New Social Order?* Amsterdam: Elsevier.

Erlenmeyer-Kimling, L., and L.F. Jarvik (1963). "Genetics and Intelligence: A Review", *Science, 142,* 1477-1479.

ETS (1957). Educational Testing Service, 1956-57. *Background Factors Relating to College Plans and College Enrolment Among Public High School Students.* Princeton: Educational Testing Service.

Eysenck, Hans J. (1971). *The IQ Argument: Race, Intelligence and Education.* London: Temple Smith.

Eysenck, Hans J. (1973). "I.Q., Social Class and Educational Policy", *Change,* No. 39, September 1973, 1-5.

Faris, Robert E.L. (1961). "Reflections on the Ability Dimension in Human Society", *American Sociological Review, 26,* Dec. 1961, 835-843.

Feldmesser, Robert A. (1957). "Social Status and Access to Higher Education: A Comparison of the United States and the Soviet Union", *Harvard Educational Review, 27,* No. 2, Spring 1957, 92-106.

Fensham, P.J. (Ed.) (1970). *Rights and Inequality in Australian Education.* Melbourne: Cheshire.

Ferguson, G.A. (1956). "On Transfer and the Abilities of Man", Canadian *Journal of Psychology, 10,* 122-131.

Finch, F.H. (1946). *Enrolment Increases and the Changes in the Mental Level.* Applied Psychology Monographs No. 10. Chicago: University of Chicago Press.

Fischer, John H. (1970). "Who Needs Schools?", *Saturday Review,* 19th September, 1970, 78-91.

Flanaghan, John C. *et al.* (1962). *Design for a Study of American Youth.* Boston: Houghton Mifflin.

Flanagan, John C., *et al.* (1964). *The American High School Student.* Cooperative Research Project No. 635. Washington, D.C.: United States Office of Education.

Fleming, Charlotte M. (1943). "Socio-Economic Level and Test Performance", *British Journal of Educational Psychology, 12,* No. 2, 1943.

Floud, Jean E. *et al.* (1956). *Social Class and Educational Opportunity.* London: Heinemann.

Frankel, Charles (1973). "The New Egalitarianism and the Old", *Commentary, 56,* No. 3, Sept., 1973, 54-66.

Fraser, Elisabeth (1959). *Home Environment and the School.* London: University of London Press.

Freeman, Richard B. (1974). *Investing in Education: Has the Bubble Burst?* Paris: OECD Directorate for Scientific Affairs (mimeo).

Frommberger, H. (1954). *Das Sitzenbleiberproblem: Untersuchungen über das Versagen von Kindern in der Volksschule.* Dortmund. Crüwell Verlagsbuchhandlung.

Furneaux W.D. (1961). *The Chosen Few.* London: Oxford University Press.

Gagné, Robert M. (1968). "Contributions of Learning to Human Development", *Psychological Review, 75,* 177-191.

Gagné, Robert M. and W.J. Gephart (Eds.) (1968). *Learning Research and School Subjects.* Itasca, Illinois: F.E. Peacock Publishers.

Galbraith, Kenneth (1973). *Economics and the Public Purpose.* Boston: Houghton Mifflin.

Gans, Herbert J. (1973). *More Equality.* New York: Pantheon Books (A Division of Random House).

Gardner, John W. (1961). *Excellence: Can We Be Equal and Excellent Too?* New York: Harper and Row.

Gartner, Alan, Colingreer and Frank Riessman (1973). *IQ and Social Stratification.* New York: Harper and Row.

Gesser, B., and E. Fasth (1973). *Gymnasieutbildning och social skiktning.* Stockholm: Universitetskanslersämbetet (Office of the Chancellor of the Swedish Universities).

Gille, René, Louis Henry, *et al.* (1954). *Le niveau intellectuel des enfants d'âge scolaire. La détermination des aptitudes. L'influence des facteurs constitutionnels, familiaux et sociaux.* Institut national d'études démographiques. Travaux et Documents, Cahier No. 23. Paris: Presses Universitaires de France.

Gintis, Herbert (1971). "Education, Technology, and the Characteristics of Worker Productivity", *American Economic Review, 61*, No. 2, May 1971, 266-279.

Girard, Alain (1953). "L'Orientation et la sélection des enfants d'âge scolaire dans le département de la Seine", *Population*, No. 4, Oct-Dec., 1953.

Girard, Alain, Henri Bastides, and Guy Pourcher (1963). "Enquête nationale sur l'entrée en sixième et la démocratisation de l'enseignement", *Population*, No. 1, Jan-March 1963.

Girard, Alain, and Henri Bastides (1969). "Orientation et sélection scolaire. Cinq années d'une promotion: de la fin du cycle élémentaire à l'entrée dans le 2e cycle du second degré", *Population*, No. 1-2.

Glass, David V. (Ed.) (1954). *Social Mobility in Britain*. London: Kegan Paul.

Glass, David V. (Ed.) (1968). *Genetics: Biology and Behavior.* New York: Russell Sage Foundation and Rockefeller University Press.

Glazer, Nathan (1970). "Are Academic Standards Obsolete?" *Change.* November-December, 1970, 38-45.

Gray, J.L. and P. Moshinski (1936). *The Nation's Intelligence.* London: Watts.

Grimm, Susanne (1966). *Die Bildungsabstinenz der Arbeiter; Eine soziologische Untersuchung.* München: Barth.

Guilford, J.P. (1967). *The Nature of Human Intelligence.* New York: McGraw-Hill.

Halsey, A.H. (1958). "Genetics, Social Structure and Intelligence", *British Journal of Sociology, 9*, No. 1, March 1958, 15-28.

Halsey, A.H. (1959). "Class Differences in General Intelligence", *British Journal of Statistical Psychology, 12*, 1-4.

Halsey, A.H. (Ed.) (1961). *Ability and Educational Opportunity.* Paris: OECD.

Halsey, A.H. (1968). "Biology and Sociology: A Reconciliation", in *Genetics: Biology and Behavior.* Proceedings of a conference under the auspices of Russell Sage Foundation, the Social Science Research Council and the Rockefeller University. New York: The Rockefeller University Press, 210-214.

Hansen, Erik Joergen (1971). *Ungdom og uddannelse: De 14-20 åriges uddannelsesituation 1965.* Vol. II. Copenhagen: Teknisk Forlag.

Hansen, Erik Joergen (1973). "The Problem of Equality in the Danish Educational Structure", *Acta Sociologica, 16*, No. 4, pp. 258-278.

Hammel, Walter (1970). *Bildsamkeit und Begabung.* Hannover: Schrödel.

Harbison, Frederik H. (1973). *Human Resources as the Wealth of Nations.* London: Oxford University Press.

Harbison, Frederick H., and Charles Myers (1964). *Education, Manpower and Economic Growth.* New York: McGraw-Hill.

Härnqvist, Kjell (1958). "Beräkning av reserver för högre utbildning", in *Reserverna för högre utbildning. 1955 års universitetsutredning.* Stockholm: Statens offentliga utredningar 1958, No. 11, Stockholm: Government Printing Office.

Härnqvist, Kjell (1959). "Intelligensutveckling och skolresultat", *Pedagogisk forskning, 2*, 57-69.

Härnqvist, Kjell (1966). "Special Factors and Educational Choice: A Preliminary Study of Some Effects of the Swedish School Reform", *International Journal of Educational Sciences, 1*, No. 2, 87-102.

Härnqvist, Kjell (1968). "Relative Changes in Intelligence from 13 to 18", *Scandinavian Journal of Psychology, 9*, 50-82.

Härnqvist, Kjell, and Ake Grahm (1963). *Vägen genom gymnasiet. Elevernas syn på valsituationer och studieformer. 1960 års gymnasieutredning*, Vol. 1. Stockholm: Government Printing Office.

179

Härnqvist, Kjell, and Jarl Bengtsson (1972). "Educational Reform and Educational Equality", in R. Scase (Ed.) *Reader on Social Stratification.*

Härnqvist, Kjell (1974). The International Study of Educational Achievement. *American Educational Research Journal.*

Hartnacke, Wilhelm (1917). "Zur Verteilung der Schultüchtigen auf die sozialen Schichten", *Zeitschrift für Pädagogische Psychologie und Experimentelle Pädagogik.* Leipzig: Quelle und Meyer, 18, Jan.-Feb. 1917, 40-44.

Havighurst, Robert J. (1973). "Opportunity, Equity, or Equality", *School Review, 81,* No. 4, August 1973, 618-33.

Heckhausen, Heinz (1974). *Leistung und Chancengleichheit.* Göttingen: Hocrafe.

Van Heek, Frederick (1968). *Het Verborgen Talent,* Meppel: van Gorcum.

Hellmuth, Jerome (Ed.) (1970). *Compensatory Education: A National Debate.* Disadvantaged Child, Vol. 3. New York: Brunner/Mazel Publishers.

Henmon, V.A.C. (1921). "Intelligence and its Measurement: A Symposium", *Journal of Educational Psychology, 12,* No. 4, April 1921, 195-210.

Henry, J. (1963). *Culture Against Man.* New York, Random House.

Henry, Louis (1954). "L'influence des divers facteurs socio-économiques et la dimension de la famille", in *Le niveau intellectuel des enfants d'âge scolaire.* Institut national d'études démographiques. Travaux et Documents. Cahier No. 23. Paris: Presses Universitaires de France. 47-96.

HER (1969a). *Environment, Heredity, and Intelligence.* Reprint Series No. 2. Cambridge; Massachusetts: Harvard Educational Review.

HER (1969b). *Science, Heritability, and IQ.* Reprint Series No. 4. Cambridge, Massachusetts: Harvard Educational Review.

Herrnstein, Richard J. (1971). "IQ", *Atlantic Monthly, 228,* No. 3, Sept., 1971, 44-64.

Herrnstein, Richard J. (1973). *IQ in the Meritocracy.* Boston: Little, Brown and Co.

Hess, Robert D., and V.C. Shipman (1965). "Early Experience and the Socialization of Cognitive Modes in Children", *Child Development, 36,* 869-886.

Heuyer, G., H. Piéron, *et al.* (1950). *Le niveau intellectuel des enfants d'âge scolaire: Une enquête nationale dans l'enseignement primaire.* Institut National d'Etudes Démographiques, Travaux et Documents, Cahier No. 13. Paris: Presses Universitaires de France.

Higgins, J.V., Elisabeth W. Reed, and S.C. Reed (1962). "Intelligence and Family Size: A Paradox Resolved", *Eugenics Quarterly, 9,* No. 1, March 1962, 84-90.

Hitpass, Josef (1963). "Begabungsreserve 1963", *Pädagogische Rundschau, 17,* No. 12.

HMSO (1954). *Early Leaving: A Report of the Central Advisory Council for Education* (England). Her Majesty's Stationery Office.

HMSO (1959). *Crowther Report. A Report of the Central Advisory Council for Education* (England), Vol. I-II. London: Her Majesty's Stationery Office.

HMSO (1963). *Half our Future.* (Newsom Report). London: Her Majesty's Stationery Office.

HMSO (1965). *Higher Education.* Report and Annexes I to V. (Robbins Report). London: Her Majesty's Stationery Office.

HMSO (1967). *Children and their Primary Schools.* A Report of the Central Advisory Council for Education (England): (Plowden Report) II: Research and Surveys. London: Her Majesty's Stationery Office.

Hodgson, Godfrey (1973). "Do Schools Make a Difference?", *Atlantic Monthly,* 231, No. 3, March 1973, 35-46.

Holland, John L. (1963). "Creative and Academic Performance Among Talented Adolescents", in Robert E. Grinder (Ed.) *Studies in Adolescence.* New York.

Holland, John L., and Alexander W. Astin (1962). "The Need for Redefining 'Talent' and 'Talent Loss'", *Journal of Higher Education.* February 1962, *32,* No. 2, 77-82.

Holland, John L., and S.W. Lutz (1968). "The Predictive Value of a Student's Choice of Vocation", *Personnel and Guidance Journal*, January 1968, *46*, No. 5, 428-436.

Holland, John L., and R.C. Nichols (1964). "Prediction of Academic and Extra-Curricular Achievement in College", *Journal of Educational Psychology*, 1964, *55*, No. 1, 55-65.

Hüfner, Klaus (Ed.) (1973). *Bildungswesen: mangelhaft. BRD-Bildungspolitik im OECD-Länderexamen*. Eine Veröffentlichung der OECD, Deutsch herasusgegeben und eigeleitet von Klaus Hüfner. Mit einem Vorwort von Hildegard Hamm-Brücher. Frankfurt am Main: Diesterweg.

Hughes, John F., and Anne O. Hughes (1972). *Equal Education: A New National Strategy*. Bloomington and London: Indiana University Press.

Hunt, J. McVicker (1961). *Intelligence and Experience*. New York: Ronald Press.

Hunt, J. McVicker (1969). *The Challenge of Incompetence and Poverty: Papers on the Role of Early Education*. Urbana: University of Illinois Press.

Hunt, J. McVicker (1973). "Heredity, Environment, and Class or Ethnic Differences", in *Assessment in a Pluralistic Society*. Proceedings of the 1972 Invitational Conference on Testing Problems. Princeton, N.J.: Educational Testing Service, 3-36.

Husén, Torsten (1946). "Intelligenskrav på olika skolutbildningsstadier", *Skola och samhälle, 27*, No. 1, 1-23.

Husén, Torsten (1947). "Begavningsurvalet och de högre skolorna", *Folkskolan-Svensk Lärartidning, 1*, No. 4, 124-137.

Husén, Torsten (1948). *Begåvning och miljö*. Stockholm: Almqvist and Wiksell.

Husén, Torsten (1950). *Testresultatens prognosvärde*. Stockholm: Almqvist and Wiksell, Gebers.

Husén, Torsten (1951). "The Influence of Schooling upon IQ", *Theoria, 17*, 61-88. Reprinted in: J.J. Jenkins and D.G. Paterson (1961) (Eds.), *Studies in Individual Differences in Search for Intelligence*, 677-693. New York: Appleton-Century-Crofts.

Husén, Torsten (1953). *Tvillingstudier*. Stockholm: Almqvist and Wiksell.

Husén, Torsten (1959). *Psychological Twin Research*. Stockholm: Almqvist and Wiksell.

Husén, Torsten (1960). "Abilities of Twins", *Scandinavian Journal of Psychology, 1*, 125-135.

Husén, Torsten (1962). *Problems of Differentiation in Swedish Compulsory Schooling*. Stockholm: Svenska Bokförlaget — Scandinavian University Books.

Husén, Torsten (1963). "Intra-Pair Similarities in the School Achievements of Twins", *Scandinavian Journal of Psychology, 4*, 108-114.

Husén, Torsten (1965). "Curriculum Research in Sweden", *International Review of Education, 11*, No. 2, 189-208.

Husén, Torsten (Ed.) (1967). *International Study of Achievement in Mathematics: A Comparison of Twelve Countries*. Vol. I-II. Stockholm and New York: Almqvist and Wiksell and Wiley.

Husén, Torsten (1968a). "Life-Long Learning in the 'Educative Society'", *International Review of Applied Psychology, 17*, No. 2, 87-99.

Husén, Torsten (1968b). "Talent, Opportunity, and Career: A Twenty-Six-Year Follow-Up", *School Review, 76*, June 1968, 190-209.

Husén, Torsten (1968c). "Educational Research and Policy-Making". In *Research and the State* (by W.D. Wall and T. Husén). London: National Foundation for Educational Research in England and Wales. 13-22.

Husén, Torsten, et al. (1969). *Talent, Opportunity and Career: A Twenty-Six-Year Follow-Up of 1,500 Individuals*. Stockholm: Almqvist and Wiksell.

Husén, Torsten (1971a). "The Comprehensive-Versus-Selective School Issue", *International Review of Education, 17*, No. 1, 1971, 3-10. Hamburg: Unesco Institute for Education.

Husén, Torsten (1971b). *Present Trends and Future Developments in Education: A European Perspective*. The Peter Sandiford Memorial Lectures. Toronto: Ontario Institute for Studies in Education. Occasional Papers No. 8.

Husén, Torsten (1973a). "Implications of the IEA Findings for the Philosophy of Comprehensive Education", Paper Presented at the Harvard Conference on Educational Achievement, Harvard Graduate School of Education, November 1973 (mimeo).

Husén, Torsten (1973b). The Standard of the Elite: Some Findings from the IEA International Survey in Mathematics and Science. Acta Sociologica, 16, No. 6, 305-323.

Husén, Torsten (1974a). The Learning Society. London: Methuen.

Husén, Torsten (1974b). Talent, Equality and Meritocracy. The Hague: Martünus Nijhoff.

Husén, Torsten, and Gunnar Boalt (1968). Educational Research and Educational Change: The Case of Sweden. Stockholm: Almqvist and Wiksell.

Husén, Torsten, and Urban Dahllöf (1960). Mathematics and Communication Skills in School and Society: An Empirical Approach to the Problem of Curriculum Content. Stockholm: Studieförbundet Näringsliv och samhälle.

Husén, Torsten, and S.E. Henricson (1951). Some Principles of Construction of Group Intelligence Tests for Adults: A Report on the Construction and Standardization of the Swedish Induction Test (the I-Test). Stockholm: Almqvist and Wiksell.

Husén, Torsten, and Sten Henrysson (1959). Differentiation and Guidance in the Comprehensive School. Stockholm: Almqvist and Wiksell.

Huth, Abert (1956)

Ingenkamp, K.(1968). "Möglichkeiten und Grenzen des Lehrerurteils und der Schultests", in H. Roth (Ed.) Begabung und Lernen, 407-432. Stuttgart: Klett.

Jackson, Brian (1964). Streaming: An Educational System in Miniature. London: Routledge and Kegan Paul.

Jackson, Brian, and D. Marsden (1968). Education and the Working Class. London: Routledge and Kegan Paul.

Jencks, Christopher, et al. (1972). Inequality: A Reassessment of the Effect of Family and Schooling in America. New York and London: Basic Books.

Jensen, Arthur R. (1969). "How Much Can we Boost IQ and Scholastic Achievement?", Harvard Educational Review, 39, No. 1, Winter 1969, 1-123.

Jensen, Arthur R. (1972). Genetics and Education. London: Methuen.

Jensen, Arthur R. (1973). Educability and Group Differences. London: Methuen.

Jensen, Arthur (1973a). "Race, Intelligence and Genetics: The Differences are Real", Psychology Today, 7, No. 7, 79-87.

Johansson, Bror A. (1965). Criteria of School Readiness: Factor Structure, Predictive Value, and Environmental Influences. Stockholm: Almqvist and Wiksell.

Juel-Nielsen, N. (1965). Individual and Environment: A Psychiatric-Psychological Investigation of Monozygous Twins Reared Apart. Acta Psychiatrica et Neurologica Scandinavica, Monograph Suppl. 183. Copenhagen: Munksgaard.

Kamin, Leon (1973). "The Misuse of IQ Testing", (Interview with Leon Kamin by John Egerton). Change, 5, No. 8, Oct. 1973, 40-43.

Kamin, Leon (1974). "Heredity, Intelligence, Politics, and Psychology", Princeton University, Psychology Department (mimeo).

Karabel, Jerome (1973a). "Open Admissions: Toward Meritocracy or Democracy", Change, No. 3, May 1972, 38-43.

Katz, I. (1968). "Academic Motivation and Equal Educational Opportunity", Harvard Educational Review, 38, No. 1, Winter 1968, 57-65.

Katz, David (Ed.) (1952). Proceedings of the 13th International Congress of Psychology in Stockholm 1951. Stockholm: Bröderna Lagerström, Boktryckare.

Keeves, John P. (1972). Educational Environment and Student Achievement. Stockholm: Almqvist and Wiksell.

La Crosse, E.R., and P.C. Lee (Ed.) (1970). "The first Six Years of Life: A Report on Current Research and Educational Practice", Genetic Psychology Monographs, 82, 1970, 161-266.

182

Lasch, Christopher (1973a). "Inequality and Education", *New York Review of Books*, May 17, 1973, 19-25.

Lasch, Christopher (1973b). "Take me to Your Leader", *The New York Review of Books*, Oct. 18, 1973, 63-66.

Levi, Edward H. (1973). "Equality through Education", *Minerva*, 157-161.

Levin, Henry M. (1972). "Schooling and Equality: The Social Science Objectivity Gap", *Saturday Review*, November 11, 1972, 49-51.

Levin, Henry M. (1973). "Vouchers and Social Equity", *Change, 5*, No. 8, Oct. 1973, 29-33.

Lewin, Kurt (1935). "The Conflict Between Aristotelian and Galilean Modes of Thought in Contemporary Psychology", in *A Dynamic Theory of Personality*. New York: McGraw-Hill.

Levine, Donald M. (1973). "Educational Policy After Inequality", *Teachers College Record, 75*, No. 2, December 1973, 149-179.

Linton, Ralph (1936). *The Study of Man: An Introduction*. New York: Appleton.

Ljung, Bengt-Olov and Sven Jansson (1970). "Recruitment to the Gymnasium in Sweden", *Pedagogisk Forskning, Scandinavian Journal of Educational Research*, No. 1, 1970, 1-14.

Lipset, Seymour Martin (1972). "Social Mobility and Equal Opportunity", *Public Interest*, No. 29, Fall 1972, 90-108.

Lundberg, George A. (1939). *Foundations of Sociology*. New York: Harper and Ross.

Marklund, Sixten (1962). *Skolklassens storlek och struktur*. Stockholm: Almqvist and Wiksell.

Maccoby, Eleanor E. (Ed.) (1966). *The Development of Sex Differences*. Stanford, Calif.: Stanford University Press.

Maccoby, Eleanor E., and Carol Nagy Jacklin (1973). "Sex Differences in Intellectual Functioning", in *Assessment in a Pluralistic Society*. Proceedings of the 1972 Invitational Conference on Testing Problems. Princeton, N.J.: Educational Testing Service, 37-55.

Machlup, Fritz (1962). *The Production and Distribution of Knowledge in the United States*. Princeton, N.J.: Princeton University Press.

Machlup, Fritz (1973). "The Growth of Knowledge Activities in the United States: Some Data Gathered in Connection with a Revision of The Production and Distribution of Knowledge in the United States (1962)", Presentation at the Autumn Meeting of the U.S. National Academy of Education.

Maxwell, James (1961). *The Level and Trend of National Intelligence: The Contribution of the Scottish Surveys*. London: University of London Press.

McClelland, William (1942). *Selection for Secondary Education*. London: University of London Press.

McIntosh, Douglas M. (1959). *Educational Guidance and the Pool of Ability*. London: University of London Press.

Medawar, P.B. (1974). "More Equal Than Others", *New Statesman, n*, Jan. 11, 1974, 50-51.

Miller, G.W. (1970). "Factors in School Achievement and Social Class", *Journal of Educational Psychology*, 1970, *61*, No. 4, 260-269.

Moberg, Sven (1951). *Vem blev student och vad blev studenten? Statistiska studier rorande fem årgangår svenska studenter under perioden 1910-1943*. Lund: Gleerups.

Moberg, Sven, and Carl-Eric Quensel (1949). *Studenternas sociala ursprung, betyg i studentexamen, vidareutbildning, yrkesval* m.m. Stockholm: Statens offentliga utredningar 1949, No. 48 (Government Printing Office).

Mood, Alexander M. (Ed.) (1970). *Do Teachers Make a Difference?* Washington, D.C.: Department of Health Education and Welfare, Office of Education.

Moran, P.A.P. (1973). "A Note on Heritability and the Correlation between Relatives", *Annals of Human Genetics, 37*, London, 217.

Moshinsky, P. (1939). "The Correlation Between Fertility and Intelligence Within Social Classes", *Sociological Review, 31*, 144-165.

Mosteller, Frederick, and Daniel P. Moynihan (Eds.) (1972). *On Equality of Educational Opportunity*. New York: Vintage Books, Random House.

Moynihan, Daniel P. (1972). "Equalizing Education: In Whose Benefit?", *Public Interest*, No. 29, Fall 1972, 68-89.

Müller, K.V. (1956). *Begabung und Soziale Schichtung*. Schriftenreihe des Instituts für empirische Soziologie, Bd. 1. Köln und Opladen: Westdeutscher Verlag.

Myrdal, Gunnar (1969). *Objectivity in Social Research*. The 1967 Wimmer Lecture, St. Vincent College, Latrobe, Pennsylvania. New York: Pantheon Books, Random House.

Nam, Charles B. (1971). "Group Disparities in Educational Participation", Background Report No. 4 in OECD (1971a), see below.

Nam, Charles B., A. Lewis Rhodes, and Robert E. Herriott (1968). "School Retention by Race, Religion, and Socioeconomic Status", *Journal of Human Resources, 3*, No. 2, Spring 1968, 171-190.

Newman, H.H., F.N. Freeman, and K.J. Holzinger (1937). *Twins: A Study of Heredity and Environment*. Chicago: University of Chicago Press.

Neymark, Ejnar (1952). "Universitetens och högskolornas rekryteringsreserv", in *Vidgat till-träde till högre studier*. Stockholm: Statens Offentliga utredningar. 1952, No.29 (Government Printing Office).

Neymark, Ejnar (1961). *Selektiv rörlighet: flyttningstendenser och yrkesval i relation till utbildning, begåvning och härkomst*. Stockholm: Personaladministrativa rådet. Rapport No.24.

OE (Office of Education) (1970). *Do Teachers Make a Difference?* A Report on Recent Research on Pupil Achievement. Washington: Government Printing Office.

OECD (1962). *Policy Conference on Economic Growth and Investment in Education*. Washington, 16th-20th October, 1961. Paris: OECD.

OECD (1965). *Reserves of Mental Abilities in the Burgenland*. Vienna: Psycho-Pedagogical Service of Austria (mimeo).

OECD (1971a). *Group Disparities in Educational Participation and Achievement*. Background Reports No. 4 and 10. Conference on Policies for Educational Growth, Paris: OECD, Vol. IV (1971).

OECD (1971b). *Development of Higher Education 1950–1967*. Paris: OECD.

OECD (1971c). *Reviews of National Policies for Education: France*. Paris: OECD.

OECD (1971d) *Educational Policies for the 1970s*. General Report, Conference on Policies for Educational Growth, Paris, June 3rd-5th 1970. Paris: OECD.

OECD (1971e). *Equal Educational Opportunity: A Statement of the Problem with Special Reference to Recurrent Education*. Paris: OECD/CERI.

OECD (1972a). *Educational Policy and Planning: France*. Paris: OECD.

OECD (1972b). *Reviews of National Policies for Education: Germany*. Paris: OECD.

Oevermann, U. (1969). *Sprache und Soziale Herkunft: Ein Beitrag zur Analyse schichtenspezifischer Sozialisationsprozesse und ihrer Bedeutung für den Schulerfolg*. Berlin: Institut für Bildungsforschung in der Max-Planck Gesellschaft.

Orring, Jonas (1959). *Flyttning, kvarsittning och utkuggning i högre skolor i relation till folkskolans betygsättning*. Statens offentliga utredningar, SOU 1959:35. Stockholm: Government Printing Office.

Örum, B. (1971). *Social Baggrund, intellektuelt niveau og placering i skolesystemet*. Copenhagen: Socialforskningsinstituttet, Studie 20;

Papadopoulos, George (1973). "The Advent of Mass Higher Education", *OECD Observer*, Paris, No. 66, 27-30.

Paulston, Rolland (1968). *Educational Change in Sweden*. New York: Teachers College Press, Columbia University.

Peaker, Gilbert F. (1974). *An Empirical Study of Education in Twenty-One Countries: A Technical Report*. Stockholm: Almqvist and Wiksell.

Peisert, Hansgert (1967). *Soziale Lage und Bildungschancen in Deutschland*. München: Piper.

Peisert, Hansgert, and Dahrendorf, Ralf (1967). *Der vorzeitige Abgang vom Gymnasium*. Schriftenreihe des Kultusministeriums Baden-Württemberg zur Bildungsforschung, Bildungsplanung, Bildungspolitik. Villingen: Neckarverlag.

Penrose, Lionel S. (1948). "The Supposed Threat of Declining Intelligence", *American Journal of Mental Deficiency, 53*, No. 1, July 1948, 114-8.

Penrose, Lionel S. (1949). "The Galton Laboratory: Its Work and Aims", *Eugenics Review, 41*, No. 1, April 1949, 17-27.

Petrat, Gerhardt (1969). *Soziale Herkunft und Schullaufbahn*. Weinheim: Beltz and Deutsches Institut für Internationale Pädagogische Forschung, Frankfurt/Main. 2nd Ed.

Pettigrew, Thomas F. (1968). "Race and Equal Educational Opportunity", *Harvard Educational Review*, Winter 1968, 38, No. 1, 66-76.

Pidgeon, Douglas A. (Ed.) (1967). *Achievement in Mathematics: A National Study in Secondary Schools*. London: National Foundation for Educational Research.

Pidgeon, Douglas A. (1970). *Expectation and Pupil Performance*. Stockholm, Almqvist and Wiksell.

Poignant, Raymond (1973). *Education in the Industrialized Countries*. Educating Man for the 21st Century. Vol. 5. The Hague: Nijhoff.

Postlethwaite, T. Neville (1967). *School Organization and Student Achievement: A Study Based on Achievement in Mathematics in Twelve Countries*. Stockholm and New York: Almqvist and Wiksell, Wiley.

Purves, Alan C. (1973). *Literature Education in Ten Countries*. International Studies in Evaluation II. Stockholm and New York: Almqvist and Wiksell and Wiley-Halsted Press.

Quensel, C.E. (1949). "Studenternas sociala rekrytering", *Statsvetenskaplig Tidskrift, 42*, Lund, Sweden, 309-322.

Radford, William (1962). *School Leavers in Australia 1959-60*. Melbourne: Australian Council for Educational Research.

Rawls, John (1971). *A Theory of Justice*. Cambridge, Massachusetts: Harvard University Press.

Reuchlin, Maurice (1964). *Pupil Guidance: Facts and Problems*. Strasbourg: Council for Cultural Co-operation.

Reuchlin, Maurice (1972). *Individual Orientation in Education*. Educating Man for the 21st Century, Vol. 2. The Hague: Nijhoff.

Reich, Charles (1970). *The Greening of America*. New York: Random House.

Rice, Berkeley (1973). "Race, Intelligence and Genetics: The High Cost of Thinking the Unthinkable", *Psychology Today, 7*, No. 7, 88-95.

Roe, Anne (1962). *The Psychology of Occupations*. 4th Printing. New York: Wiley.

Rosenthal, Robert (1973). "The Pygmalion Effect Lives", *Psychology Today, 7*, No. 4, Sept. 1973, 56-58.

Roth, Heinrich (Ed.) (1968). *Begabung und Lernen*. Stuttgart: Klett.

Rutkewitch, M.N. (Ed.) (1969). *The Career Plans of Youth*. White Plains, New York: International Arts and Sciences Press.

Sauvy, Alfred and Alain Girard (1965). "Les diverses classes sociales devant l'enseignement: mise au point générale des résultats", *Population*, 20e année, March-April, No. 2, 205-232.

Sauvy, Alfred and Alain Girard (1970). "Les diverses classes sociales devant l'enseignement", *Population et l'enseignement*. Paris: l'Institut National d'Etudes Démographiques.

185

Sauvy, Alfred with the cooperation of Alain Girard, Albert Jaquard and Janina Lagneau-Markiewicz (1973). *Access to Education: New Possibilities.* Educating Man for the 21st Century, Vol. 4. The Hague: Nijhoff.

Scarr, Sandra (1968). "Environmental Bias in Twin Studies", in: Steven G. Vanderberg (Ed.) *Progress in Human Behavior Genetics.* Baltimore, Md: The John Hopkins Press, 205-209.

Scarr-Salapatek, Sandra (1971). "Race, Social Class, and IQ", *Science, 174,* 24 December, 1971, 1285-1295.

Scarr-Salapatek, Sandra (1973). "Heritability of IQ by Social Class", *Science,* Vol. 182, 7 December, 1045-1047.

Schacht-Breland, N. (1971). *A New Approach to Estimates of Heritability from Twin Data.* Research Qualifying Paper, Dept. of Educational Psychology, State University of New York at Buffalo.

Schrag, Peter (1970). "End of the Impossible Dream", *Saturday Review,* 19th September, 1970, 68-96.

Schultz, Theodore W. (1962). *Economic Value of Education.* New York: Columbia University Press.

Scottish Council for Research in Education (1933). *The Intelligence of Scottish Children: A National Survey of an Age Group.* London: University of London Press.

Scottish Council for Research in Education (1949). *The Trend of Scottish Intelligence: A Comparison of the 1947 and 1932 Surveys of the Intelligence of Eleven-Year-Old Pupils.* London: University of London Press.

Scottish Council for Research in Education (1953). *Social Implications of the 1947 Scottish Mental Survey.* London: University of London Press.

Senna, Carl (Ed.) (1973). *The Fallacy of IQ.* New York: The Third Press — Joseph Okpaku Publishing Co.

Sewell, William H. (1971). "Inequality of Opportunity for Higher Education", *American Sociological Review, 36,* No. 5, October 1971, 793-809.

Sewell, William S., and Vimal P. Shah (1967). "Socioeconomic Status, Intelligence, and the Attainment of Higher Education", *Sociology of Education, 40,* No. 1, Winter 1967, 1-23.

Sewell, William H., Archibald O. Haller, and George W. Ohlendorf (1970). "The Educational and Early Occupational Status Attainment Process: Replication and Revision", *American Sociological Review, 35,* No. 6, December 1970, 1014-27.

Shaycoft, M.F. (1967). *Project Talent: The High School Years: Growth in Cognitive Skills.* Pittsburgh: American Institute for Research and School of Education, University of Pittsburgh.

Shields, J. (1962). *Monozygotic Twins Brought Up Together.* London: Oxford University Press.

Shockley, William (1972a). "Dysgenics, Geneticity, Raceology: A Challenge to the Intellectual Responsibility of Educators", *Phi Delta Kappan, 53,* 297-307.

Shockley, William (1972b). "A Debate Challenge: Geneticy is 80% for White Identical Twins' IQ's", *Phi Delta Kappan, 53,* 415-419.

Smith, Marshall S. (1968). "Equality of Educational Opportunity: Comments on Bowles and Levin", *Journal of Human Resources, 3,* No. 3, 384-89.

SNS (1950). *Skolreformen och näringslivet: Synpunkter på försöksverksamheten.* Stockholm: Norstedt.

Sjöstrand, Wilhelm (1970). *Frihet och jämlikhet: Tva grundbegrepp inom 60-talets svenska pedagogik.* Stockholm: Gebers.

Sjöstrand, Wilhelm (1973). *Freedom and Equality as Fundamental Educational Principles in Western Democracy: From John Locke to Edmund Burke.* Studia Scientiae Paedagogicae Upsaliensia No. 12. Stockholm: Almqvist and Wiksell.

Sokolov, J.M. (1970). Torsten Husén's Educational Points of View. (In Russian) *Sovjetskaja Pedagogika,* 1970, No. 7, 126-135.

SOU (1944). *Sambandet mellan folkskolan och den högre skolan*. Stockholm: Statens offentliga utredningar 1944, No. 21 (Government Printing Office).

SOU (1948a). *Betänkande och förslag angaende studentsociala stödåtgärder avgivet av 1946 års utredning om den högre undervisningens demokratisering* (Student-sociala utredningen). Statens offentliga utredningar, SOU 1948:42. Stockholm: Government Printing Office.

SOU (1948b). *Betänkande med förslag till riktlinjer för det svenska skolväsendets utveckling, avgivet av 1946 års skolkommission*. Statens offentliga utredningar, SOU 1948:27. Stockholm: Government Printing Office.

SOU (1973). *Högskolan: Betänkande av 1968 års utbildningsutredning*. Stockholm: Statens offentliga utredningar, No. 2 (Government Printing Office).

Spearman, Charles (1927). *The Abilities of Man: Their Nature and Measurement*. London: MacMillan.

Spitz, J.C. (1959). "De Reserve aan Hoger Intellect in Nederland", *Universiteit en Hogeschool No. 6*, Dec. 1959, 77-93.

Spitz, J.C. (1962). "Reserves for Higher Education in the Netherlands Estimated by a Simple Method", in *Yearbook of Education 1962 (The Gifted Child)*. Ed. by George Z.F. Bereday and J.A. Lauwerys. London: Evans Brothers. 481-496.

Stern, William (1911). *Die differentielle Psychologie in ihren methodischen Grundlagen*. Leipzig: Barth.

Stern, William (1920). *Die Intelligenz der Kinder und Jugendlichen*. Leipzig : Barth.

Stern, William (1935). *Allgemeine Psychologie auf personalistischer Grundlage*. The Hague: Nijhoff.

Stice, G., W.G. Mollenkopf, and W.S. Torgerson (1957). *Background Factors and College-Going Plans Among High-Aptitude Public High-School Seniors*. Princeton: Educational Testing Service.

Stoddard, George D. (1945). *The Meaning of Intelligence*. New York: MacMillan.

Sussman, L. (1968). "Democratization and Class Segregation in Puerto Rican Schooling: The U.S. Model Transplanted", *Sociology of Education*. *41*, Fall 1968, 321-341.

Svensson, Allan (1971). *Relative Achievement. School Performance in Relation to Intelligence, Sex and Home Environment*. Stockholm: Almqvist and Wiksell.

Svensson, Nils-Eric (1962). *Ability Grouping and Scholastic Achievement*. Stockholm: Almqvist and Wiksell.

"A Symposium on Intelligence and its Measurement", *The Journal of Education Psychology, 12*, No. 3, March 1921, 123-147.

"A Symposium on Equality of Educational Opportunity", *Harvard Educational Review*, 1968, *38*, No. 1, 1-184.

Szczepanski, Jan (1963). *Problèmes sociologiques de l'enseignement supérieur en Pologne*. Paris: Editions Anthropos.

Tawney, R.H. (1951). *Equality*. London: Allen and Unwin. 4th Ed.

Terman, Lewis M. (1919). *The Intelligence of School Children*. Boston: Houghton Mifflin.

Terman, Lewis M. (1921). "Intelligence and its Measurement: A Symposium", in *The Journal of Educational Psychology, 12*, No. 3, March 1921, 127-133.

Terman, Lewis M. and Merrill, Maud A. (1937). *Measuring Intelligence*. New York: Houghton-Mifflin.

Thomson, Godfrey H. (1946). "The Trend of National Intelligence", *Eugenics Review*, *38*, 9-18.

Thomson, Godfrey H. (1947). "The Reserve of Intelligence outside the Universities", in *Proceedings of the Conference of the Home Universities*. London: Association of Universities of the British Commonwealth.

Thomson, Godfrey H. (1950). "Intelligence and Fertility", *Eugenics Review, 41*, No. 4, 163-170.

Thorndike, Edward L. (1903). *Educational Psychology*. New York: The Science Press.

187

Thorndike, Robert L. (1973). *Reading Comprehension Education in Fifteen Countries: An Empirical Study*. Stockholm and New York: Almqvist and Wiksell, and Wiley-Halsted Press.

Thurow, Lester C. (1972). "Education and Economic Equality", *Public Interest*, Summer 1972, No. 28, 66-81.

Thurstone, Louis L. (1938). *Primary Mental Abilities*. Psychometric Monographs No. 1. Chicago: University of Chicago Press.

Thurstone, Louis L. (1946). "Theories of Intelligence", *Scientific Monthly*, February 1946.

Tomasson, Richard F. (1965). "From Elitism to Egalitarianism in Swedish Education", *Sociology of Education, 38*, No. 3, 203-223.

Trow, Martin (1973). "Problems in Transition from Elite to Mass Higher Education", Paper presented at the Conference on Future Structures of Post-Secondary Education. Paris: OECD, June 1973 (mimeo).

Tuddenham, R.D. (1948). "Soldier Intelligence in World Wars I and II ", *American Psychologist, 3*, 54-56.

Undeutsch, Udo (1955). "Auslese für und durch die höhere Schule", in *Bericht über den 22. Kongress der deutschen Gesellschaft für Psychologie*. Göttingen: Hogrefe. 175-196

Undeutsch, Udo (1960). "Die Sexta-Aufnahmeprüfung", *Der Gymnasial-Unterricht*, No. 2. Stuttgart: Klett.

United Nations, Dept. of Social Affairs, Population Division (1953). *The Determinants and Consequences of Populations Trends*. New York: United Nations.

United Nations, Dept. of Social Affairs (1955). *Proceedings of the World Population Conference in Rome, 1954*. New York: United Nations.

Vandenberg, Steven G. (1966). "Contributions of Twin Research to Psychology", *Psychological Bulletin, 66*, No. 5, November 1966, 327-352.

Vandenberg, Steven G. (Ed.) (1968). *Progress in Human Behavior Genetics: Recent Reports on Genetic Syndromes, Twin Studies, and Statistical Advances*. Baltimore, Md.: The John Hopkins Press.

Vandenberg, Steven G., Richard E. Stafford, and Anne M. Brown (1968). "The Louisville Twin Study", in Steven G. Vandenberg (Ed.), *Progress in Human Behavior Genetics*. Baltimore, Md.: The Johns Hopkins Press, 153-204.

Vernon, Philip E. (1950). *The Structure of Human Abilities*. London: Methuen.

Vernon, Philip E. (Ed.) (1957). *Secondary School Selection: A British Psychological Society Inquiry*. London: Methuen.

Vernon, Philip E. (1963). "The Pool of Ability", *Sociological Review*. Monograph No. 7: Sociological Studies in British University Education. Ed. by Paul Halmost. Keele: University of Keele, 45-57.

Vernon, Philip E. (1969). *Intelligence and Cultural Environment*. London: Methuen.

Warner, W. Lloyd, and R.J. Havighurst, and Martin B. Loeb (1946). *Who Shall be Educated? The Challenge of Unequal Opportunities*. New York, London: Harper.

Wechsler, David (1944). *The Measurement of Adult Intelligence*. 3rd ed. Baltimore: Williams and Wilkins.

Westergaad, John and Alan Little (1967) in "Social Objectives in Educational Planning". Paris: OECD. 215-232.

Weiss, Joel (1970). *The Development and Measurement of Home Environmental Models for Personality Characteristics*. Paper Read at the Annual Meeting of the American Educational Res. Asso., Minneapolis, March 1970.

Wilson, A.B. (1968). "Social Class and Equal Educational Opportunity", *Harvard Educational Review, 38*, No. 1, Winter 1968, 77-84.

Wolf, Richard M. (1964). *The Identification and Measurement of Environmental Process Variables Related to General Intelligence*. University of Chicago: Unpublished doctoral dissertation.

De Wolff, P. (1960). " Intellectual Resources and the Growth of Higher Education ", *Forecasting Manpower Needs for the Age of Science*. Paris: OEEC.

De Wolff, P., and Kjell Härnqvist (1961). "Reserves of Ability: Size and Distribution ", *Ability and Educational Opportunity*. Ed. by A.H. Halsey, 137-175, Paris: OECD.

De Wolff, P., and A.R.D. Van Slijpe (1973). "The Relation Between Income, Intelligence, Education and Social Background ", *European Economic Review, 4*, 235-264.

Wolfle, Dael (1954). *America's Resources of Specialized Talent*. New York: Harper.

Yanowitch, Murray and Norton Dodge (1968). "Social Class and Education: Soviet Findings and Reactions ", *Comparative Education Review*, 1968, 248-267.

Yanowitch, Murray, and Norton T. Dodge (1969). "The Social Evaluation of Occupations in the Soviet Union ", *Slavic Review*, December, 1969.

Yates, Alfred (Ed.) (1966). *Grouping in Education*. Stockholm: Almqvist and Wiksell.

Yates, Alfred, and Douglas A. Pidgeon (1957). *Admission to Grammar Schools*. London: Newnes.

Young Michael (1958). *The Rise of the Meritocracy*. London: Penguin.

OECD SALES AGENTS
DEPOSITAIRES DES PUBLICATIONS DE L'OCDE

ARGENTINA – ARGENTINE
Carlos Hirsch S.R.L.,
Florida 165, BUENOS-AIRES.
☎ 33-1787-2391 Y 30-7122
AUSTRALIA – AUSTRALIE
B.C.N. Agencies Pty. Ltd.,
161 Sturt St., South MELBOURNE, Vic. 3205.
☎ 69.7601
658 Pittwater Road, BROOKVALE NSW 2100.
☎ 938 2267
AUSTRIA – AUTRICHE
Gerold and Co., Graben 31, WIEN 1.
☎ 52.22.35
BELGIUM – BELGIQUE
Librairie des Sciences
Coudenberg 76-78, B 1000 BRUXELLES 1.
☎ 13.37.36/12.05.60
BRAZIL — BRESIL
Mestre Jou S.A., Rua Guaipá 518,
Caixa Postal 24090, 05089 SAO PAULO 10.
☎ 256-2746/262-1609
Rua Senador Dantas 19 s/205 - 6, RIO DE
JANEIRO GB. ☎ 232-07. 32
CANADA
Information Canada
171 Slater, OTTAWA. K1A 0S9.
☎ (613) 992-9738
DENMARK – DANEMARK
Munksgaards Boghandel
Nørregade 6, 1165 KØBENHAVN K.
☎ (01) 12 69 70
FINLAND — FINLANDE
Akateeminen Kirjakauppa
Keskuskatu 1, 00100 HELSINKI 10. ☎ 625.901
FRANCE
Bureau des Publications de l'OCDE
2 rue André-Pascal, 75775 PARIS CEDEX 16.
☎ 524.81.67
Principaux correspondants :
13602 AIX-EN-PROVENCE : Librairie de
l'Université. ☎ 26.18.08
38000 GRENOBLE : B. Arthaud. ☎ 87.25.11
31000 TOULOUSE : Privat. ☎ 21.09.26
GERMANY – ALLEMAGNE
Verlag Weltarchiv G.m.b.H.
D 2000 HAMBURG 36, Neuer Jungfernstieg 21
☎ 040-35-62-501
GREECE – GRECE
Librairie Kauffmann, 28 rue du Stade,
ATHENES 132. ☎ 322.21.60
ICELAND – ISLANDE
Snaebjörn Jónsson and Co., h.f.,
Hafnarstræti 4 and 9, P.O.B. 1131,
REYKJAVIK.. ☎ 13133/14281/11936
INDIA – INDE
Oxford Book and Stationery Co.:
NEW DELHI, Scindia House. ☎ 47388
CALCUTTA, 17 Park Street. ☎ 24083
IRELAND – IRLANDE
Eason and Son, 40 Lower O'Connell Street,
P.O.B. 42, DUBLIN 1. ☎ 01-41161
ISRAEL
Emanuel Brown :
35 Allenby Road, TEL AVIV. ☎ 51049/54082
also at :
9, Shlomzion Hamalka Street, JERUSALEM.
☎ 234807
48 Nahlath Benjamin Street, TEL AVIV.
☎ 53276
ITALY – ITALIE
Libreria Commissionaria Sansoni :
Via Lamarmora 45, 50121 FIRENZE. ☎ 579751
Via Bartolini 29, 20155 MILANO. ☎ 365083
Sous-dépositaires :
Editrice e Libreria Herder,
Piazza Montecitorio 120, 00186 ROMA.
☎ 674628
Libreria Hoepli, Via Hoepli 5, 20121 MILANO.
☎ 865446
Libreria Lattes, Via Garibaldi 3, 10122 TORINO.
☎ 519274
La diffusione delle edizioni OCDE è inoltre assicurata dalle migliori librerie nelle città più importanti.

JAPAN – JAPON
OECD Publications Centre,
Akasaka Park Building,
2-3-4 Akasaka,
Minato-ku
TOKYO 107. ☎ 586-2016
Maruzen Company Ltd.,
6 Tori-Nichome Nihonbashi, TOKYO 103,
P.O.B. 5050, Tokyo International 100-31.
☎ 272-7211
LEBANON – LIBAN
Documenta Scientifica/Redico
Edison Building, Bliss Street,
P.O.Box 5641, BEIRUT. ☎ 354429 – 344425
THE NETHERLANDS – PAYS-BAS
W.P. Van Stockum
Buitenhof 36, DEN HAAG. ☎ 070-65.68.08
NEW ZEALAND – NOUVELLE-ZELANDE
The Publications Officer
Government Printing Office
Mulgrave Street (Private Bag)
WELLINGTON, ☎ 46.807
and Government Bookshops at
AUCKLAND (P.O.B. 5344). ☎ 32.919
CHRISTCHURCH (P.O.B. 1721). ☎ 50.331
HAMILTON (P.O.B. 857). ☎ 80.103
DUNEDIN (P.O.B. 1104). ☎ 78.294
NORWAY – NORVEGE
Johan Grundt Tanums Bokhandel,
Karl Johansgate 41/43, OSLO 1. ☎ 02-332980
PAKISTAN
Mirza Book Agency, 65 Shahrah Quaid-E-Azam,
LAHORE 3. ☎ 66839
PHILIPPINES
R.M. Garcia Publishing House,
903 Quezon Blvd. Ext., QUEZON CITY,
P.O. Box 1860 – MANILA. ☎ 99.98.47
PORTUGAL
Livraria Portugal,
Rua do Carmo 70-74. LISBOA 2. ☎ 360582/3
SPAIN – ESPAGNE
Libreria Mundi Prensa
Castello 37, MADRID-1. ☎ 275.46.55
Libreria Bastinos
Pelayo, 52, BARCELONA 1. ☎ 222.06.00
SWEDEN – SUEDE
Fritzes Kungl. Hovbokhandel,
Fredsgatan 2, 11152 STOCKHOLM 16.
☎ 08/23 89 00
SWITZERLAND – SUISSE
Librairie Payot, 6 rue Grenus, 1211 GENEVE 11.
☎ 022-31.89.50
TAIWAN
Books and Scientific Supplies Services, Ltd.
P.O.B. 83, TAIPEI.
TURKEY – TURQUIE
Librairie Hachette,
469 Istiklal Caddesi,
Beyoglu, ISTANBUL, ☎ 44.94.70
et 14 E Ziya Gokalp Caddesi
ANKARA. ☎ 12.10.80
UNITED KINGDOM – ROYAUME-UNI
H.M. Stationery Office, P.O.B. 569, LONDON
SE1 9 NH, ☎ 01-928-6977, Ext. 410
or
49 High Holborn
LONDON WC1V 6HB (personal callers)
Branches at: EDINBURGH, BIRMINGHAM,
BRISTOL, MANCHESTER, CARDIFF,
BELFAST.
UNITED STATES OF AMERICA
OECD Publications Center, Suite 1207,
1750 Pennsylvania Ave, N.W.
WASHINGTON, D.C. 20006. ☎ (202)298-8755
VENEZUELA
Libreria del Este, Avda. F. Miranda 52,
Edificio Galipán, Aptdo. 60 337, CARACAS 106.
☎ 32 23 01/33 26 04/33 24 73
YUGOSLAVIA – YOUGOSLAVIE
Jugoslovenska Knjiga, Terazije 27, P.O.B. 36,
BEOGRAD. ☎ 621-992

Les commandes provenant de pays ou l'OCDE n'a pas encore désigné de dépositaire
peuvent être adressées à :
OCDE, Bureau des Publications, 2 rue André-Pascal, 75775 Paris CEDEX 16
Orders and inquiries from countries where sales agents have not yet been appointed may be sent to
OECD, Publications Office, 2 rue André-Pascal, 75775 Paris CEDEX 16

OECD PUBLICATIONS, 2, rue André-Pascal, 75775 Paris Cedex 16 - No. 34.039 1975
PRINTED IN FRANCE